FUTURISTIC

© 2011 DAAB MEDIA GMBH
All rights reserved. No part of this publication may be reproduced or transmitted in any form or by any means, electronic or mechanical, including photocopy, recording or any information storage and retrieval system, without permission in writing from the copyright owner(s).

Published and distributed worldwide by
DAAB MEDIA GMBH
Scheidtweilerstrasse 69
50933 Cologne/Germany
fon + 49 221 690 48 210
fax + 49 221 690 48 229
www.daab-media.com

Join our community
www.edaab.com and present your work to a worldwide audience

Edited by Caroline Klein
Text by Stefanie Lieb
Concept by Ralf Daab
Corporate Design by Meiré und Meiré, Cologne
Layout by Sonia Mion, Nicola Iannibello, Milan, www.ventizeronove.it

Managing Editor: Christiane Blass, redaktionsbüro, Cologne
Copy Editors: Christiane Blass, Claudia Grönemeyer, Cologne; Caroline Klein, Milan

German translations by Norma Kessler, Aschaffenburg; Rainer Remmel, Berlin; Michael Wachholz, Berlin
English translation by Karin Dufner, Meerbusch; Gaines Translations, Frankfurt/Main; Lisa Ronan, Milan
Copy proofreading by Nicole Bilstein-Brok, Malmö; Michael Scuffil, Leverkusen

Lithographie by fgv Group, Milan
www.fgvgrafica.it

Printed in Italy
www.graficheflaminia.com

ISBN 978-3-942597-09-8

VISIONS OF FUTURE LIVING
FUTURISTIC

Edited by CAROLINE KLEIN
Text by STEFANIE LIEB

CONTENT / INHALT

8	INTRODUCTION	
10	FUTURISTIC? Essay: Kas Oosterhuis	
12	**URBAN**	
14	B+U City Futura, 2010	
20	THE WHY FACTORY (T?F) City Pig, 2009 Hanging Food Gardens, 2009	
24	CONSTRUCTING URBAN FUTURES Essay: The Why Factory (t?f)	
26	MAD Beijing 2050, 2006 Superstar: A Mobile China Town, 2008 Urban Forest, 2009	
38	LET'S HEAD FOR UTOPIA Essay: Florian Heilmeyer	
40	JOHN WARDLE ARCHITECTS AND STEFANO BOSCUTTI Multiplicity, 2010	
44	RAG URBANISM Sydney 2050: Fraying Ground, 2010	
48	ARCHI-TECTONICS NYC 2106: A Coastal Megalopolis, 2007	
52	A SYSTEMATIC APPROACH TO THE FUTURE Essay: Winka Dubbeldam	
54	RAUMLABORBERLIN Snuggle, 2009	
58	J. MAYER H. ARCHITEKTEN A. Way, 2010	
64	SUSTAINABILITY Essay: J. Mayer H.	
66	**TOWER**	
68	NABITO Stairscraper, 2010	
72	JOANNA BOREK-CLEMENT Sky-Terra, 2009	
74	LAVA Tower Skin, 2010 Bionic Tower, 2009	
78	WHY I AM IN LOVE WITH HIGH-RISES Essay: Christoph Ingenhoven	
80	FAULDERS STUDIO GEOtube, 2010	
86	LABSCAPE Tree Plug, 2005	
88	LUCA D'AMICO / LUCA TESIO Nomad Skyscraper, 2011	
92	MASS STUDIES Seoul Commune 2026, 2005	
100	**ATMOSPHERE**	
102	PAUL-ERIC SCHIRR-BONNANS Flat Tower, 2011	
106	WERNER SOBEK R129, 2001–2012	
110	PHILIPPE RAHM Domestic Astronomy, 2009	
114	TOWARDS A METEOROLOGICAL ARCHITECTURE Essay: Philippe Rahm	
116	ARCHITECTURE AND VISION Moon Ville, 2009 Moon Base Two, 2007	

120	FOSTER + PARTNERS Spaceport, 2006–2011	
124	CARLORATTIASSOCIATI The Cloud, 2009	
130	STUDIO MASSAUD Manned Cloud, 2005–2008	

134 GREEN

- **136** CDMB ARCHITECTS
  Vardø's Arks, 2009
  Green Desert Mine, 2007
- **142** MARCOSANDMARJAN
  Khataba (Al Jadida), Agropolis, 2009
- **148** MVRDV
  Gwanggyo Power Centre, 2007–2011
- **154** VINCENT CALLEBAUT
  Hydrogenase, 2010; The Perfumed Jungle, 2007; Lilypad, 2008
- **164** IWAMOTOSCOTT
  Hydro-Net, 2008
- **170** VERTICAL FARM
  Essay: Dickson Despommier
- **174** LUC SCHUITEN
  Vegetal City, 2008; The City of the Waves, 2003; Urbacanyon, 2009; The Hollow City, 2009
- **178** ANTOINE DAMERY
  Biospace, 2009
- **182** BIG – BJARKE INGELS GROUP
  Zira Island, 2008
  Amagerforbrænding, 2008
  (Driver)less is more, 2010

190 WATER

- **192** ARUP
  Ocean City, 2010
- **196** JACQUES ROUGERIE
  SeaOrbiter, 1999–2013
- **200** UNDERWATER CITY
  Essay: Caroline Klein
- **204** KOKKUGIA / EMERGENT
  Oceanic Pavilion, 2010
- **210** PHU HOANG OFFICE
  No Man's Land, 2007
- **214** BIOTHING
  FissurePort, 2010
- **220** SCOTT LLOYD / ROOM 11 / KATRINA STOLL
  The Island Proposition 2100, 2010
- **224** OFF ARCHITECTURE
  Bering Strait, 2009
- **230** MGS / BILD ARCHITECTURE / DYSKORS / MATERIAL THINKING
  Saturation City, 2010

234 BIONIC

- **236** R & SIE(N)
  Isobiot®ope, 2010
- **240** DIGITAL TECTONICS
  Essay: Alberto T. Estévez
- **242** TERREFORM ONE
  Peristaltic City, 2008
  Fab Tree Hab, 2008
- **248** DESIGN AS A RESOURCE FOR ALL RESOURCES
  Essay: Mitchell Joachim and Maria Aiolova
- **250** ONL
  Digital Pavilion, 2006
- **254** DCA – DESIGN CREW FOR ARCHITECTURE
  Freshwater Factory, 2010
- **258** HWKN
  MEtreePOLIS, 2008
- **264** A POSSIBLE MANIFESTO
  Luca Molinari
- **268** BIBLIOGRAPHY
- **269** PHOTO CREDITS
- **270** INDEX

"THE FUTURE BELONGS TO THOSE WHO

BELIEVE IN THE BEAUTY OF THEIR DREAMS."

ELEANOR ROOSEVELT

INTRODUCTION

On the necessity of visionary living

Gaston Berger, the French philosopher and statesman, in the 1950s clad the development of human civilization in the following metaphor: "Our civilization can be compared to a car moving down an unknown street at an increasingly faster speed while it is getting dark. Its headlights have to reach further and further into the nights, if a catastrophe is to be avoided." Data and facts in regard to the enormous growth of population, the uncontrollable conurbation, the imminent ultimate snarl-up, and man-made pollution were available even in those days. It was young experimental teams of architects like Archigram or the Japanese Metabolists who, with their visionary concepts, reacted to this deplorable state of affairs already in the 1960s. Their drafts and fictional architectural cityscapes were radical, shrill, colorful, provocative, and sometimes a little crazy, but, as it turned out in the following decades, paved the way to innovation. Anagram´s Plug-In-City, a stationary scaffolding to which mobile housing-capsules could be attached, has gained more immediacy than ever in our era of global nomadism. The same is true for the concepts of the Metabolists whose high-rises with cellular structures, suggesting an organic metabolism, surely will have an impact on contemporary concepts of urban living.

It does not come as a surprise that the architectural visions of the 1960s were marked by a rather uncritical approach to progress and an obsession with modern technology, as their creators still were convinced of the beneficial effects the newly invented synthetic materials and "clean" nuclear energy would have on mankind. Thus, the idea was to introduce technology into all areas of life in order to solve future social, economic, and environmental problems. There were even plans to air-condition the earth on a large scale: Richard Buckminster Fuller intended to cover the entire island of Manhattan with a plastic dome, while Frei Otto wanted to control the world´s climate with the help of climatic hoods.

Although reality has since caught up with these utopias, it was not these creative minds who positively influenced the global climate by means of technology. Instead, the human race has managed to dramatically alter the world´s climate in such a way that it has become a threat to our civilization. Therefore, the ongoing global warming with all its consequences has moved into the focus of contemporary futuristic architctical visions. Sustainability and an ecological approach have replaced the blind belief in technology and the careless consumption of energy and meanwhile play a major role in regard to future conceptualizing and construction. To ignore them will not remain unpunished as we recently had occasion to observe on Dubai´s famous artificial palm island, a holiday resort whose edges have already been eroded by floods.

In spite of having to consider the consequences brought about by the world´s current ecological situation, contemporary futuristic concepts devised by young architects and designers are no less innovative and imaginative than they were 50 years ago. Roughly classified by the categories "Urban", "Tower", "Atmosphere", "Green", "Water", and "Bionic", almost all concepts for our future lives reflect the need to return to nature with its sustainable sources of energy. However, the feats of digital technology and computer controlled systems are integrated into the process of planning and production as well.

In our future cities highrises will reach into the skies like plants and feed by photosynthesis, while supplying their inhabitants with fresh air. In the few remaining streets of these cities, which are surrounded by various jungle zones, computer controlled transportation systems with driverless electric vehicles will shuttle people from A to B. And if our cities should indeed be flooded by oceans, the human race will survive in floating structures, underwater metropolises or settlements on other planets somewhere in space. Promising visions and constructive plans that deal with these scenarios are already waiting to be put to the test.

Stefanie Lieb

EINLEITUNG

Von der Notwendigkeit visionärer Lebensentwürfe

Der französische Philosoph und Staatsmann Gaston Berger formulierte in den 1950er-Jahren die Weiterentwicklung der menschlichen Zivilisation folgendermaßen: „Unsere Zivilisation ist vergleichbar mit einem Auto, das immer schneller auf unbekannter Straße fährt, während die Nacht hereinbricht. Seine Scheinwerfer müssen immer weiter reichen, wenn die Katastrophe verhindert werden soll."

Bereits zu dieser Zeit lagen Daten und Fakten zur stark anwachsenden Weltbevölkerung, zu unkontrollierten Ballungen in den Großstädten, zum bevorstehenden Verkehrskollaps und sogar zur menschenverursachten Umweltverschmutzung vor. Es waren die visionären Entwürfe junger experimenteller Architekturteams wie Archigram oder die Metabolisten in Japan, die in den 1960er-Jahren auf diese Missstände reagierten. Ihre Planungen und fiktiven Stadt- und Architekturbilder für die Zukunft waren radikal, schrill, bunt, provokativ und ein wenig verrückt. Aber sie waren auch wegweisend, wie sich in den Folgejahrzehnten herausstellen sollte. Die Plug-In-City von Archigram als stationäres Trägersystem, an das mobile Wohnkapseln angedockt werden können, hat in unserer heutigen Zeit des globalen Nomadentums mehr Aktualität denn je. Oder auch die Entwürfe der Metabolisten für Hochhäuser mit Zellstrukturen, die einen organischen Stoffwechsel suggerieren, sind für zeitgenössische Stadt- und Wohnkonzepte hochinteressant.

Sicherlich waren die Architekturvisionen der 1960er-Jahre noch fortschrittsgläubiger und technikbesessener ausgerichtet. Man war von dem Nutzen neu entwickelter Kunststoffe und der „sauberen" Atomenergie für den Menschen überzeugt. Die angestrebte Technisierung aller Lebensbereiche sollte zur Lösung der zukünftigen Probleme auf gesellschaftlichem, wirtschaftlichem und ökologischem Gebiet führen. Es gab sogar Planungen hinsichtlich einer großräumigen künstlichen Klimatisierung der Erde: Richard Buckminster Fuller wollte ganz Manhattan mit einer Kunststoffkuppel überdecken, Frei Otto strebte gar die Weltklimatisierung mit entsprechenden Klimahüllen an.

Diese Utopien sind allerdings tatsächlich von der Realität eingeholt worden. Nicht die Menschheit und kreative Planer können das Weltklima durch Technologien zu ihren Gunsten bestimmen, vielmehr wird das durch die Menschheit zerstörte natürliche Erdklima zur akuten Bedrohung der menschlichen Zivilisation. So ist denn auch der bereits eingesetzte globale Klimawandel mit all seinen Konsequenzen das zentrale Thema aktueller futuristischer Architekturvisionen. Statt blinder Technikgläubigkeit und Energieverschwendung sind nun Nachhaltigkeit und Umweltschutz wichtige Prämissen für ein zukünftiges Planen und Bauen geworden. Wenn diese nicht eingehalten werden, sind die Folgen unabsehbar: so jüngst zu beobachten bei Dubais berühmter künstlicher Palminsel, einem Urlaubsdomizil, das an den Rändern bereits durch Überflutungen beschädigt wurde.

Trotz dieser Konsequenzen, die die heutige ökologische Situation weltweit mit sich bringt, fallen die aktuellen futuristischen Entwürfe junger Architektur- und Designbüros nicht weniger innovativ und fantasievoll aus als vor 50 Jahren. Grob sortiert in die sechs Themengruppen „Urban", „Turm", „Atmosphäre", „Grün", „Wasser" und „Bionik" ist bei fast allen dieser Planungen für das Leben von morgen eine Rückbesinnung auf die Natur mit ihren nachhaltigen Energiesystemen erkennbar. Aber auch die Errungenschaften digitaler Techniken und computergesteuerter Systeme werden im Entwurfs- und Produktionsprozess mit einbezogen.

In der zukünftigen Stadt werden Hochhäuser wie Pflanzen emporwachsen, sich durch Fotosynthese ernähren und den Bewohnern darüber hinaus noch Frischluft liefern. Auf den wenigen Straßen dieser Stadt, die ansonsten von vielen Dschungelzonen umgeben ist, wird ein computergesteuertes Verkehrssystem mit fahrerlosen Elektromobilen den Verkehrsteilnehmer von A nach B transportieren. Sollten unsere Städte in der Zukunft tatsächlich durch einen Anstieg der Meeresspiegel überflutet werden, kann die Menschheit in Architekturen, die auf dem Wasser schwimmen, in Unterwassermetropolen oder in Siedlungen auf anderen Planeten des Weltalls überleben. Die vielversprechenden Visionen und produktiven Entwürfe für all diese Szenarien liegen auf jeden Fall schon bereit.

Stefanie Lieb

FUTURISTIC?

I have always avoided the word futuristic when it comes to describe my own work, strongly embedded in the here and the now, both technologically and socially, and in that sense not at all futuristic. But in the common usage of the word futuristic it is true that the selection of architects who are brought together in this book under this common denominator are indeed innovative and revolutionary. Architects who are in some way ahead of their times, expressing a vision of the future that is thought likely to be current or fashionable at some future time. It is almost impossible to find another common denominator for the selected architects other then the view of the future of architecture. The internal nature of the work of Terreform One cannot be more different than the work of Norman Foster or Mass Studies.

Now Werner Sobek, Vincent Callebaut and MVRDV are in one and the same collection. Are we all futurists then? Is that what binds us together? Indeed all of the selected architects are breeding followers, most of them are active in the process of displaying their view on the future to become fashionable. But mind you, all of these views are intrinsically unique and actually advocating only their personal view of the future. There is not just one future, in extremo according to quantum physics there is a multitude of possible futures, all of them happening at the same time. Some of these visions are deeply conflicting with each other, trying to pull the reader in complete opposing directions. In the end this collection is a pool of potential new conflicts between the visionary architects rather than the presentation of one big happy family. Any visionary architect typically propagates a clear, distinctive and specific vision of the future, usually connected with advances in technology and/or social/political arrangements. Visionaries want to breed offspring, and whether they are conscious of this ambition or not, their design proposals and their realized buildings function as their propaganda vehicles. Visionaries typically wish to create and inspire followers. Now we all are presented as futurists in this fine collection, the arena is open for debate. Debate is exactly what I have been missing in the last decades. I wish the architects would stand up and argue for their vision in an open debate, seriously questioning the vision of their colleagues, and eventually step out of the happy family and win votes for their vision of the future.

May this book function as the driver of a refreshed debate!

Kas Oosterhuis

FUTURISTISCH?

Das Wort futuristisch versuche ich immer zu vermeiden, wenn es um die Beschreibung meiner eigenen Arbeit geht. Denn sie ist technologisch wie auch gesellschaftlich fest im Hier und Jetzt eingebunden und in diesem Sinne in keinster Weise futuristisch. Aber nach dem allgemeinen Verständnis des Wortes futuristisch sind viele Projekte der Architekten, die in diesem Buch unter dem gemeinsamen Nenner futuristisch zusammengefasst wurden, in einigen Aspekten innovativ und revolutionär. Diese Architekten sind in gewisser Weise ihrer Zeit voraus, und ihre jeweilige Vision von Zukunft könnte irgendwann einmal üblich oder modern sein. Es ist fast unmöglich, einen anderen gemeinsamen Nenner für die ausgewählten Architekten zu finden, als den Blick auf die Zukunft der Architektur. Zwischen den wesentlichen Elementen der Arbeiten von Terreform One und denen von Norman Foster oder Mass Studies liegen Welten.

Nun finden sich Werner Sobek, Vincent Callebaut und MVRDV in ein und derselben Sammlung. Sind wir also alle Futuristen? Verbindet uns genau das? In der Tat haben alle ausgewählten Architekten ihre Anhänger, die meisten stellen aktiv ihre Ansichten über die Zukunft dar, um ins Gespräch zu kommen. Alle hier vertretenen Ansichten sind absolut individuell und geben eine persönliche Sicht auf die Zukunft wieder. Es gibt nicht nur eine Zukunft, im Extrem gibt es nach der Quantenphysik eine Vielzahl möglicher Zukünfte, die alle zur gleichen Zeit stattfinden. Manche dieser Visionen sind absolut gegensätzlich und versuchen den Leser in eine jeweils andere Richtung zu beeinflussen. Die Sammlung zeigt eine Reihe möglicher neuer Konflikte zwischen visionären Architekten auf, statt eine große glückliche Familie zu präsentieren. Jeder visionäre Architekt vertritt in der Regel eine klare, unverwechselbare und besondere Sicht der Zukunft, die üblicherweise mit technischen Fortschritten und/oder gesellschaftlichen/politischen Konstellationen verbunden ist. Visionäre möchten Motivation für andere sein; vielleicht sind sie sich dessen nicht bewusst, aber ihre Entwürfe und ihre realisierten Gebäude sind ihr Propagandamaterial. Visionäre wollen in der Regel Anhänger haben und sie inspirieren. Jetzt werden wir alle in dieser erlesenen Sammlung als Futuristen präsentiert, und die Diskussion kann beginnen. Genau diese Diskussion habe ich in den vergangenen Jahrzehnten vermisst. Ich hoffe, die Architekten treten für ihre Sicht in einer offenen Diskussion ein, stellen die Visionen ihrer Kollegen in Frage und setzen sich schließlich von der glücklichen Familie ab, um Stimmen für ihre Vision der Zukunft zu gewinnen.

Möge dieses Buch eine wiedererstarkte Diskussion fördern!

Kas Oosterhuis

URBAN

Since antiquity the word "city" has connoted a certain way of life. As opposed to "village", "city" stands for clustering and centralization. Here, the seats of government, administration, and economy are located. Here, business and trade are conducted. Here, the centers of religion, education, and culture can be found. In the course of the millennia the parameters of urbanity have remained more or less the same, even if the conditions and dimensions of a modern mega-city differ dramatically from those of a city around the year 1800, the early phase of industrialization. In those days there was not a single city with more than one million inhabitants, while 38 cities has reached the size already in 1940. Today, 23 metropolises worldwide were home to over ten million people. By 2050 there will be more than 27 mega-cities like this on the map, which means a massive increase. When talking about urban development, the growing tendency to migrate from the countryside into the cities worldwide also has to be taken into account. Asia's booming cities in particular will experience an increase in population of about 300% within the next 40 years.

The wildly expanding metropolises, however, are only one of the many aspects urban planners and architects have to consider when devising cities fit for the future. The daily chaos in our streets and the ensuing pollution, especially due to CO_2 and micro dust, as well as the currently poor energy efficiency have to be remedied as quickly as possible, if we want to avert the threat of climatic catastrophes caused by global warming. Intelligent and courageous concepts of urban planning are called for to make the perfectly green and clean city come true. Foster + Partners have taken a first step in this direction with Masdar City in Abu Dhabi, which is the world's first CO_2-free city with an energy consumption cut by 70%. However, the question remains how our present cities can be restructured to achieve a higher degree of sustainability, an issue many teams of architects introduced in this book have intensively pondered on.

The post-fossil city of the future, the "Post Oil City", should not only possess a computer controlled and driverless transportation system, but also make room for nature in the shape of many parks, designed either as energy storing junglescapes or cultivated meadows and fields, located in the center of town. This vision is not as strange as it sounds, because there already are serious surveys and concepts for an urban agriculture to bring the farm, maybe even housed in a highrise, into the city. This way city dwellers would have the option to grow their own food, a new urban agriculture, accompanied by the respective "agritecture" that could lay the foundation of rural social structures in the middle of the city. Instead of living in inner-city slums, ghettos, and individual isolation, people would become members of agricultural rural communities, while still taking part in a digital, nomadic, global, and networking culture.

Even for the worst-case scenario of global warming with mega-waves flooding our large cities, constructive visionary concepts of new floating cities, underwater metropolises, and urban settlements in space have been devised.

URBAN

Mit dem Bild der Stadt ist seit der Antike auch eine spezifische menschliche Lebensform verbunden. Im Unterschied zum Leben auf dem Land ist in der Stadt alles zentriert und verdichtet; hier ist der Sitz von Regierung, Verwaltung und Wirtschaft, hier finden Handel und Warenaustausch statt, und hier befinden sich die Zentren von Religion, Bildung und Kultur. Über die Jahrtausende hat sich bis heute an diesen Parametern des Urbanen nicht viel geändert. Dennoch sind die Konditionen und vor allem Dimensionen der modernen Großstadt vollständig andere als z.B. die der frühindustriellen Stadt um 1800: Zu diesem Zeitpunkt überschritt keine Stadt der Welt die Einwohnerzahl von einer Million. Bereits 1940 zählte man global 38 Städte, die mehr als eine Million Einwohner besaßen. Heute gibt es weltweit 23 Metropolen mit über zehn Millionen Menschen, für das Jahr 2050 werden mehr als 27 Megastädte dieser Größe prognostiziert. Die Tendenz steigt also frappant, und auch die weltweite Zunahme der Abwanderung vom Land in die Städte muss man als Tatbestand der nahen urbanen Zukunft registrieren. Besonders in den boomenden Städten Asiens wird sich in den nächsten 40 Jahren die Stadtbevölkerung um 300 % erhöhen.

    Die wuchernden Megastädte sind aber nur ein Aspekt unter vielen, die Stadtplaner und Architekten in ihren Visionen einer zukunftsfähigen Stadt berücksichtigen müssen. Das tägliche Verkehrschaos in unseren Großstädten und die damit verbundene enorme Luftverschmutzung, besonders die hohe CO_2- und Feinstaubbelastung, sowie die mangelnde Energieeffizienz sind Entwicklungen, auf die in Anbetracht drohender Klimakatastrophen aufgrund der Erderwärmung schnellstmöglich Einfluss genommen werden muss. Hierzu benötigt man intelligente und mutige Stadtentwicklungsplanungen, die eine neue, grüne und saubere Idealstadt Realität werden lassen. Ein erster Schritt in diese Richtung wurde bereits von Foster + Partners mit Masdar City in Abu Dhabi, der weltweit ersten CO_2-freien Stadt mit 70 % reduziertem Energieverbrauch, gemacht. Aber es geht insbesondere auch um die Fragestellung, wie man bereits bestehende Großstädte mit nachhaltigeren Strukturen versehen kann. Viele der hier vorgestellten Architektenteams setzen sich in ihren Masterplänen intensiv mit dieser Thematik auseinander.

    In der postfossilen Stadt der Zukunft, der „Post Oil City", sollte neben einem computergesteuerten und fahrerlosen öffentlichen Verkehrsnetz auch die Natur wieder Einzug halten, mit vielen Grünflächen, z.B. in Form energiespeichernder Dschungellandschaften, und mit zu bewirtschaftenden Wiesen und Äckern, die mitten in der Innenstadt platziert werden. Diese Vision ist gar nicht so abwegig, denn es existieren bereits ernst zu nehmende Studien und Planungen hinsichtlich einer urbanen Landwirtschaft, die den Bauernhof, eventuell sogar als Hochhausstruktur, in die Großstadt holt. Damit wäre eine direktere und autarke Stadtversorgung mit frischen Nahrungsmitteln gewährleistet. Vielleicht würde mit dieser neuen städtischen Agrikultur und der entsprechenden „Agritecture" auch der Boden für dörfliche Sozialstrukturen mitten in der Stadt bereitet. Statt urbaner Verslumung, Ghettoisierung und Vereinsamung wären die Stadtbewohner, neben ihrem digitalisierten Nomadendasein und globalen Networking, in agrikulturelle Dorfgemeinschaften eingebunden.

    Selbst wenn das Worst-Case-Szenario der Klimakatastrophe die Weltstädte mit meterhoher Überflutung heimsuchen sollte, liegen bereits heute durchgeplante visionäre Entwürfe für schwimmende Städte, Unterwassermetropolen und urbane Siedlungen im All vor.

B+U
LOS ANGELES, USA

"It always requires a leap of faith for a culture to move forward. If something is new, it always seems too complex, too unusual, too out of context, impossible to build… If we can't develop a vision for our future, we don't know where we are going. Thus it is important to imagine what architecture will look like in 200 years from now, so it can inform what we are designing and building today."

„Wenn sich eine Kultur weiterentwickeln will, gelingt ihr das nur mit neuem Denken. Etwas völlig Neues gilt immer als zu komplex, zu ungewöhnlich, zu zusammenhanglos, nicht umsetzbar… Wenn wir keine Vision für unsere Zukunft entwickeln können, wissen wir nicht, wohin wir gehen. Deshalb ist es wichtig sich vorzustellen, wie die Architektur in 200 Jahren aussehen wird und sich davon für die heutigen Entwürfe und Bauten inspirieren zu lassen."

CITY FUTURA, 2010

Proposition for Milan 2210, Italy

- View from the City Futura of the original city beneath.
- Blick aus der City Futura auf die darunterliegende, ursprüngliche Stadt.

PAGE/SEITE 18–19
- Like an organic network City Futura soars over the city of Milan in 2210.
- Wie ein organisches Geflecht erhebt sich die City Futura im Jahr 2210 über der Stadt Mailand.

● ENGLISCH City Futura is a visionary design concept, suggesting a solution for the expansion of Milan in the year 2210. The project is part of a development plan for fifteen locations along the outer edge of the ring road around town. City Futura is meant to be an addition to the present city, which will leave most buildings intact. Today´s infrastructure will be integrated and expanded. The structure, which will soar 600 meters over the city and cover an area of about one million square kilometers, will be divided into nine sections according to their purpose, like administration, entertainment and leisure, art and culture, and fashion and production. At first, these nine sections seem to be empty spheric spaces, scattered over the area at random and floating above ground. They are plate warmers of different sizes, representing enormous stages with a diameter of up to 250 meters that offer space for citizens´ activities, for example a future amphitheater with 5,000 seats. These public super-centers form a scaffolding and the core of a new kind of urban texture. This arrangement, however, will neither be subject to the usual building regulations nor be confined to the boundaries of a two-dimensional map, but is based on a model of growth and the concept of integrating individual structures into larger sub-systems between and around public junctions. These, again, will be connected in order to form an even larger system that will cover the entire city. While soaring over the city, the structure shows its bottom side like yet another, a sixth, facade, thus making it possible to rethink the city "from below". B+U also takes into consideration how people would move about in this floating city, thereby changing their perception of space. The sections can be described best as public outdoor spaces, stretching vertically and horizontally like spheres with large openings to let in the daylight and to offer a view around the "old" city.

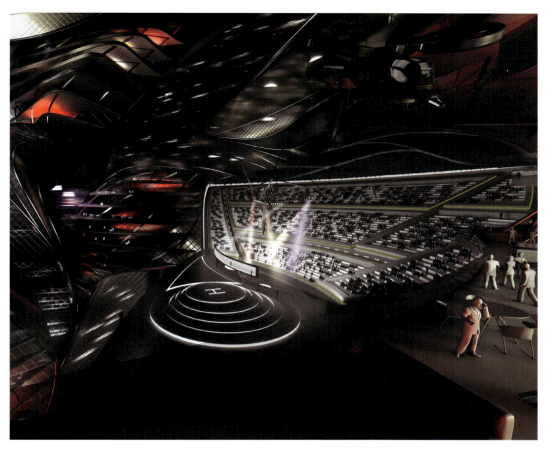

- The design concept offers enormous space for citizens' activities.
- Der Gestaltungsentwurf bietet Raum für gewaltige Bürgerspielstätten.

● The architectural firm B+U is located in Los Angeles, California, and was founded by Herwig Baumgartner and Scott Urio in 1999. Today it is involved in major international projects (Nam June Paik Museum in Kyonggi, Korea; Grand Egyptian Museum in Cairo, Egypt; New Opera in Oslo, Norway). The team sees its mission in constantly expanding the boundaries of architecture and urban planning, while experimenting with artistic and technical elements that leave the confines of traditional architecture. In order to illustrate its visionary concepts, B+U uses 3D digital technology and also traditionell models. The architectural firm especially concentrates on sustainable concepts and the use of thermal and solar energy systems as well as environmental-friendly materials.

● Das Architekturbüro B+U mit Sitz in Los Angeles, Kalifornien, wurde 1999 von Herwig Baumgartner und Scott Urio gegründet und ist inzwischen weltweit mit großen Projekten (Nam June Paik Museum in Kyonggi, Korea; Grand Egyptian Museum in Kairo, Ägypten; Neues Opernhaus in Oslo, Norwegen) vertreten. Seine Aufgabe sieht das Team vor allem darin, die Grenzen von Architektur und Stadtplanung ständig zu erweitern sowie mit künstlerischen und technischen Bereichen zu experimentieren, die eigentlich außerhalb des architektonischen Rahmens liegen. Um seine visionären Entwürfe zu veranschaulichen, nutzt B+U 3D-Digitaltechnologien sowie traditionelle Modelle. Schwerpunkte in der Arbeit des Architekturbüros bilden nachhaltige Konzepte sowie der Einsatz von thermalen und solaren Energiesystemen sowie neuen, umweltschonenden Baumaterialien.

● DEUTSCH City Futura ist ein visionärer Gestaltungsentwurf einer Stadterweiterung für Mailand im Jahr 2210. Das Projekt ist Teil eines Entwicklungsplans für 15 Standorte entlang des äußeren Stadtrings. City Futura wird so auf die existierende Stadt aufgesetzt, dass die meisten bestehenden Gebäude intakt bleiben. Die bereits vorhandene Infrastruktur wird aufgegriffen und erweitert. Die 600 m hohe Konstruktion über der Stadt bedeckt eine Fläche von rund einer Million m². Das Baugefüge ist in neun Stadtbezirke aufgeteilt, die unterschiedlichen Nutzungen, wie Verwaltung, Unterhaltung und Erholung, Kunst und Kultur sowie Mode und Produktion entsprechen. Zunächst erscheinen diese neun Bezirke als leere sphärische Räume, die, willkürlich auf den Standort verteilt, über der Erde schweben. Sie sind unterschiedlich große Platzhalter für gewaltige Bürgerspielstätten mit einem Durchmesser von bis zu 250 m, so z. B. für ein geplantes Amphitheater mit 5.000 Sitzplätzen. Die öffentlichen Superzentren bilden das Gerüst, um das herum eine neue Art von städtischer Textur geschaffen werden soll. Diese Formation wird allerdings nicht von den üblichen Bauvorschriften innerhalb eines zweidimensionalen Stadtplans festgelegt. Vielmehr beruht sie auf einem Wachstumsmodell und auf dem Gedanken, Baukörper zusammenzufassen, die größere Subsysteme zwischen den öffentlichen Knotenpunkten und um sie herum bilden. Diese wurden wiederum miteinander verbunden, um ein noch größeres System entstehen zu lassen, das sich großflächig über die Stadt erstreckt. Die sich über ihr erhebende Struktur zeigt ihre Unterseite als eine weitere, sechste Fassade. So kann die Stadt „von Grund auf" neu erdacht werden. B+U stellt Überlegungen an, wie sich ein Mensch in dieser schwebenden Stadt bewegen und wie sich dementsprechend seine Raumwahrnehmung verändern würde. Die Bezirke lassen sich am besten als öffentliche Räume im Freien beschreiben, die sich vertikal und horizontal wie Sphären mit großen Öffnungen für das Tageslicht ausdehnen und einen Rundumblick auf die „alte" Stadt gewähren.

THE WHY FACTORY (T?F)
DELFT, THE NETHERLANDS

"It is our demand that the urban future has to be explored, theorized, and politicized as the true territory of architecture."

„Wir fordern, die urbane Zukunft als wahres Terrain der Architektur zu erforschen, zu theoretisieren und zu politisieren."

CITY PIG, 2009

The Hague, The Netherlands

• In City Pig pig sties could also be stacked on top of each other for lack of space. It also would be possible to house pigs in the many empty office buildings.
• In der City Pig könnten aus Platzmangel die Schweineställe übereinandergestapelt werden. In der Stadt wäre die Unterbringung der Tiere auch in den vielen leer stehenden Bürogebäuden möglich.

● ENGLISCH   Breeding pigs, in the old days, used to be a routine part of urban life, but meanwhile has become an industry located the outskirts of our settlements and hardly noticed by the public. The project City Pig explores the possibility to again make breeding pigs a visible part of urban life with an ecological impact. To this end, a number of concepts have been explored: pig bridges, stacked sties, and the use of office buildings to produce pork. The biogas emitted by the animals supplies the city with energy. Another option would be to house the pigs in municipal parks – with nearby butcher shops and restaurants, where customers could see where the meat comes from. The many empty office and commercial buildings also could be used to breed pigs in order to productively recapture these urban spaces. With their project The Why Factory wants to weigh the pros and cons of bringing pigs back into our cities.

● DEUTSCH   Die Schweinezucht war früher ein normaler Bestandteil des städtischen Lebens. Heute dagegen ist sie eine außerhalb der Städte angesiedelte Industrie, die kaum wahrgenommen wird. Bei dem Projekt City Pig wird eruiert, ob man aus der Schweinezucht wieder einen sichtbaren, ökologisch wirksamen Bestandteil des Stadtlebens machen kann. Dafür werden verschiedene Typologien getestet: Schweinebrücken, gestapelte Ställe und Bürogebäude, in denen Schweinefleisch produziert wird. Das aus den Exkrementen der Tiere erzeugte Biogas würde die Stadt mit Energie versorgen. Die Schweine könnten auch in innerstädtischen Parks gehalten werden – mit begleitenden Schlachtereien und Gaststätten, sodass die Konsumenten die Herkunft des Schweinefleisches direkt vor Augen haben. Es wäre auch möglich, die städtische Schweinezucht in die vielen leerstehenden Büro- und Geschäftshäuser zu verlagern; so würden diese urbanen Räume wieder sinnvoller genutzt. The Why Factory stellt mit ihrem Projekt die Frage: Was kostet es uns, und was können wir gewinnen, wenn wir die Schweine wieder in die Städte holen?

HANGING FOOD GARDENS, 2009

Barcelona, Spain

- Produce like grain, fruit, and vegetables are grown in hothouses, hanging over the city of Barcelona.
- Der Anbau von Nahrungsmitteln wie Getreide, Obst und Gemüse erfolgt in über der Stadt Barcelona hängenden Gewächshäusern.

• ENGLISCH   For the series Dream Green-Projects The Why Factory has developed a system of hothouses, hanging over the Spanish city of Barcelona, to provide plenty of produce for its population. As meat production would be discontinued due to its high costs, people would have to adopt a vegetarian lifestyle. In the hothouses above the roofs of Barcelona, also called "food shelves", sufficient amounts of grain, fruit, and vegetables would be grown. These "food shelves" consist of light-weight materials. At harvest time helium balloons are used to take weight off the machines. The plants form a floating field, accessible by a number of skyways, which are also used for harvesting and transporting the produce.

• DEUTSCH   In der Reihe der Dream-Green-Projekte schlägt The Why Factory am Beispiel der spanischen Stadt Barcelona ein System von über der Stadt hängenden Gewächshäusern vor, die die City ausreichend mit Nahrungsmitteln versorgen. Die Ernährung der Bewohner müsste auf rein vegetarische Kost umgestellt werden, denn die Fleischproduktion würde aus Kostengründen abgeschafft. In den Gewächshäusern über den Dächern Barcelonas würde hinreichend Getreide, Obst und Gemüse angebaut. Diese sogenannten „Nahrungsregale" bestehen aus Leichtbaumaterialien. Um auch die Maschinen möglichst leicht zu machen, hilft ein Heliumballon bei der Ernte. Die Pflanzen wachsen zu einem schwebenden Getreidefeld heran. Ein Netzwerk aus Skyways bildet den Zugang zu den Nahrungsmittelfabriken. Über diese Skyways wird auch geerntet und das Erntegut abtransportiert.

• The Why Factory (t?f) is a new global and urban think tank and a joint research facility founded by the architectural firm MVRDV and the technical university of Delft, Netherlands. It is headed by Winy Maas. The Why Factory explores options to create better ecological conditions in our cities by developing models and visionary illustrations of future ones.

• The Why Factory (t?f) ist eine neue globale und urbane Denkfabrik, eine gemeinsame Forschungseinrichtung des Architekturbüros MVRDV und der Technischen Universität Delft in den Niederlanden. Geleitet wird sie von Winy Maas. The Why Factory lotet aus, wie sich unsere Städte unter besseren ökologischen Bedingungen entwickeln könnten, indem sie sich auf die Erarbeitung von Modellen und visionären Darstellungen zukünftiger Städte konzentriert.

CONSTRUCTING URBAN FUTURES

The Why Factory (t?f) is an exploratory body that analyzes, theorizes and constructs future cities. t?f operates from the purity and beauty of science and fiction. It thus studies the future cityscapes through a direct activation and envisioning of urban and architectural interventions. t?f sees its goal in confronting immediate actualities of our world with their urban implications. It wants to advocate the necessity to research, theorize and politicize the urban future as the actual territory of architecture.

t?f investigates within the given world and produces future scenarios beyond it; from universal to specific and global to local. It wants to intervene and act as direct as possible to encourage potentials and possibilities of the actual. t?f proposes, constructs and envisions hypothetical societies and cities, from science to fiction and vice versa. The research program of The Why Factory aims at revealing possible directions of our urban future. It concentrates on the production of models and visualizations for future cities.

STRATEGY
The Why Factory critically addresses the role of the architect in our society. It encourages closer collaboration with all parties involved in the making of the city. t?f thus raises issues and questions which concern a variety of disciplines; from philosophy and sociology to urban planning, architecture and product design. It wants to enlarge the argumentative power of the architectural and urbanistic profession.

THE TRIPOD
The future city is evidently not one city. It is built out of many future cities. Each based on its own set of parameters. In the program they are positioned in a classical research triad of models, views and a controller, of model cities, applications and storage which will be accompanied in time with evaluations and discussions, the Why Talks. Each resulting in a series of books, films and games.

MODEL CITIES
In the model city program, abstract cities appear by focusing each on its own limited set of parameters that allow for maximal exploration of a specific subject in order to engage with possible futures. t?f seeks for a refined combination of 'science' and 'fiction' in order to bring our dreams and desires closer to reality.

APPLICATIONS
In the applications program model cities are tested in real cities. The different models become counter proposals for existing cities. t?f collaborates with local institutions to test different hypotheses and discusses them with local governments and population.

STORAGE
How can we store all the information that derives from the model city and applications program? Can we create a library that is not only passive but can behave actively? Maybe we can better store all this in gigantic software, an evolutionary game that not only collects this data but as well positions it and makes it visible, comparable and in the end even productive? It combines the role as a 'library' with the one as a 'connector' or a 'communicator' and even 'generator'. It becomes a 'city' itself. An evolutionary city. Such a tool combines the more collective agendas with the individualistic tendencies of current societies; a developing series of 'urban software' is imagined.

The Why Factory (t?f)

ZUKÜNFTIGE STÄDTE BAUEN

The Why Factory (t?f) ist eine Forschungseinrichtung für die Städte der Zukunft. Sie entwirft zukünftige Stadtbilder, im Hinblick darauf, welche urbanen und architektonischen Eingriffe vorgenommen werden müssen. The Why Factory konfrontiert die Realitäten unserer Welt mit deren urbanen Auswirkungen. Sie fordert, die urbane Zukunft als wahres Terrain der Architektur zu erforschen, zu theoretisieren und zu politisieren.

t?f forscht im Heute und bringt Szenarien hervor, die darüber hinausweisen: vom Universellen zum Spezifischen und vom Globalen zum Lokalen. The Why Factory will intervenieren und ist bemüht, so direkt wie möglich zu handeln, um so Potenziale und Chancen des Gegebenen auszuloten. t?f entwirft, erträumt und baut hypothetische Gesellschaften und Städte, vom Wissenschaftlichen zum Fantastischen und umgekehrt. Das Forschungsprogramm der Why Factory will mögliche Richtungen unserer urbanen Zukunft offenlegen. Schwerpunkt ist die Erarbeitung von Modellen und anschaulichen Darstellungen zukünftiger Städte.

STRATEGIE

The Why Factory hinterfragt die Rolle des Architekten in unserer Gesellschaft. Sie regt eine enge Zusammenarbeit mit allen am Stadtwerdungsprozess Beteiligten an. t?f stellt Fragen, die in vielen Disziplinen behandelt werden können, von der Philosophie und Soziologie über die Stadtplanung und Architektur bis hin zum Produktdesign. Sie möchte insbesondere den Berufen, die sich mit Architektur und Städtebau beschäftigen, mehr Gehör verschaffen.

DIE DREI SÄULEN

Die Stadt der Zukunft ist nicht eine Stadt, sondern setzt sich aus mehreren Städten zusammen, von denen jede auf eigenen Parametern beruht. Diese werden in einem klassischen dreigliedrigen Forschungsansatz positioniert: Modelle, Ansichten und Kontrollinstanz beziehungsweise Modellstädte, Anwendungen und Archivierung, die von Überprüfungsphasen und Diskussionen, den Why Talks, begleitet werden. Letztere schlagen sich in Büchern, Filmen und Spielen nieder.

MODELLSTÄDTE

Im Modellstädte-Programm erscheinen abstrakte Städte, von denen jede auf ihren eigenen begrenzten Faktoren basiert, die die bestmögliche Erforschung eines Themas im Hinblick auf eine mögliche Zukunft erlauben. t?f sucht nach einer präzisen Kombination von Wissenschaft und Fiktion, um unsere Träume und Wünsche einen Schritt näher an die Realität heranzuführen.

ANWENDUNGEN

Im Anwendungs-Programm werden Modellstädte in realen Städten getestet. Die verschiedenen Modelle werden zu Gegenvorschlägen für bestehende Städte. t?f arbeitet mit lokalen Institutionen zusammen, um verschiedene Hypothesen zu überprüfen und sie mit lokalen Entscheidungsgremien und der Bevölkerung zu diskutieren.

ARCHIVIERUNG

Wie können wir all die Informationen speichern, die im Modellstädte- und im Anwendungs-Programm anfallen? Ist es möglich, eine „Bibliothek" zu schaffen, die nicht nur passiv ist? Vielleicht sollten wir alles in einem riesigen Speicher archivieren, in einem sich ständig weiterentwickelnden Spiel, das nicht nur die Daten sammelt, sondern sie auch selbstständig produktiv weiterverarbeitet. Ein solches Werkzeug würde die „Bibliothek" zu einem „Vermittler" oder gar „Generator" erweitern – es würde selbst zu einer „Stadt", einer evolutionären Stadt. Und es würde eher kollektive Vorhaben mit den individualistischen Tendenzen unserer heutigen Gesellschaften in Einklang bringen. Vorstellbar wäre eine sich entwickelnde „urbane Software".

The Why Factory (t?f)

MAD
BEIJING, CHINA

"At a time when sustainable ecology and energy savings are driven by the demand for comfort, we are afraid that the yearning of a return to nature is ignored."

„Zu einer Zeit, in der nachhaltiges Handeln und Energiesparen in erster Linie vom Verlangen nach Komfort gesteuert werden, beobachten wir mit Sorge, die Ignoranz gegenüber der Sehnsucht nach einer Rückkehr zur Natur."

BEIJING 2050, 2006

Beijing, China

● ENGLISCH   The Olympic Games of 2008 in Beijing fuelled the dream of turning the city into the perfect metropolis in the years that followed. Thus, for MAD the time has come to devise a concept for the city´s future. With past, present, and future in view, they introduce three projects to bring about Beijing´s imminent change. This step, however, is not meant to be a radical act of rebellion, but rather an attempt to suggest innovation without turning one´s back on tradition. The changes Tianamen Square underwent during the last decades reflect this attitude that prevails in modern China. By the year 2050 China will have become a mature democracy, making large squares as stages for political parades superfluous. What will Tianamen Square look like when it has no more political and traffic-related function? Will it, perhaps, be a park for Beijing´s population? In 2050 Tianamen will be an urban space teeming with life, the green heart in the center of Beijing.

The business dstrict, which dates from the last century and was planned following a Western model, will be turned into a downtown area, reflecting the needs of a post-Western and post-industrial society. New solutions for the densely populated Chinese city as such have to be found. Therefore, the new Beijing has to be designed as an entity instead of randomly setting up individual "glass boxes", each one trying to tower over its neighbor. Computer labs, multi-media centers, theaters, restaurants, libraries, touristic landmarks, gyms, and even an artificial lake will soar over today´s business district like gigantic mushroom-like plateaus, thus creating a new horizontal connection.

- Beijing in 2050: mushroom-like plateaus soar over the business district, offering space for natural reserves as well as for cultural and athletic facilities.
- Peking im Jahr 2050: Pilzähnliche Plateaus erheben sich über der Geschäftsstadt und bieten Platz für Naturparks, Kultur- und Sporteinrichtungen.

● DEUTSCH

Die Olympischen Spiele 2008 in Peking waren während der letzten Jahre das Symbol schlechthin für die Träume von einer idealen Metropole Peking. Für MAD scheint es nun an der Zeit, die weitere Zukunft dieser Stadt zu entwerfen. Mit der Vergangenheit, Gegenwart und Zukunft vor Augen stellen sie drei Projekte vor, die Pekings anstehende Veränderungen aufgreifen. Sie verstehen das weder als einen rebellischen noch radikalen Akt. Sie wollen vielmehr etwas Neues vorschlagen und nicht Altes kritisieren. Die Veränderungen, die am Tiananmen-Platz in den letzten Jahrzehnten vorgenommen wurden, spiegeln diese geistige Haltung der chinesischen Nation wider. Bis zum Jahr 2050 wird ein reifes und demokratisches China entstehen, Plätze für große politische Aufmärsche werden nicht mehr nötig sein. Wie wird der Tiananmen-Platz aussehen, wenn er keine politische oder verkehrstechnische Funktion mehr hat? Wie wäre es mit einem Park für die Bevölkerung Pekings? 2050 wird Tiananmen ein mit Leben gefüllter städtischer Ort sein, das grüne Herz im Zentrum der Metropole.

Der zentrale Geschäftsbezirk, der im letzten Jahrhundert nach westlichen Vorbildern geplant wurde, soll in ein Stadtzentrum für eine postwestliche und postindustrielle Gesellschaft umgewandelt werden. Wie wird die dicht besiedelte chinesische Stadt der Zukunft aussehen? Die urbane Zukunft Pekings muss zusammenhängend geplant werden, sie darf nicht aus einzelnen „Glaskästen" bestehen, von denen jeder der höchste sein will. Computer-Studios, Multimedia-Zentren, Theater, Restaurants, Bibliotheken, Sehenswürdigkeiten, Sporthallen und selbst ein künstlicher See werden sich in Form von gigantischen Pilzplateaus über den heutigen Geschäftsbezirk erheben und eine neue horizontale Verbindung schaffen.

PAGE/SEITE 28–29
- The mushroom-like plateaus serve as the metropolis´s green lungs and are accessible by zeppelins.
- Die Pilzplateaus sind die grüne Lunge der Metropole und sollen durch Zeppeline erreichbar sein.

SUPERSTAR:
A MOBILE CHINA TOWN, 2008

● ENGLISCH   The traditional Chinatown, marked by stores, gas stations, and fast-food establishments, has become redundant and looks the same all over the world. Today, it mostly consists of restaurants and pseudo-historical buildings, presenting a sentimental image of China that no longer bears any relation to contemporary life. The old part of town has morphed into a historical theme-park, an urban eyesore that calls for a radical approach. Superstar, a "mobile Chinatown" by MAD, is the answer to a hybrid and obsolete concept of Chinatown. It is a mobile structure and a thoroughly designed and modern solution, where high-quality products and cultural events can be enjoyed and creativity and education will thrive. Therefore, the way this new community functions is as important as its essence. Superstar works as a "benign virus", setting free the unknown energies that float between random changes and structured continuity. Like a spaceship it is able to land anywhere on earth to infect the world with the "new Chinese energy". Superstar is an autonomous unit: it produces its own food, does not consume any of its host´s resources, and recycles its garbage. It is a space with an authentic Chinese atmosphere, offering facilities for leisure and sports as well as freshwater reservoirs. There even is a digital cemetery to commemorate the dead. Superstar is a dream and could be home to 15,000 people – without hierarchies and without making distinctions between its citizens. It just wants to be a fusion of technology and nature, future, and the mere fact of being human.

● DEUTSCH   Mit Einkaufszentren, Tankstellen und Schnellimbiss-Filialen ist das klassische Modell „Chinatown" in den Städten der Welt langweilig und austauschbar geworden. Im Wesentlichen besteht es heute aus Restaurants und pseudo-historischen Gebäuden. Hier wird ein verkitschtes Bild Chinas gezeigt, das nichts mehr mit dem heutigen Leben zu tun hat. Diese Stadtbezirke sind zu historischen Themenparks verkommen, die den städtischen Raum vergiften. Superstar, eine Art „mobiles Chinatown" von MAD, ist die Antwort auf ein hybrides und überholtes Chinatown-Konzept. Er soll ein Ort sein, an dem man hochwertige Produkte und kulturelle Veranstaltungen genießen kann und wo sich Kreativität und Bildung entfalten können. Ebenso wichtig wie die Inhalte dieser neuen Community ist ihre Funktionsweise. MAD versteht Superstar als einen „gutartigen Virus", der unbekannte Energien freisetzt, die zwischen prinzipienlosen Veränderungen und prinzipientreuer Beständigkeit pendeln. Er kann als Raumschiff überall auf der Welt landen und die „neue chinesische Energie" auf die Umwelt übertragen. Superstar ist autark: Er produziert seine Nahrung selbst, braucht keine Ressourcen von seinem Gastgeber und recycelt seinen Müll. Er ist ein Quartier von authentischem chinesischen Charakter, mit Erholungseinrichtungen, Sportanlagen und Trinkwasser-Reservoirs. Es gibt sogar einen digitalen Friedhof, der an die Toten erinnert. Superstar ist ein Traum, der 15.000 Menschen eine Heimstatt verspricht – ohne Hierarchien, ohne Unterschiede zwischen seinen Bürgern, einfach nur eine Fusion aus Technik und Natur, aus Zukunft und Menschsein.

• Superstar, a new mobile Chinatown, will be an autonomous city and an entity in itself, which can be placed anywhere in the world like an oversize star.
• Superstar, eine Art neues mobiles Chinatown, soll eine autarke Stadt sein, die als überdimensionaler Stern an verschiedenen Orten der Welt platziert werden kann.

• Superstar, as a mobile section of town, will blend with any landscape like a star fallen from heaven.
• Wie ein vom Himmel gefallener Stern soll sich Superstar als mobile Stadteinheit in jede Landschaft einfügen.

URBAN FOREST, 2009

Proposal for Chongqing, China

● ENGLISCH MAD suggests a new architectural concept for urban development in China: a sustainable, multi-dimensional highrise in Chongqing, China's newest city. The philosophy behind it is to reintegrate nature into a densely populated urban space to enable city dwellers to form a relationship with their environment in the way it went without saying in traditional China. Chongqing's urbanization, which is taking place on a large scale, is not meant to only promote economic growth and the generation of wealth, but also the city's cultural development. Many Chinese cities have been designed on the drawing board, following the path of modern Western urbanization. Currently, the expansion of the economic infrastructure focuses on China's interior region. Which chances lie in the future of China's cities? What to do about densely populated Chinese cities like Chongqing, surrounded by a picturesque landscape?

The project Urban Forest draws its inspiration from the view Eastern philosophy takes on nature and man, and links city life with outdoor nature experience. The building's shape resembles a mountain-range that moves in a dynamic rhythm, while becoming the extension of an exuberant nature. Urban Forest symbolizes the great dream of Chinese architecture: an urban landmark that has its roots in embracing nature – not a static monument, but an organic shape that constantly changes with human perception.

● DEUTSCH MAD schlägt ein neues architektonisches Konzept für die Stadtentwicklung in China vor: ein nachhaltiges, mehrdimensionales Hochhaus, entwickelt für Chongqing, der jüngsten Stadtgründung Chinas. In naher Zukunft soll dort die Natur wieder in die hochverdichtete städtische Umwelt eingegliedert werden, damit der Stadtmensch von heute erneut einen Bezug zur Natur findet, wie es in der alten asiatischen Welt noch selbstverständlich war. Die im großen Maßstab stattfindende Urbanisierung von Chongqing soll nicht nur zum Wirtschaftswachstum und zur Schaffung von Wohlstand beitragen, sondern auch die kulturelle Entwicklung der Stadt fördern. Viele chinesische Städte wurden am Reißbrett entworfen und sind den Weg der zeitgenössischen westlichen Urbanisierung gegangen. Zurzeit orientiert sich der Ausbau der ökonomischen Infrastruktur auf das chinesische Binnenland. Welche Chancen liegen in der Zukunft der Städte? Wie soll mit den neu entstehenden, hochverdichteten chinesischen Städten wie beispielsweise dem landschaftlich reizvollen Chongqing umgegangen werden?

Das Projekt Urban Forest bezieht seine Inspiration aus der Betrachtung von Natur und Mensch in der fernöstlichen Philosophie und verbindet das Stadtleben mit der unmittelbaren Naturerfahrung. Die Form des Gebäudes erinnert an einen Gebirgszug, der sich in einem dynamischen Rhythmus bewegt und zu einer Fortsetzung der wuchernden Natur wird. Urban Forest steht für einen großen Traum in der zeitgenössischen chinesischen Architektur: als ein städtisches Wahrzeichen, das aus der Hinwendung zur Natur entsteht – kein statisches Symbol, sondern eine organische Form, die sich mit der Wahrnehmung der Menschen ständig verändert.

• The individual floors of Urban Forest are designed as exuberant natural units, offering new organic spaces with lots of plant-life, light, and air.
• Die einzelnen Geschosse von Urban Forest sind als wuchernde Natureinheiten konzipiert, die neue organische Räume mit viel Grün, Licht und Luft schaffen.

• Urban Forest, a special highrise among the skyscrapers of Chongqing, China
• Urban Forest liegt als spezielle Hochhauseinheit zwischen den Skyscrapern im chinesischen Chongqing.

• The view of Urban Forest and the city beyond illustrates the philosophy of "woodlands in the city".
• Der Blick auf Urban Forest und die dahinter liegende Stadt verdeutlicht die Idee des „Waldes in der Stadt".

● The architectural firm MAD in Beijing is headed by Ma Yansong, Yosuke Hayano, and Qun Dand. Its visionary concepts are the harbingers of a new era, promoting the architectural realization of concepts taken from contemporary art, reflecting the current lifestyle, and applying multimedia formats to the urban structures of modern China. MAD looks out for the flexibility contained in simple and traditional processes and tries to transport them into the future. By using new forms of organization and innovative approaches, the values, aims, cultural influences, and political conditions of contemporary China are analyzed. Because these factors, in the view of MAD, are in an ever dynamic flow, their concepts and buildings are not isolated objects, but natural elements that blend in with everyday life and the urban environment.

● Das Architekturbüro MAD in Peking wird von Ma Yansong, Yosuke Hayano und Qun Dand geführt. Ihre visionären Entwürfe künden vom Beginn einer neuen Ära. Sie propagieren die architektonische Umsetzung von Konzepten aus der zeitgenössischen Kunst, reflektieren den aktuellen Lifestyle und übertragen Multimediaformate auf die urbanen Strukturen des heutigen China. MAD sucht nach der Flexibilität in einfachen und traditionellen Funktionen und versucht sie in die Zukunft zu transformieren. Dazu werden neue Formen der Organisation und des Denkens genutzt, mit denen Werte, Wünsche, Kultur und politische Macht des heutigen China analysiert werden. Die Architekten fassen diese Faktoren als fließend und dynamisch auf; dadurch sind ihre Entwürfe und Bauten keine isolierten Objekte mehr, sondern werden zu natürlichen und stimmigen Elementen des Alltags und des Stadtumfeldes.

LET'S HEAD FOR UTOPIA

Utopia is often said to be a silly waste of time, far removed from reality, and at best a romantic dream. But do we not precisely in an age of climate change need an idea of what our life could be like in a century's time?

Architecture is home to a long and colorful series of images of the future – and the list grew longer and more radical, more contradictory and different as the 20th century progressed. Starting with the smooth Renaissance drawings of ideal cities the line moved on to the zestful highways of cities designed for cars and then to the interlocking high-rise cities of the Futurists, Metabolists and Structuralists or the floating city-spheres that were the stuff of Buckminster Fuller's dreams, for one.

Are architects the born utopians? As part of their work they are always producing ideal drawings of a more or less remote future any way. But on paper the cities always look more ideal and the houses more perfect as usually there are no people. Architectural utopias are almost always shaped by a robust rejection of the present. They are (counter) notions of a different world. Extending the timeline to 100 years or more serves to point things up. Future scenarios take up current processes or technologies and think them through to their logical conclusions. Will we be producing our own electricity in our cellars and own flying cars driven by hydrogen in 100 years' time? What will our cities then look like? What must we already factor in given the rising sea level and temperatures? Where do these ideas go?

In fact, utopia is not so much a romantic dream. For such a visualization of the future is extremely important in order to gain a clearer picture of things and to drive the collective imagination. It provides substance for debate and serves to highlight the impact of our actions today. And of course it also drives that thoroughly pleasant and ongoing human effort to create a better world. At the beginning of the 21st century, in the age of cities and climate change, proposed solutions in the sense of potentialities are more important than ever. And alternatives are definitely called for in the context of the ever broader discussion of the problematic concept of sustainability. But now that we turn to face utopia we are forced to concede that it has a far harder time of it. There is no longer anything that does not already exist. We are already planning cities for millions of people, travel into outer space and down into the depths of the oceans.

Future visions are essentially reflections that we hold up in order to understand the present. The intention is to think the impossible and show it. We do not after all know how our world will look 100 or 1,000 years from now. But we can try to be aware of the consequences of our actions. The question is not: How will we live? The question is: How do we wish to live? The best way of predicting the future is to actively shape it. And there's a certain need to dream in this regard. Perhaps it is specifically the architects who must find images for these dreams in order to sharpen our eye for the present.

Florian Heilmeyer

UTOPIA VOR AUGEN

Der Utopie wird oft nachgesagt, sie sei versponnene Zeitverschwendung, eine realitätsferne, bestenfalls romantische Träumerei. Aber brauchen wir nicht gerade in Zeiten des Klimawandels eine Vorstellung davon, wie unser Leben in 100 Jahren aussehen könnte?

Die Reihe der Zukunftsbilder in der Architektur ist bunt und lang – und wird bis ins 20. Jahrhundert hinein stets länger und radikaler, widersprüchlicher und unterschiedlicher: Von den glatten Idealstadtzeichnungen der Renaissance geht die Reise zu den schwungvollen Highways der autogerechten Städte und weiter zu den verschachtelten Hochhaus-Städten der Futuristen, Metabolisten und Strukturalisten oder den schwebenden Stadtkugeln, von denen etwa Buckminster Fuller träumte.

Sind Architekten die geborenen Utopisten? Im Rahmen ihrer Arbeit produzieren sie sowieso andauernd ideale Zeichnungen einer mehr oder weniger weit entfernten Zukunft. Aber auf dem Papier sehen die Städte stets idealer aus und die Häuser perfekter. Denn meist fehlen die Menschen. Architektonische Utopien sind fast immer von einer starken Ablehnung der Gegenwart geprägt. Sie sind (Gegen-)Vorstellungen einer anderen Welt. Das Strecken des Zeithorizonts auf eine Distanz von 100 Jahren oder mehr dient der Überzeichnung. Zukunftsszenarien greifen gegenwärtige Prozesse oder Technologien auf und denken sie konsequent weiter. Werden wir in 100 Jahren alle unseren eigenen Strom im Keller produzieren und Flugautos besitzen, die Wasserstoff tanken? Wie sehen dann unsere Städte aus? Was müssen wir wegen des steigenden Meeresspiegels und der Temperatur heute schon bedenken? Wohin führen diese Ideen?

Tatsächlich ist die Utopie also nicht so sehr romantische Träumerei. Denn eine solche Visualisierung der Zukunft ist für die Meinungsbildung und die kollektive Vorstellungskraft extrem wichtig. Sie liefert Diskussionsstoff und dient der Bewusstmachung der Konsequenzen unseres gegenwärtigen Handelns. Und natürlich ist sie Motor des grundsympathischen und andauernden Strebens des Menschen nach einer besseren Welt. Zu Beginn des 21. Jahrhunderts – im Zeitalter der Städte und des Klimawandels – sind Lösungsvorschläge im Sinne von Möglichkeitsräumen wichtiger denn je. Im Zusammenhang mit der immer breiter geführten Diskussion um den schwierigen Begriff der Nachhaltigkeit werden Alternativen geradezu erwartet. Aber nun, da wir uns der Utopie zuwenden, müssen wir feststellen, dass sie es heute viel schwerer hat. Es gibt ja nichts mehr, was es nicht gibt. Wir planen bereits Städte für Millionen Menschen, wir reisen ins All und in die Tiefsee.

Zukunftsvisionen sind letztlich die Spiegelbilder, die wir uns vorhalten, um unsere Gegenwart zu verstehen. Es gilt, das Unmögliche zu denken – und zu zeigen. Wir wissen ja nicht, wie unsere Welt in 100 oder 1.000 Jahren aussehen wird. Aber wir können versuchen, uns der Konsequenzen unserer Handlungen bewusst zu werden. Die Frage lautet nicht: Wie werden wir leben? Die Frage lautet: Wie wollen wir leben? Denn die beste Art die Zukunft vorherzusagen ist, sie aktiv zu gestalten. Dabei gibt es eine gewisse Notwendigkeit, zu träumen. Vielleicht ist es speziell an den Architekten, diesen Träumen Gestalt zu geben, um den Blick auf unsere Gegenwart zu schärfen.

Florian Heilmeyer

JOHN WARDLE ARCHITECTS AND STEFANO BOSCUTTI

LOS ANGELES, USA
MELBOURNE, AUSTRALIA

"Our work as architects will become more complex, interweaving many strands of thinking, whilst yearning for intimate detail and clarity more than ever before."

„Die Arbeit der Architekten wird komplexer werden und viele Gedankengänge miteinander verknüpfen, während das Verlangen nach feinsten Details und größter Klarheit stark zunimmt."

MULTIPLICITY, 2010

Proposition for the City of Melbourne, Australia

Shown at the Australian Pavilion,
12th International Architecture Exhibition,
La Biennale di Venezia 2010.

● ENGLISCH   For a future Melbourne, Australia, in the year 2110 John Wardle, together with Stefano Boscutti, designed Multiplicity as a fictional and speculative project that covers the already high-density upper downtown region with a tent-like structure. This cover, which is grounded in the townscape by substructures equipped with supply units, provides on its surface plots for agriculture, the generation of energy, the collection of rainwater, and air transport. This new green urban zone aims at combating Melbourne's future problems like global warming, air pollution, traffic, and sealed ground surfaces.

● DEUTSCH   Für die Zukunft des australischen Melbourne im Jahr 2110 entwarf John Wardle zusammen mit Stefano Boscutti Multiplicity. Bei diesem fiktionalen, hypothetischen Projekt wird die bereits im oberen Bereich stark verdichtete Innenstadt Melbournes von einer zeltartigen Hülle überfangen. Diese Hülle, die nach unten durch Substruktionen mit Versorgungseinheiten im Stadtbild verankert ist, bildet auf ihrer Oberfläche Parzellen für Landwirtschaft, Energieerzeugung, Regenwassergewinnung und Lufttransport aus. Mit dieser neuen grünen Stadtzone soll den zukünftig anstehenden Problemen für Melbourne wie Klimawandel, Luftverschmutzung, Verkehrschaos und Flächenversiegelung entgegengesteuert werden.

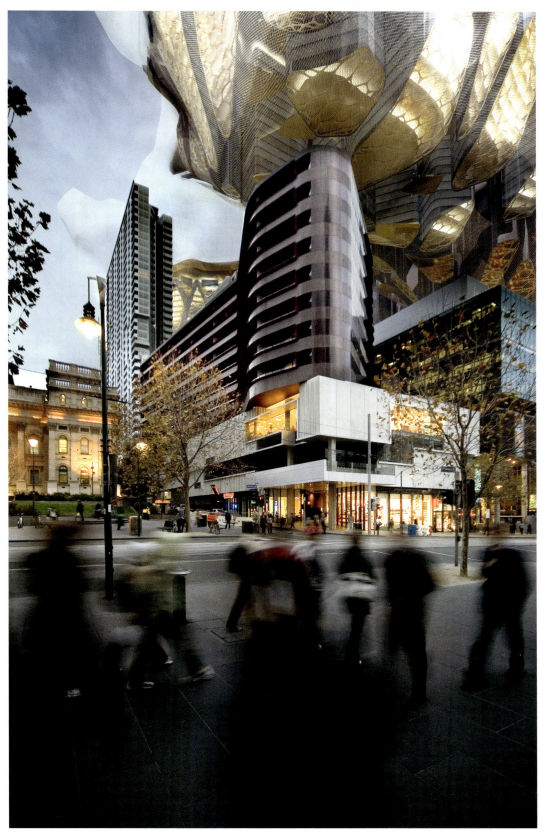

- In 2110 Multiplicity will cover Melbourne´s center like a protective green blanket.
- Multiplicity soll sich im Jahr 2110 wie eine schützende grüne Hülle über die Innenstadt von Melbourne legen.

PAGE/SEITE 42–43
- Multiplicity, Melbourne 2110, a new agricultural zone soars over the city.
- Multiplicity, Melbourne 2110 – eine neue landwirtschaftliche Zone erhebt sich über der Stadt.

- John Wardle Architects, Melbourne, was founded in 1986 and is one of Australia´s most renowned architectural firms. Besides planning and designing family homes, business structures, apartment buildings (QV1-Wardle Tower in Melbourne, 2005), and universities, Wardle´s team is famous for its visionary urban planning, where sustainability and ecology play a major role. The Multiplicity project was realized by John Wardle in association with the award-winning writer and director Stefano Boscutti (photo right).

- John Wardle Architects in Melbourne existiert seit 1986 und ist eines der bekanntesten australischen Architekturbüros. Neben Planungen und Entwürfen für Einfamilienhäuser, Geschäftsbauten, Appartmenthäuser (QV1-Wardle Tower in Melbourne, 2005) und Hochschulgebäude zeichnet sich das Wardle-Team durch seine visionären Stadtentwürfe aus, bei denen Nachhaltigkeit und Ökologie eine große Rolle spielen. Das Projekt Multiplicity hat John Wardle zusammen mit dem preisgekrönten Schriftsteller und Regisseur Stefano Boscutti (Foto rechts) realisiert.

RAG URBANISM
SYDNEY, AUSTRALIA

"The potential energy of buildings acts as an armature for new sustainable systems and the gutting of existing obsolescence, in a fraying urban ground. Landscape becomes urban agriculture and the external vanities of building units collapse into a coral reef of possibility."

„Die potenzielle Energie von Gebäuden dient als Gerüst für neue, nachhaltige Systeme und das Aufbrechen überalterter Strukturen auf ausfransendem urbanen Grund. Landschaft wird zu städtischer Agrikultur und die äußeren Vergänglichkeiten mancher Gebäude kollabieren in ein Korallenriff der Möglichkeiten."

SYDNEY 2050: FRAYING GROUND, 2010

Sydney, Australia

Shown at the Australian Pavilion,
12th International Architecture Exhibition,
La Biennale di Venezia 2010.

- Old city and building structures are broken up, thus making new creative urban designs possible.
- Alte Stadt- und Gebäudestrukturen werden aufgebrochen und ermöglichen die Freisetzung neuer kreativer, urbaner Formen.

● ENGLISCH Already today Sydney gives us a taste of what it might look like in 2050. Thus, Team Rag Urbanism focuses on the potential of change in the status quo rather than developing utopic visions. A remapping of the city, a block, or a building illustrates the different options. After exploring the existing economic, social, ecological, and national network of relationships the city is based on, these structures are broken up, resulting in new urban patterns. In this vision the lines that hold the city together begin to fray, suggesting new forms of control. This can result in the configuration of new buildings, urban spaces, and thoroughfares that meet people´s ever changing economic, environmental, and economic needs.

● DEUTSCH Eine Ahnung davon, wie Sydney im Jahr 2050 aussehen kann, ist bereits in der heutigen Stadt angelegt. Folglich beschäftigt sich das Team Rag Urbanism weniger mit einer utopischen Vision der Stadt, sondern eher mit dem Veränderungspotenzial dessen, was bereits vorhanden ist. Eine Neukartierung der Stadt oder auch eines Blocks oder Gebäudes zeigt diese Möglichkeiten auf. Geht man auf das bereits vorhandene ökonomische, soziale, ökologische und nationale Beziehungsgeflecht ein, das der Stadt zugrunde liegt, ergeben sich durch das Aufbrechen dieser Strukturen neue urbane Muster. In dieser Vision beginnen die Linien, die die Stadt zusammenhalten, auszufransen (fraying), und suggerieren neue Formen der Steuerung. Das kann zur Konfiguration neuer Gebäude, urbaner Plätze und der Verkehrswege führen, die den sich verändernden Bedürfnissen der Bevölkerung, der Umwelt und der Wirtschaft entsprechen.

● The team Rag Urbanism consists of the architects, artists and philosophers Richard Goodwin, Gerard Reinmuth (Terroir Sydney), and Andrew Benjamin, who, coming from different spheres of interest, have made urban development their priority. The model of "Fraying Ground" has been devised by Andrew Benjamin. Richard Goodwin added the concept of a public space, growing out of the old buildings as parasitical architecture. Gerard Reinmuth contributed the presentation of different sliding tectonic elements in an architectural system.

● Das Team Rag Urbanism setzt sich aus den Architekten, Künstlern und Philosophen Richard Goodwin, Gerard Reinmuth (Terroir, Sydney) und Andrew Benjamin zusammen. Sie beschäftigen sich, jeweils aus unterschiedlichen Arbeitsgebieten kommend, mit dem übergeordneten Thema der Stadtentwicklung. Das Modell des Fraying Ground, also des „ausfransenden Stadtkerns", stammt von Andrew Benjamin. Richard Goodwin lieferte dazu das Konzept eines öffentlichen Raums, der als parasitäre Architektur aus den alten Gebäuden erwächst. Gerard Reinmuths Beitrag schließlich liegt in der Darstellung der unterschiedlichen, sich verschiebenden tektonischen Elemente in einem architektonischen Gefüge.

ARCHI-TECTONICS

NEW YORK, USA
ROTTERDAM, THE NETHERLANDS

"The future of the urban metropolis lies in a drastic rethinking of its infrastructures."

„Die Zukunft städtischer Metropolen liegt in einer völligen Neuausrichtung ihrer Infrastrukturen."

NYC 2106: A COASTAL MEGALOPOLIS, 2007

New York City, USA

Three-day competition by invitation from The History Channel to envisage the future of New York City in 100 years.
Exhibition at Grand Central Terminal, NYC

● ENGLISCH When thinking about New York´s future, there is one thing that cannot be ignored: the city´s obsolete infrastructures are beyond repair and will have to be completely replaced. Archi-Tectonics has developed two major projects to take pressure off the island of Manhattan: a chain of artificial floating islands and a dual off-shore traffic concept, which at the same time will supply the region with renewable energy. An automated regional transportation system leading across the water shortens trips between the coasts, while connecting the islands with one another. The result would be a Manhattan as one of many islands, embedded in a natural seascape, where it could finally be the thing it always wanted to be: a pleasant urban environment with comfortable living conditions and a tourist attraction. As a group, the islands have various local and international functions – from eco-tourism in an artificial new landscape to world travel, leisure, and global business relations. This international island hub off New York´s shore is designed to offer a large variety of business and economic facilities and allow stopovers without visa formalities – a chance for New York City to become an international hub in an era of global turbo-mobility.

● DEUTSCH Wenn man über die Zukunft New Yorks nachdenkt, ist eines vollkommen klar: Die veralteten Infrastrukturen der Stadt müssen komplett ersetzt und nicht nur repariert werden. Archi-Tectonics schlägt zwei Großprojekte vor, um die Insel Manhattan zu entlasten: eine Kette künstlicher schwimmender Inseln und ein der Küste vorgelagertes duales Verkehrssystem, das gleichzeitig erneuerbare Energien für die Region zur Verfügung stellt. Ein automatisches Nahverkehrsnetz, das „übers Wasser" führt, sorgt für kurze Wege zwischen den Küsten und verbindet die Inseln untereinander. Manhattan wäre so eine von vielen Inseln in einer natürlichen Wasserlandschaft und endlich das, was sie sein will: eine schöne urbane Umwelt, in der es sich angenehm leben lässt – ein Anziehungspunkt für Touristen. Die Inseln erfüllen gemeinsam viele verschiedene Funktionen mit lokaler und internationaler Bedeutung: vom Ökotourismus in einem künstlichen Neuland bis hin zu Weltreisen, von lokaler Freizeitgestaltung bis hin zu globalen Geschäftsbeziehungen. Der internationale Insel-Verkehrsknotenpunkt vor New York soll alle Geschäfts- und Wirtschaftseinrichtungen umfassen und Zwischenstopps ohne Reisebeschränkungen möglich machen. Auf diese Weise würde New York City in der Ära der globalen Turbomobilität zu einem internationalen Reiseumschlagplatz.

• New York City 2106 as an international island metropolis
• New York City 2106 als internationale Inselmetropole

- New York City 2160, masterplan of the New York islandscape.
- New York City 2160, Masterplan der New Yorker Insellandschaft

● Archi-Tectonics, founded by Winka Dubbeldam, 1994 in New York and 1997 in Rotterdam, is an architectural and design laboratory keen on experiments and focused on innovative concepts. The firm´s philosophy is blending theory with practical use to create product and structural design. Archi-Techtonics analyzes and researches new sustainable programs and materials for future structural and urban concepts, using digital project management and the parametric software FTF (file to factory), which allows a direct communication between design and the industrial production of structural elements.

● Archi-Tectonics, 1994 in New York und 1997 in Rotterdam von Winka Dubbeldam gegründet, ist ein experimentierfreudiges Architektur- und Design-Laboratorium, dessen Fokus auf der Entwicklung innovativer Konzepte liegt. Die Philosophie des Büros beinhaltet die Verbindung von Theorie und Praxis, um daraus Produkt- und Baugestaltungen entstehen zu lassen. Archi-Tectonics analysiert und erforscht neue nachhaltige Programme und Materialien für zukünftige Bau- und Stadtsysteme. Hierbei arbeiten sie mit digitalem Projektmanagement und der parametrischen Software FTF (file to factory), die eine direkte Kommunikation zwischen dem Entwurf und der fabrikmäßigen Herstellung von Bauelementen erlaubt.

A SYSTEMATIC APPROACH TO THE FUTURE

The future of the urban metropolis lies in a drastic rethinking of its infrastructures. Most fundamentally for a long-term innovation one must focus not on buildings but on its systems: transit systems, floodscapes, waste management, and alternative energy must all be reinvented for the near future.

With the city centers and urban cores reserved for housing, culture and tourism, the edge zones are to be dedicated to the new uses. Most importantly, these new zones will constitute productive landscapes that provide renewable energy resources while simultaneously capturing opportunities for urban recreation. Unlike the spoiled industrial landscapes of twentieth-century energy production, the energy sources of the future amplify the productivity of existing natural processes. The industrial factory, for example, becomes the energy farm. Wind power, wave energy, geothermal power, and bio-fuel will radically transform urban energy production in the next hundred years. Bio-fuel ecologies will process unwanted biomass such as urban garbage, transforming waste into energy. Capturing energy from the city's prevailing winds, channels of artificial reefs support wind turbines that form an iconic gateway to the city. Larger, high-altitude turbine structures are flown above the city like kites. Meanwhile, wave farms utilize the motion of the sea as one of the greatest potential sources of renewable energy. Floating networks of articulated buoys capture energy from the dynamic movements of waves, creating a stunning visual landscape at a city's harbor.

In an era of global warming, rather than fighting rising water levels, we designate floodplains as recreational areas to accommodate the overflow of water. The introduction of wetlands with phyto-remediation creates lush green landscapes and opportunities for residential development and bioscience research campuses.

An automated intra-urban transit system will ease congestion at the heart of the city, and intelligent vehicle highway systems provide dual-mode vehicles that operate on parts of the rapid transit network. Propulsion on the guideway, as in the case of the personal transit system, would almost certainly be electric, probably using third-rail power distribution. Within the city, guidance of the personal rapid transit vehicles can be automated or augmented by on-board computers to safely navigate the busy streets and connect fluidly to the multiplicity of small (private) airports.

This clean energy and smooth transport offers a relaxed atmosphere with urban beaches for the city's new urbanites. From Grid City to a city off the grid, the future is here.

Winka Dubbeldam

EINE SYSTEMATISCHE ANNÄHERUNG AN DIE ZUKUNFT

Die Zukunft städtischer Metropolen liegt in einer Neuausrichtung ihrer Infrastrukturen. Eine langfristig angelegte innovative Planung darf sich nicht auf Gebäude konzentrieren, sondern muss die Systeme der Stadt im Blick haben: Verkehrssysteme, Hochwasserprävention, Abfallmanagement und alternative Energien müssen neu gedacht werden.

Während Stadtzentren und urbane Kerngebiete für Wohnen, kulturelles Leben und Tourismus reserviert bleiben, gilt es, die Randzonen für die neuen Nutzungen zu erschließen und sie zu produktiven Landschaften umzugestalten, wo gleichzeitig Anlagen für erneuerbare Energien und stadtnahe Erholungsräume entstehen. Anders als die zerstörten Landschaften, die die industrielle Energieerzeugung des 20. Jahrhunderts zurückließ, verstärken die Energiequellen der Zukunft die Produktivität bestehender natürlicher Prozesse. Aus Industriebetrieben werden Energieparks; mit Wind- und Wellenkraft, geothermischer Energie und Biotreibstoffen lässt sich die urbane Energieerzeugung der nächsten 100 Jahre revolutionieren. Biokraftstoffanlagen verarbeiten überschüssige Biomassen wie den Müll der Städte und verwandeln so Abfall in Energie. Auf künstlichen Riffen montierte Windturbinen, jeweils nach der vorherrschenden Windrichtung ausgerichtet, werden die Zufahrtsrouten der Städte ikonenhaft markieren. Noch höher ragende Turbinen lassen sich wie Winddrachen über den Städten auftürmen. Parallel dazu nutzen Wellenkraftwerke die Bewegungen des Meeres als eine der bedeutendsten Quellen für erneuerbare Energie überhaupt. Teppiche aus beweglichen, durch Gelenke verbundenen Bojen erzeugen, vom Wellenschlag angetrieben, Elektrizität und verwandeln zugleich Häfen in beeindruckende Landschaften.

Die globale Erwärmung erfordert die Vorbereitung auf Überschwemmungen, nicht den Kampf gegen den steigenden Meeresspiegel. Dazu gilt es, Überflutungsflächen auszuweisen, die zugleich als Erholungsräume dienen. Mit dem Anlegen von Feuchtgebieten durch Phytoremediation kann man gleichzeitig üppige Grünflächen und neue Areale für Wohnungen und biowissenschaftliche Forschungseinrichtungen schaffen.

Automatisierte intra-urbane Verkehrssysteme und intelligente Schnellstraßen entlasten die verstopften Innenstädte; die Fahrzeuge der Zukunft verfügen über zwei Betriebsmodi und können auch das Schnellbahnsystem nutzen. Der Antrieb solcher Personennahverkehrs-Fahrzeuge wird voraussichtlich elektrisch sein, die Stromversorgung erfolgt über eine dritte Schiene. In den Innenstädten lassen sich die Fahrzeuge automatisch führen. Mittels Bordcomputer werden die Wagen sicher über vielbefahrene Straßen gelenkt und verbinden eine Vielzahl kleiner (privater) Flughäfen mit der Stadt.

Dergestalt reibungslose und mit sauberer Energie betriebene Verkehrssysteme nehmen den Innenstädten ihre Hektik; Stadtzentren werden zu entspannenden Stadtstränden. Der energiefressende Moloch der Moderne wird zu einem urbanen „Niedrigenergieraum". Diese Zukunft hat bereits begonnen.

Winka Dubbeldam

RAUMLABORBERLIN
BERLIN, GERMANY

"We don´t want to conquer space at all. We want to expand Earth endlessly. We don´t need other worlds; we need a mirror. … Man needs man!"

„Wir wollen den Weltraum gar nicht erobern. Wir wollen die Erde ins Unendliche erweitern. Wir brauchen keine anderen Welten, wir brauchen einen Spiegel. … Der Mensch braucht den Menschen."

Stanislav Lem, Solaris, 1972

SNUGGLE, 2009

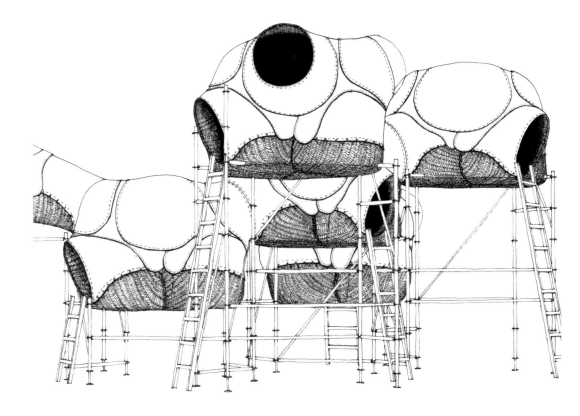

● ENGLISCH Snuggle, a mobile hotel, is a concept developed by Raumlaborberlin especially for festivals, seminars, and conventions as a solution of the problem that it is usually not easy to find the right accommodation for everyone, because local hotels are either too low in standard, have a bad location, or are too expensive. Owing to their own experiences as organizers and participants, Raumlaborberlin has often resorted to building temporary lodgings in the past. They can be set up in special places with a breathtaking view. Snuggle is a hotel made of wickerwork. It takes three days to set up and totally blends in with its environment. Structure and the number of rooms are flexible, as required by the size and location of the event. The rooms consist of a platform attached to a scaffolding. On this platform a mattress rests in a wicker basket which is covered with a rainproof tarpaulin. The individual parts of the basket are joined on site. Three identical floor elements can be combined with three variable ceiling elements. The rooms are equipped with pockets, hooks, and eyelets that are attached to the basket. Every room has its own entrance, which can be sealed with a lid. A separate mobile module unit contains showers and toilets. Depending on location, weather, and demand, there is the option to add an inflatable common room, which serves as kitchen, breakfast room, and convention center. Snuggle can also be set up in existing buildings like farms, parking structures, empty supermarkets, or caves.

• Snuggle is a mobile hotel made from wickerwork, meant for festivals or conventions. It takes three days to set up.
• Snuggle ist ein mobiles Hotel aus Weidengeflechtkörben für Festivals oder Workshops, das in drei Tagen aufgebaut werden kann.

● Raumlaborberlin is a network-collective, consisting of eight Berlin architects, that was founded in 1999. Project-oriented teams of Raumlaborberlin work together with external partners and specialists, depending on the task in hand. The projects are interdisciplinary with an emphasis on architecture, urban construction, art, and performance. Raumberlin focuses on questions concerning urban transformation as well as the line that divides public and private spaces. Artistic and architectonic interventions are their tools of communication and the shaping of processes at the interface of culture and planning.

● Raumlaborberlin ist ein Netzwerk-Kollektiv aus acht Berliner Architekten, das seit 1999 besteht. Projektbezogene Teams von Raumlaborberlin arbeiten, abhängig von der Aufgabe, mit externen Partnern und Spezialisten zusammen. Die Bereiche sind genreübergreifend und interdisziplinär, mit den Schwerpunkten Architektur, Städtebau, Kunst und Performance. Inhaltlich beschäftigt sich Raumlaborberlin besonders mit Fragestellungen zu städtischen Transformationen sowie den Grenzen zwischen öffentlichen und privaten Räumen. Künstlerische und architektonische Interventionen dienen ihnen als Werkzeuge der Kommunikation und Prozessgestaltung an der Schnittstelle von Kultur und Planung.

● DEUTSCH Das mobile Hotel Snuggle ist ein Entwurf, den Raumlaborberlin speziell für Festivals, Workshops und Kongresse entwickelt hat. Passende Unterkünfte für die Teilnehmer solcher Veranstaltungen zu finden, ist generell nicht einfach; oft sind die zur Verfügung stehenden Hotels schlecht ausgestattet, ungünstig gelegen oder zu teuer. Aufgrund der eigenen Erfahrungen als Veranstalter und Teilnehmer hat Raumlaborberlin daher schon häufiger temporäre Unterkünfte gebaut. Diese können an besonderen Orten mit atemberaubenden Aussichten errichtet werden. Snuggle ist ein Hotel aus Weidengeflecht, das in drei Tagen aufgebaut werden kann und sich komplett der Umgebung anpasst. Je nach Größe, Anlass und Ort ändern sich der Aufbau und die Zimmeranzahl. Die Zimmer bestehen aus einer Plattform, die an einem Gerüst befestigt ist; auf dieser liegt die Matratze, umhüllt von einer Schale aus Weidengeflecht mit einem regenfesten Textilüberzug. Die Einzelteile der Korbschale werden vor Ort miteinander verknüpft. Drei identische Bodenelemente werden mit drei variablen Deckenelementen kombiniert. Zur weiteren Ausstattung der Zimmer werden Taschen, Haken und Ösen an der Korbschale befestigt. Grundsätzlich hat jedes Zimmer einen eigenen Zugang, der mit einem Deckel verschließbar ist. Duschen und Toiletten befinden sich in einer separaten, mobilen Moduleinheit. Je nach Lage, Wetter und Bedarf wird das Hotel durch einen pneumatischen Gemeinschaftsraum ergänzt, der sowohl Küche und Frühstücksraum als auch Kongresszentrum sein kann. Snuggle kann auch in oder an bestehenden Bauten wie Bauernhöfen, Parkhäusern, leer stehenden Supermärkten oder Höhlen aufgebaut werden.

J. MAYER H. ARCHITEKTEN
BERLIN, GERMANY

"The debates on climate change, limited natural resources and issues of distributive justice are increasingly moving to the center of public attention. Extreme weather conditions with at times catastrophic effects sharpen our eye for future challenges and lead to a discourse of sustainability that dominates almost every aspect of our everyday lives."

„Die Diskussion um Klimawandel, begrenzte Ressourcen und Fragen globaler Verteilungsgerechtigkeit rückt immer stärker ins öffentliche Bewusstsein. Wetterextreme mit zum Teil katastrophalen Auswirkungen schärfen den Blick für unsere Zukunft und führen zu einem Nachhaltigkeitsdiskurs, der fast jeden Aspekt des Alltags dominiert."

A. WAY, 2010

Winner of the Audi Urban Future Award 2010 competition ran by the Audi Urban Future Initiative. The initiative aims to establish a dialog on the synergy of mobility, architecture and urban development by means of a view into the future and is curated by Stylepark AG.

● ENGLISCH

For the Audi Urban Future Award 2010 the architectural firm J. Mayer H. presented their concept A. Way, a visionary study on an environment-friendly infrastructure controlled by digital technology. They describe their project as follows:

"A long time ago, around 1985, the world found out that there was a hole in the ozone layer, which changed our approach to the future. From this moment on, consumption, production, and mobility were endangered. Thanks to the rise of digital technology in the early 21st century and electricity as our main source of energy, our cities will grow without pollution and congested streets: green, clean, peaceful, and efficient. The individual mobility of the future will be closely linked with digitally expanded urban spaces, with driverless vehicles and with an individual exchange of data between the human body and its environment. Then, traffic will be in constant motion and a steady flow. Parked vehicles will be a thing of the past. Pedestrian zones will reclaim the space they had to yield to cars. The change will have social, economic, and ecological effects. Monitoring technologies will turn the city and its inhabitants into a data stream. From digital technologies new forms of perception will rise, which will allow every individual to accept or reject certain aspects of the city. The car will be transformed from a viewing machine into a perception vehicle, which deftly and 'intelligently' finds its own way around town, while creating sensuous experiences. On our travels through the city, our experiences will be in the foreground and the result will be a new interaction with the urban environment. Even though the danger of a sudden collapse of all systems always remains, it will urge us on and force us to improvise, to invent, and to look ahead. If our cities once more prove to be flexible, adaptable, changeable, and ready to survive until then, we will live a closed and undamaged ozone layer again, happily ever after".

• The car of the future is driverless and finds its way through the city intelligently and independently.
• Das zukünftige Auto ist fahrerlos und sucht sich intelligent und eigenständig seinen Weg durch die Stadt.

PAGE/SEITE 60
• In the city of the future infrastructures and traffic are controlled by digital data streams.
• In der Stadt der Zukunft werden Infrastrukturen und Verkehrsführungen durch digitale Datenströme gelenkt.

• DEUTSCH   Für den Audi Urban Future Award 2010 legte das Architekturbüro J. Mayer H. den Entwurf A. Way vor, eine visionäre Studie über die durch digitale Technologien gesteuerte, umweltfreundliche städtische Infrastruktur. Sie beschreiben ihr Projekt wie folgt:

„Vor langer Zeit, um 1985, entdeckte die Welt das Ozonloch, und so wandelte sich unser Denken über die Zukunft. Von nun an stehen Konsum, Produktion und Mobilität auf dem Spiel. Mit dem Aufkommen digitaler Technologien zu Beginn des 21. Jahrhunderts und mit Elektrizität als Hauptenergieversorgungsquelle werden unsere Städte ohne Umweltverschmutzung und Staus wachsen; grün, sauber, ruhig und effizient. Die individuelle Mobilität der Zukunft wird eng mit der Entwicklung von digital erweiterten städtischen Räumen verbunden sein, mit fahrerlosem Verkehr und individuell angepasstem Datenaustausch zwischen dem menschlichen Körper und seiner Umgebung. Der Verkehr ist nun in ständiger Bewegung, ein fortlaufender Strom, parkende Fahrzeuge sind überflüssig. Fußgängerzonen gewinnen den Raum zurück, den sie an Autos abtreten mussten. Dies wird soziale, wirtschaftliche und ökologische Auswirkungen haben. Monitoring-Technologien werden die Stadt und ihre Bewohner in einen Datenstrom verwandeln und so die Grenzen zwischen Körper, Auto und Architektur weitgehend auflösen. Aus den digitalen Technologien werden sich neue Formen der Wahrnehmung entwickeln, die jedem Einzelnen erlauben, ausgewählte Aspekte der Stadt zuzulassen oder abzulehnen. Das Auto wird sich wandeln von einer Blickmaschine hin zu einem Wahrnehmungsvehikel, das sich geschickt und intelligent seinen Weg sucht und für sinnliche Erfahrungen sorgt. Bei Fahrten durch die Stadt rückt unser Erleben in den Vordergrund, sodass wir auf ganz neue Weise mit dem städtischen Umfeld interagieren können. Und dennoch, es besteht immer die Chance, dass alle Systeme überraschend kollabieren, doch das treibt uns an und zwingt uns dazu, zu improvisieren, Neues zu erfinden und nach vorne zu schauen. Wenn sich Städte bis dahin erneut als flexibel, anpassungsfähig, verwandelbar und überlebensfähig erwiesen haben, dann werden wir wieder unter einer geschlossenen schützenden Ozonschicht leben, glücklich bis ans Ende."

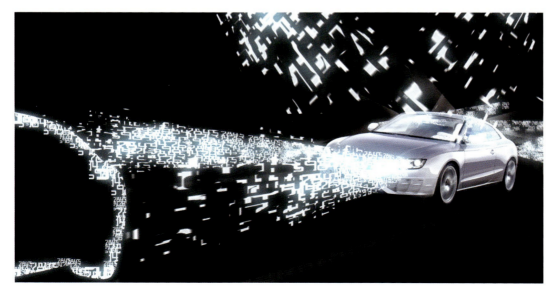

● The firm J. Mayer H. Architekten was founded in Berlin in 1997. Its head, Jürgen Mayer, studied architecture at the university of Stuttgart, the Cooper Union in New York, and Princeton University. His team, which meanwhile has grown considerably, is involved in the interface of architecture, communications design, and new technologies. Interactive media and responsive materials play a central role in the creation of space. Everything, from installations to concepts in urban construction, international competitions, and multi-disciplinary spacial research in regard to the relation between body, nature, and technology, is compiled in cooperative groups. Famous buildings and projects include the Stadthaus in Stuttgart-Ostfildern, the Mensa Moltke at the technical university of Karlsruhe, or Metropole Parasol, a new design for a city square in Seville.

● Das Büro J. Mayer H. Architekten wurde 1996 in Berlin gegründet. Der Leiter Jürgen Mayer studierte Architektur an der Universität Stuttgart, der Cooper Union in New York und an der Princeton University. Das inzwischen auf etliche Mitarbeiter angewachsene Team arbeitet an den Schnittstellen von Architektur, Kommunikationsdesign und neuen Technologien. Dabei spielt der Einsatz interaktiver Medien und responsiver Materialien eine zentrale Rolle bei der Produktion von Raum. In kooperativen Gruppen wird – von Installationen über städtebauliche Entwürfe bis hin zu internationalen Wettbewerben – multidisziplinäre Raumforschung mit Bezug zum Verhältnis von Körper, Natur und Technologie erarbeitet und realisiert. Bekannte Bauten und Projekte des Büros sind u. a. das Stadthaus in Stuttgart-Ostfildern, die Mensa Moltke der FH Karlsruhe oder Metropole Parasol, eine Neugestaltung für einen Stadtplatz in Sevilla.

SUSTAINABILITY
NACHHALTIGKEIT

The concept of sustainability is characterized by its high degree of complexity and by continuous re-evaluations brought about through rapid gains in knowledge. Sustainable practice is possible only if ecological, economic and social demands are mutually balanced, and argues among other aspects for ecologically intelligent technologies as a necessity for future survival. This perspective is enacted by means of an environment creating an all-encompassing atmosphere in which digital and material spaces merge to become a unit. It is especially noteworthy how the striving for sustainability has become transformed since the 1970s from the back-to-nature attitude of a small minority that was hostile towards business and economic progress, to a popular consensus. Thus the notion of sustainability has become one of the leading catchwords of marketing rhetoric and functions nowadays as a driving force of modern business and of comprehensive technological innovation. In the course of this development the framework for the evaluation of sustainable practice has been continuously redefined. Practices claiming to be sustainably correct today may be exposed to be the very opposite tomorrow. We must not overtax consumers and decision makers with an overabundance of information and constantly changing instructions of how to behave and proceed, and thus cause people to become indifferent to the subject. A certain measure of uncertainty in this field is productive, however, as it motivates aware citizens to contribute their own ideas, continuously question existing practices and critically weigh their options and choices.

J. Mayer H.

Der Begriff der Nachhaltigkeit ist bestimmt durch ein hohes Maß an Komplexität und fortwährender, durch raschen Erkenntnisgewinn bedingter Neubewertung. Nachhaltiges Handeln ist nur möglich, wenn ökologische, ökonomische und soziale Anforderungen ausgeglichen sind, und zeigt, dass unter anderem ökologisch-intelligente Technologien für ein Überleben in der Zukunft wichtig sind. Inszeniert wird diese Haltung als gesamtatmosphärisches Environment, in dem digitale und materielle Räume zu einer Einheit verschmelzen. Die Wandlung des Strebens nach Nachhaltigkeit von einer wirtschafts- und fortschrittsfeindlichen back-to-nature-Haltung einer klaren Minderheit in den 1970er-Jahren hin zum populären Konsens ist hierbei besonders bemerkenswert. So hat es das Thema „Nachhaltigkeit" als Schlagwort an die Spitze der Marketing-Rhetorik geschafft und fungiert unlängst als wirtschaftstreibende Kraft und als Motor umfangreicher technischer Innovationen. Dabei werden die Bewertungsgrundlagen für nachhaltiges Handeln fortlaufend neu definiert. Was heute noch im Sinne der Nachhaltigkeit korrektes Verhalten proklamiert, könnte morgen als das Gegenteil entlarvt werden. Es gilt in diesem Fall, den handelnden Menschen nicht durch eine unüberschaubare Fülle an Informationen und ständig wechselnden Handlungsanweisungen zu überfordern und dem Thema gegenüber gleichgültig werden zu lassen. Ein gewisses Maß an Unsicherheit in diesem Bereich ist jedoch produktiv, sensibilisiert es einen wachen Bürger doch mitzudenken, kontinuierlich zu hinterfragen und die Optionen seines Handelns kritisch abzuwägen.

J. Mayer H.

TOWER

Highrises and skyscrapers have always been more than just high buildings, but rather metaphors for man´s desire to reach for the skies and also symbols of power, realized in the shape of tower-structures. Apart from that, skyscrapers also are masterworks of architecture and engineering, built with the help of the newest technologies and materials. Since the first skyscrapers were built in Chicago and New York in the late 19th century, there has been an ongoing competition for the highest building of the world between continents, countries, and owners. In 2010, the skyscraper Burj Dubai in Dubai, which is about 820 meters tall, broke a new record of superlatives.

Even in times of sustainable construction and ecological awareness highrises have not lost their importance for large cities, as only residential towers can prevent an uncontrollable urban spread. Thus, the new urban housing of the future has to be devised as high-quality clusters to protect or even recapture green zones and forests, and to combat sealed ground surfaces.

Current visions in regard to the construction of highrises mostly focus on the following two aspects: first to plan sustainable skyscrapers with the help of high-tech methods and second to create residential clusters that meet the modern city-dweller´s needs for individuality on the one and community on the other hand. Tomorrow´s highrises are anything but gray and monotonous: they have organic round shapes, equipped with overgrown terrace gardens, and autonomous in regard to water and energy supply. Their facades are covered in green plants and can be intelligent computer controlled screens that send information, signals, or pictures as needed. The highrise-dweller of the future will be able to live in the center of town, while being surrounded by a green eco-system.

TÜRME

Hochhäuser und Wolkenkratzer sind mehr als nur hohe Architekturen. Sie gelten als Metaphern für den Wunsch des Menschen, in den Himmel zu bauen, und für seinen Machtanspruch, dem das Turmgebäude symbolische Form verleiht. Wolkenkratzer sind darüber hinaus architektonische und ingenieurtechnische Meisterleistungen, bei denen neueste Technologien und Materialien eingesetzt werden. Seitdem die ersten Skyscraper in Chicago und New York am Ende des 19. Jahrhunderts entstanden, gibt es einen Wettstreit zwischen Kontinenten, Staaten und Auftraggebern, wer das höchste Gebäude der Welt errichten kann. 2010 wurde in Dubai mit der Eröffnung des Wolkenkratzers Burj Dubai, der eine Höhe von rund 820 m aufweist, ein neuer Rekord der Superlative aufgestellt.

Hochhäuser gehören, auch in Zeiten von nachhaltigem Bauen und ökologischem Bewusstsein, nach wie vor zu wichtigen Bestandteilen der Großstadt. Denn nur durch die Errichtung hoher Wohnhäuser in der Stadt kann man die ausufernde Zersiedlung in der Peripherie verhindern. Urbaner Wohnungsneubau sollte in der Zukunft ein qualitativ verdichteter sein, um auf diese Weise langfristig Grün- und Waldflächen zu schützen oder sie sogar zurückzugewinnen und so der Flächenversiegelung entgegenzuwirken.

Die aktuellen Zukunftsvisionen zum Thema Hochhausbau orientieren sich vor allem an zwei zentralen Zielvorstellungen: Zum einen sollen mit Hightech-Verfahren nachhaltige Wolkenkratzer konzipiert und zum anderen verdichteter Wohnraum so gestaltet werden, dass er den heutigen Bedürfnissen nach Individualität, aber auch nach sozialer Gemeinschaft entspricht. Die Hochhäuser von morgen sind alles andere als grau und eintönig: Sie haben organisch runde Formen, üppig wuchernde Terrassengärten und sind in Bezug auf Wasser- und Energiehaushalt autark. Ihre Außenfassaden können grüne Pflanzenhüllen, intelligente, computergesteuerte Screens sein, die je nach Bedarf Informationen, Signale oder Bilder aussenden. Der Hochhausbewohner der Zukunft kann mitten in der Großstadt leben und gleichzeitig von einem grünen Ökosystem umgeben sein.

NABITO
BARCELONA, SPAIN

"We need to pass from theory to strategy, from drawing to a planned plot, and from a personal concept to a general criteria. We need to liberate the form from the concept; we need to manipulate it with other multiple relations dictated by the economic, social and cultural contest."

„Wir müssen von der Theorie zur Strategie kommen, vom Zeichnen zum geplanten Ablauf und von persönlichen Auffassungen zu generellen Kriterien. Wir müssen die Form vom Konzept befreien; wir müssen sie durch andere Wechselwirkungen beeinflussen, die der ökonomische, soziale und kulturelle Kontext diktieren."

STAIRSCRAPER, 2010

Proposal for New York City, USA

• The Stairscraper soars into the skies above New York City like a giant spiral staircase.
• Der Stairscraper schraubt sich wie eine riesige Wendeltreppe in den Himmel New Yorks.

● ENGLISCH Nabito´s search for the urban residential highrise of the future led to a building shaped like a spiral staircase, whose individual housing modules reach up into the skies as "steps". Besides opting for this rather symbol-laden metaphor of the "stairway to heaven", Nabito aims at realizing a rather down-to-earth approach to social living in tomorrow´s New York City.

These modules, one-family bungalows with gardens, are stacked on top of each other at a 36-degree angle. The concept is based on the idea of a village community, arranged not horizontally, but vertically, right in the middle of the metropolis of New York. The stairway highrise will include not only private and commercial spaces, but also public rooms and facilities.

● DEUTSCH Auf der Suche nach dem städtischen Wohnhochhaus der Zukunft hat Nabito ein Gebäude in Form einer Wendeltreppe entworfen, deren einzelne „Stufen" als Wohnmodule spiralförmig in den Himmel steigen. Neben dieser symbolträchtigen Metapher der „Himmelsleiter" verfolgt Nabito mit dem Stairscraper aber auch ganz bodenständige Visionen des sozialen Lebens und Wohnens im New York von morgen. Die Module sind als Einfamilienbungalows mit Garten ausgebildet, die jeweils um 36° gedreht, übereinandergesetzt werden. Dem Stairscraper liegt die Idee einer sozialen Dorfgemeinschaft zugrunde, die statt in der Fläche inmitten der Metropole New York in der Vertikalen angeordnet ist. Neben Wohn- und Gewerbeflächen sollen auch öffentliche Einrichtungen und Räume in das Treppenhochhaus integriert werden.

• The Stairscraper consists of individual bungalows with gardens, which are not arranged side by side, but vertically at an angle of 36 degrees.
• Der Stairscraper besteht aus einzelnen Wohnbungalows mit Garten, die, statt in der Fläche nebeneinander, in der Vertikalen und mit einer Drehung von 36° übereinandergesetzt werden.

• Nabito was founded in 2006 in Barcelona by the architects Alessandra Faticanti and Roberto Ferlito. Their concepts focus on the different aspects of sustainable and territorial construction. Their visionary concepts especially emphasize the relation between private and public spaces in a future urban context.

• Nabito wurde 2006 von der Architektin Alessandra Faticanti und dem Architekten Roberto Ferlito in Barcelona gegründet. Ihre Entwurfsstrategie konzentriert sich auf Fragestellungen von nachhaltigem und territorialem Bauen. Einen Schwerpunkt ihrer visionären Planungen bilden Überlegungen hinsichtlich des Verhältnisses von privaten und öffentlichen Räumen im zukünftigen urbanen Kontext.

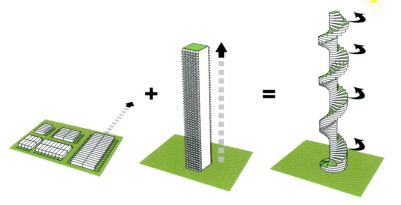

JOANNA BOREK-CLEMENT

SAN FRANCISCO, USA

"It is in moments when we are capable of breaking from our comfort zone that there is opportunity to discover the new, continuously reinventing the way we approach the world."

„Es sind die Momente, in denen es uns gelingt, aus der Bequemlichkeit auszubrechen, die uns Gelegenheit geben, Neues zu entdecken und dabei die Art, wie wir die Welt begreifen, neu zu erfinden."

SKY-TERRA, 2009

Conceptual project for any congested metropolis

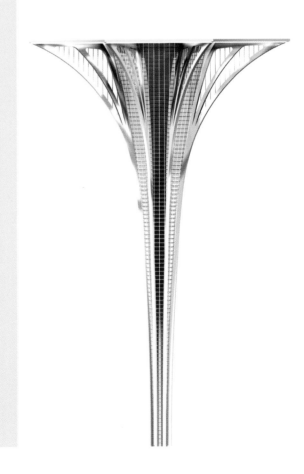

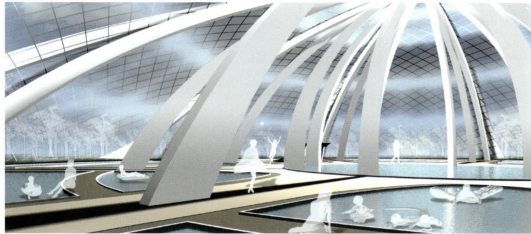

- Sky-Terra is a platform that soars over the roofs of Tokyo, offering people green spaces for work and recreation.
- Sky-Terra ist eine sich über den Dächern von Tokio erhebende Plattform, die großflächige grüne Arbeits- und Freizeitbereiche für die Bevölkerung bereitstellt.

● ENGLISCH   Sky-Terra is a mounted plateau that soars 500 meters over Tokyo, offering public and green spaces for work and leisure. At the moment, public recreational spaces for walking, running, or cycling in Tokyo are restricted to little parks amid roaring traffic and towering highrises. The new public green zone will reach up on high, funnel-like plateaus, linked by a multi-stranded web, which was inspired by the organic neural network.

Each unit of Sky-Terra consists of three elements: a core controlling vertical circulation, office spaces surrounded by supporting "ribs", and outdoor lawns. The individual plateaus are connected by pedestrian paths and narrow lanes for bicycles and electric vehicles, which provide maximum room for green zones and reduce the thermal-island effect. The generous public spaces thus created become gathering places for the inhabitants and therefore not only meet individual physical needs, but also create a feeling of community and enhance the quality of life in our society.

● DEUTSCH   Sky-Terra ist eine in 500 m Höhe über Tokio errichtete, aufgeständerte Ebene mit öffentlichen und grünen Flächen für Arbeit und Freizeit. Die Flächen zum Spazierengehen, Joggen oder Fahrradfahren beschränken sich in Tokio bisher auf kleine Parkgelände inmitten von Verkehr und Wolkenkratzern. Das neue öffentliche Grün soll sich auf trichterförmigen Plateaus erheben, die horizontal durch ein mehrsträhniges Geflecht wie ein organisches System von Nervenbahnen miteinander verbunden sind. Jede Einheit besteht aus drei Elementen: dem die vertikale Zirkulation regulierenden Kern, den von tragenden „Rippen" umschlossenen Büroflächen sowie den außen liegenden Grünflächen. Fußwege und schmale Straßen für Fahrräder und Elektroautos verbinden die Plateaus; das schafft Raum für Grünflächen und reduziert den Wärmeinseleffekt. Die großzügigen öffentlichen Räume dienen als Versammlungsorte, die nicht nur den physischen Bedürfnissen des Einzelnen, sondern auch einem Gemeinschaftsgefühl gerecht werden und so die Qualität des sozialen Lebens verbessern.

● Joanna Borek-Clement works as a designer in San Francisco, California. She holds an M.A. in architecture and urban planning from the technical university of Cracow. Her multifacetted concepts deal with the fields of architecture, urban planning, interior decoration, digital graphic arts, and goldsmith's works.

● Joanna Borek-Clement lebt als Designerin in San Francisco, Kalifornien; sie hat einen Masterabschluss im Fach Architektur und Stadtplanung der Technischen Universität Krakau. In ihrer vielfältigen konzeptionellen Arbeit beschäftigt sie sich mit den Themenbereichen Architektur, Stadtplanung, Innenarchitektur, digitale Grafik und Goldschmiedekunst.

LAVA
STUTTGART, GERMANY
SYDNEY, AUSTRALIA

"We see architecture as a field for research and strive to contribute to the future of architecture. The guiding principle for our work inspired by natural principles is 'more with less': more architectural quality using less resources."

„Wir verstehen Architektur als ein Forschungsgebiet und möchten zu ihrer Entwicklung beitragen. Der Leitgedanke unserer Arbeit ‚mehr mit weniger' ist von naturnahen Prinzipien inspiriert: mehr architektonische Qualität bei geringerem Verbrauch natürlicher Ressourcen."

TOWER SKIN, 2010

Sydney, Australia

- Tower Skin in Sydney is a highrise dating from the 1960s, which is optically and energetically enhanced by a fabric media cover.
- Tower Skin in Sydney ist ein Hochhaus aus den 1960er-Jahren, das durch eine textile Gebäudehülle optisch und energetisch aufgewertet wird.

● ENGLISCH The idea, which originally started as a mere speculative suggestion LAVA made for the modification of the UTS Broadway Tower in Sydney, which dates from the 1960s, over the years turned into a major architectural concept of converting inefficient or technically obsolete buildings into ecological and economically profitable units instead of pulling them down and replacing them with something new. LAVA has developed simple low-cost building-covers that are easy to set up and enhance the identity of the present structure, while improving its sustainability and the quality of the indoor space. The translucent cocoon generates its own micro-climate, produces energy by photovoltaic means, collects rainwater, lets more natural daylight in, and uses the available convective energy to power the building´s ventilation system. A membrane made of a light-weight and durable compound-fabric is stretched over a framework of light-weight steel that is set up around the building. Thus, with a minimum use of material a maximum optical effect is achieved. LED-slats are integrated into the membrane, turning the building´s cover into an illuminated intelligent media façade that can be used as a digigal screen for animations and as a public bulletin board. The "Re-Skin" concept is the result of LAVA´s research in the field of sustainable public architecture. It uses state-of-the-art light-weight materials and the newest digital methods of production to accomplish more (architecture) with less (material, energy, time).

● DEUTSCH Was ursprünglich als rein spekulativer Vorschlag von LAVA zum Umbau des UTS Broadway Towers in Sydney aus den 1960er-Jahren begann, hat sich zu einem breit angelegten architektonischen Konzept entwickelt, das ineffiziente oder technisch überholte Gebäude neuen ökologisch und ökonomisch vertretbaren Verwendungen zuführt, statt diese abzureißen und durch einen Neubau zu ersetzen. LAVA hat eine einfache, kostengünstige und leicht zu konstruierende Gebäudehülle entwickelt, mit der sich die Identität eines bestehenden Gebäudes aufwerten und seine Nachhaltigkeit und Innenraumqualität verbessern lassen. Der transluzente Kokon generiert sein eigenes „Mikroklima": Er erzeugt mittels Fotovoltaik seine eigene Energie, sammelt Regenwasser, verbessert die Zufuhr des natürlichen Tageslichts und nutzt die verfügbare konvektive Energie, um das Belüftungssystem des Gebäudes mit Strom zu versorgen. Eine Membran aus leichtem und leistungsstarkem gewebten Verbundtextil umgibt, über einen Leichtbau-Stahlrahmen gespannt, das Gebäude und erzeugt mit minimalem Materialaufwand eine maximale optische Wirkung. Durch die in die Membran integrierten LED-Leisten wird die Gebäudehülle zur intelligenten leuchtenden Medienfassade und kann als digitale Leinwand für Animationen und Screen für öffentliche Informationsdienste genutzt werden. Das „Re-Skin"-Konzept ist ein Ergebnis der Forschungen von LAVA über Modelle für nachhaltige öffentliche Architekturen. Bei diesem Konzept werden modernste Leichtbaumaterialien mit den neuesten digitalen Herstellungsverfahren verbunden, um „Mehr" (Architektur) mit „Weniger" (Material-, Energie-, Zeitaufwand) zu schaffen.

BIONIC TOWER, 2009

Proposal for Abu Dhabi, United Arab Emirates

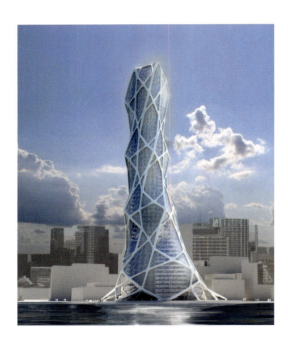

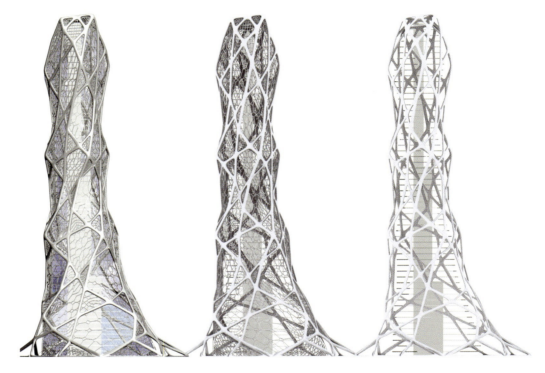

• Bionic Tower is a highrise meant for Abu Dhabi. Its construction and technology follow bionic rules of growth; its body is covered with an organically shaped facade.
• Der Bionic Tower ist ein Hochhaus für Abu Dhabi, dessen Konstruktion und Technologie nach bionischen Wachstumsregeln entwickelt wurden; eine organisch geformte Fassade überzieht den Baukörper.

● ENGLISCH Bionic Tower is a highrise projected for Abu Dhabi, its structure following shapes that can be found in nature. The building's technical systems imitate the efficiency of natural mechanisms and cycles. The façade will be an intelligent automated surface that takes into account practical aspects like ventilation, the intensity of the sunlight, and the collection of rainwater. Taking the pattern from organic mechanisms of regeneration, the building will be equipped with a system of structuring and reorganization that resembles nature. The things we have learned from observing nature, combined with highly developed methods of calculation, make it possible today to construct buildings of an astounding lightness, efficiency, and elegance. New materials and technologies enable us to increase the ability of buildings to adapt and react, while making them more durable and sensitive in the interaction with their environment. The building is not just a collection of individual structural elements, but works like an organism or an eco-system. Façade and technical systems are equipped with a control mechanism that reacts to external influences like air pressure, temperature, humidity, pollution, and sunlight. These aspects, of course, influence the Bionic Tower's outward appearance: It soars from the city like an organically grown entity; its surface with its irregular texture resembles the wings of an insect.

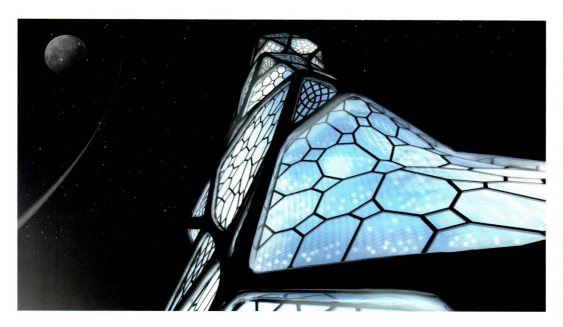

- LAVA (Laboratory for Visionary Architecture) was founded in 2007 by Chris Bosse, Tobias Wallisser, and Alexander Rieck. It is the only think tank operating from Stuttgart and Sydney. Using the motto "Green is the New Black", LAVA works with the most modern materials and high-tech applications to create a future architecture that is as close to nature as possible, follows bionic principles, and, by being environment-friendly, also has a positive effect on the individual and society as a whole.

- LAVA (Laboratory for Visionary Architecture) wurde 2007 von Chris Bosse, Tobias Wallisser und Alexander Rieck gegründet. Als einzigartiger Thinktank operiert das Büro von Stuttgart und Sydney aus. Unter dem Motto „Green is the new black" arbeitet LAVA mit neuesten Baumaterialien und Hightech-Verfahren, um die zukünftige Architektur möglichst naturnah, nach bionischen Prinzipien, umweltgerecht und dadurch auch menschenfreundlich und sozial verträglich zu gestalten.

● DEUTSCH   Der Bionic Tower ist ein für Abu Dhabi geplantes Hochhaus, das in seinem strukturellen Aufbau an Formen angelehnt ist, die in der Natur vorkommen. Die Systemtechnik des Gebäudes ahmt dabei Mechanismen und Kreisläufe nach, die aus der Natur bekannt sind. Für die Fassade ist bezüglich pragmatischer Aspekte wie Belüftung, Sonneneinstrahlung und Regenwassersammlung eine intelligente Automatisierung der Oberfläche vorgesehen. In Anlehnung an organische Regenerationsmechanismen soll das Gebäude mit einem naturähnlichen System zur Strukturierung und Reorganisation ausgestattet werden. Die Lehren, die man aus dem Studium der Natur gezogen und durch hochentwickelte Rechenverfahren entwickelt hat, ermöglichen es heutzutage, Bauten von verblüffender Leichtigkeit, Effizienz und Eleganz zu konstruieren. Neue Materialien und Technologien erlauben es, die Anpassungs- und Reaktionsfähigkeit von Gebäuden zu steigern und sie in ihrer Interaktion mit der Umwelt sensibler und belastbarer zu machen. Das Gebäude besteht nicht mehr nur aus einer Anordnung einzelner Bauelemente, sondern funktioniert wie ein Organismus oder Ökosystem. Gebäudehülle und Gebäudesystemtechnik verfügen über eine Steuerung, die auf äußere Einflüsse wie Luftdruck, Temperatur, Luftfeuchtigkeit, Luftverschmutzung und Sonneneinstrahlung reagiert. Diese Aspekte beeinflussen auch das äußere Erscheinungsbild des Bionic Towers: Er erhebt sich wie ein organisch gewachsenes Gebilde über der Stadt; seine Oberfläche erinnert mit ihrer unregelmäßigen Gewebestruktur an Insektenflügel.

WHY I AM IN LOVE WITH HIGH-RISES

Towers were once the crowning glory of architecture, the highest achievable level of difficulty, a mathematical and technical, structural and logistical masterly performance. Reaching for perfection, power, artistic brilliance, political religious positioning, there were many reasons which convinced people to build tall buildings. Towers were the tools for putting up a fight, providing protection, serving the purposes of defense, offering an overview and orientation and – less frequently – space for living and working.

In the major ports and delta cities of the world, Shanghai, Hong Kong, Sao Paulo, New York, Cairo, London, Marseille, Lagos, Osaka, Tokyo, Singapore, Sydney it has been possible for hundreds of years to study increasing population density patterns, some of which have been dramatic. The explosion in the population figures, regional and global migrations, as well as the concentration of communication-intensive jobs in the financial economy that depend on every form of city infrastructure are all reasons today for the towers to shoot up practically unchecked. There is no possible way of solving this ever-growing task other than through the construction of high-rises. Anyone who has ever seen the thousands of residential high-rise buildings when coming into land at the old Hong Kong airport will understand that architects and engineers, sociologists, communication experts and many others have to try to further develop this type of building as quickly as possible.

Seen from the central European dual income-oriented perspective of a relative reduction in the size of the population with – at the moment at least – its desperate defense of its prosperity, high-rise buildings and skyscrapers might appear to be uninteresting and the technologies required for their planning and construction of no interest. It may well also be that the type of American, fully air-conditioned box-shaped high-rise that was so successful in the 1970s to 1990s – whose origins were devised and exported by German architects, above all Mies van der Rohe – and whose worldwide triumphal march was accompanied by enormous energy consumption and a terrible (in part) flattening of the urban building culture, has cdistorted our appreciation of these necessities. Nevertheless, a view across the borders towards Europe presents us with growing cities such as Istanbul, Moscow, London, Paris, Marseille and Milan in which debates are held not only about high-rises and architectural style (sic!) – productively accompanied by strong arguments – but also increasing building densities are planned and constructed on a grand scale.

While we are still debating whether structural engineers ought to be involved in the training of architects, technology and know-how pools like Arup and SOM as well as Japanese giants of design such as Kajima, Obsajashi, and others have already begun to offer solutions to the problems related to these needs.

High-rise buildings and the solutions to the associated infrastructural, town planning, constructional and logistical problems offer – like only a few other projects such as airports, bridges, railway stations and clinics – opportunities for experimentation and technological advances. The concentration of money, time and expertise makes it possible to progress with big steps and supply blueprints for the world market from key innovative projects.

The construction of high buildings is a key technology of the 21st century. Like the aerospace industry, biotechnology and genetic engineering, computer science, communications technology, the automobile and health industries, it is the mastery that made it possible to build, for example, the Minster in Ulm, the Eiffel Tower and the Chrysler Building that is again required today in order to enable people to survive in towns and cities and structure their lives as pleasantly as possible.

Christoph Ingenhoven

WARUM ICH WOLKENKRATZER LIEBE

Türme waren einst die Krönung der Baukunst, höchster Schwierigkeitsgrad, mathematische und technische, konstruktive und logistische Meisterleistung. Streben nach Vollendung, Macht, künstlerische Brillanz, politisch-religiöse Positionierung, vieles brachte Menschen dazu, in die Höhe zu bauen. Türme waren Werkzeuge der Wehrhaftigkeit, gewährten Schutz, dienten der Verteidigung, boten Überblick und Orientierung, seltener auch Räume zum Wohnen und Arbeiten.

In den großen Hafen- und Delta-Städten der Welt, Schanghai, Hongkong, São Paulo, New York, Kairo, London, Marseille, Lagos, Osaka, Tokio, Singapur, Sydney, lassen sich seit 100 Jahren teils dramatische Verdichtungsmuster studieren. Die Explosion der Bevölkerungszahlen, regionale und globale Wanderungsbewegungen, aber auch die Konzentration finanztechnologisch-wirtschaftlicher, kommunikationsintensiver, von jeder Form großstädtischer Infrastruktur abhängiger Arbeitsplätze lassen bis heute praktisch ungebremst Türme in die Höhe schießen. Es ist kein Weg vorstellbar, der am Hochhaus zur Lösung dieser noch anwachsenden Aufgabe vorbeiführt. Wer jemals auch nur im Landeanflug auf den alten Hongkonger Flughafen die Tausenden von Wohnhochhäusern auf dem Gebiet der damaligen Kronkolonie gesehen hat, wird verstehen, dass Architekten und Ingenieure, Soziologen, Kommunikationsexperten und viele mehr sich um die zügige Weiterentwicklung dieses Bautyps bemühen müssen.

Aus der mitteleuropäischen doppelverdiener-orientierten Perspektive relativen Bevölkerungsrückgangs mit – noch – verzweifelt verteidigtem Wohlstand betrachtet, mögen hohe Häuser entbehrlich und die zu ihrer Planung und Errichtung notwendigen Technologien uninteressant erscheinen. Es mag auch sein, dass der Typus des in den 1970er- bis 1990er-Jahren so überaus erfolgreichen, amerikanischen, vollklimatisierten Schachtelhochhauses – in seinen Ursprüngen von deutschen Architekten, vor allem von Mies van der Rohe, erdacht und exportiert –, dessen weltweiter Siegeszug mit immensem Energieverbrauch und einer teilweise schrecklichen Verflachung der Stadtbaukultur einherging, uns eine vernünftige Sicht auf diese Notwendigkeiten verstellt. Jedoch bereits der Blick über die Grenzen nach Europa zeigt uns mit Istanbul, Athen, Moskau, London, Paris, Marseille und Mailand wachsende Städte, in denen durchaus – von heftigen Auseinandersetzungen auch produktiv begleitet – nicht nur Hochhaus- und Architekturstil-[sic!]Debatten geführt werden, sondern auch Verdichtung im großen Stil geplant und gebaut wird.

Während wir noch darüber nachdenken, ob bei der Architektenausbildung Tragwerksingenieure eine Rolle spielen sollten, haben sich längst Technologie- und Know-how-Pools wie Arup und SOM oder die japanischen Planungsriesen wie Kajima, Obajashi und andere daran gemacht, für diese Bedürfnisse Problemlösungen anzubieten.

Hochhäuser und die Lösung der mit ihnen verbundenen infrastrukturellen, städtebaulichen, konstruktiven und logistischen Probleme bieten wie nur wenig andere Projekte – Flughäfen, Brücken, Bahnhöfe, Kliniken – die Möglichkeit zum Experiment, zum Technologiesprung. Die Konzentration von Geld, Zeit und Know-how macht es möglich, in großen Schritten vorwärtszugehen und aus innovativen Schlüsselprojekten, Blaupausen für die Generika-Produkte des Weltmarktes zu liefern.

Das Bauen hoher Häuser ist eine Schlüsseltechnologie des 21. Jahrhunderts, wie Luft- und Raumfahrt, Bio- und Gentechnologie, Computer Science, Kommunikationstechnologie, Automobil- und Gesundheitsindustrie. Die Meisterschaft, die es ermöglicht, das Ulmer Münster, den Eiffelturm und das Chrysler Building zu bauen, ist auch heute vonnöten, um das Überleben von Menschen in Städten zu ermöglichen und so angenehm wie möglich zu gestalten.

Christoph Ingenhoven

FAULDERS STUDIO

SAN FRANCISCO, USA

"The future will be exponentially different from what we expect it to be."

„Die Zukunft wird exponentiell anders sein, als wir sie uns vorstellen."

GEOTUBE, 2010

Dubai, United Arab Emirates

● ENGLISCH GEOtube is a concept for a highrise in Dubai. The innovative aspects of this sculptural urban tower are its construction and the texture of its façade. An external vascular system of pipes constantly sprays the open pillars and the membrane cover with salt water from the Persian Gulf nearby. When the water evaporates, the salty residue turns the façade from a translucent blanket into a hard and white crust. The result is a permanent and regular growth of saline crystals on the building´s large visible façade, forming a layer or flaking off in bits. Thus, GEOtube becomes a special biotope for those animals which consider this type of environment their natural habitat. At the same time it offers the option to harvest crystalline salt from an easily accessible surface. The project uses a geological and non-organic material to interact with its natural environment.

PAGE/SEITE 82—84
- The façade of the highrise GEOtube consists of a pipe-system spraying salt-water, thus creating a crust of salt.
- Die Fassade des GEOtube-Hochhauses besteht aus einem Rohrleitungssystem, das Salzwasser sprüht und so eine Salzkruste entstehen lässt.

- GEOtube is characterized by is membrane-like façade, which consists of an ever-changing crust of salt.
- GEOtube hat eine membranartige Fassade, die aus einer sich ständig verändernden Salzhülle besteht.

- Faulders Studio has its seat in San Francisco, California, and is headed by Thom Faulder. It concerns itself with application-oriented concepts as well as with speculative research. The drafts take into consideration the innovative reaction of materials, the users´ perception, and the urban network as well as ecological requirements. Architecture is considered a dynamic open situation, not a static form or a preconditioned room. The firm enjoys an international reputation due to its comprehensive experience in regard to developing new methods of construction, production processes, and uses of materials, one of them being the "growing" of architecture, that is searching for ways to "program" architecture in a way that it will develop autonomously, thus "constructing itself".

- Faulders Studio im kalifornischen San Francisco wird von Thom Faulders geleitet und widmet sich der anwendungsorientierten Entwurfspraxis sowie der spekulativen Forschung. In die Entwürfe fließen innovatives Materialverhalten, Wahrnehmungen der Nutzer, urbane Vernetzung und ökologische Erfordernisse ein. Architektur wird als dynamische und offene Situation aufgefasst, nicht als statische Form oder vorprogrammierter Raum. Die internationale Reputation des Büros beruht insbesondere auf seiner großen Erfahrung bei der Entwicklung neuer Baumethoden, Fabrikationsprozesse und Materialanwendungen. Dazu gehört auch das Konzept des „Züchtens" von Architektur, bei dem nach den Möglichkeiten gefragt wird, wie Architektur so „programmiert" werden kann, dass sie sich autonom entwickelt und „selbst konstruiert".

- DEUTSCH GEOtube ist ein Entwurf für ein Hochhaus in Dubai. Das Neuartige an diesem skulpturalen, städtischen Tower sind seine Konstruktion und Gebäudeoberfläche. Das offen liegende Tragwerk aus Stahlrohren und die Membranhülle werden über ein externes, vaskuläres Rohrleitungssystem fortwährend mit Salzwasser aus dem nahe gelegenen Persischen Golf besprüht. Durch die Wasserverdunstung und die Salzablagerungen an den Gebäuderohren wandelt sich die Fassade von einer transparenten Hülle zu einer festen weißen Salzmembran. Es entsteht auf den großflächigen Außenseiten des Gebäudes ein permanentes, gleichförmiges Wachstum von Salzkristallen, die eine Schicht bilden oder in Stücken abplatzen. Für Tierarten, deren natürlicher Lebensraum dieser Art von Umgebung entspricht, wird der GEOtube zu einem speziellen Biotop. Gleichzeitig bietet er die Möglichkeit, an einer gut zugänglichen Oberfläche kristallines Salz zu ernten. Das Projekt macht sich ein geologisches, nicht-organisches Material zunutze, um mit der natürlichen Umwelt zu interagieren.

LABSCAPE

MILAN, ITALY
BRUSSELS, BELGIUM
NEW YORK, USA

"Architecture will be a new way to connect the world and share experiences. Architecture will take its role by creating experiences for its users. Architecture will then be actively integrated in human society."

„Architektur wird ein neuer Weg sein, die Welt zu verbinden und Erfahrungen zu teilen. Architektur wird eine Rolle übernehmen, wenn es darum geht, Erfahrungen für ihre Nutzer zu schaffen. Architektur wird dann aktiv in die menschliche Gesellschaft integriert sein."

TREE PLUG, 2005

Masterplan for Kuopio, Finland

● ENGLISCH   Tree Plug is a masterplan for Kuopio, Finland. It is based on a system of urban development that takes up the binary tree Y. The result of this natural ramification is the perfect ratio between surface and volume. Ramification links architectural elements simply and effectively and distributes buildings in the landscape in a natural way. The street pattern also is based on a fractal system, which includes an infinite self-reproduction with variable dimensions and the rotating axis of the binary tree. This way it is possible to arrange the city´s throughways in three hierarchical layers, while outdoor spaces can be developed at will. The residential buildings´ vertical orientation initiates a process which will make them blend in totally with their surroundings.

● DEUTSCH   Tree Plug ist ein urbaner Masterplan für Kuopio in Finnland. Er basiert auf einem System zur Stadtentwicklung nach dem Vorbild des Binärbaums Y. Diese natürliche Verästelungsstruktur ermöglicht, das Verhältnis von Oberfläche und Volumen zu optimieren. Durch die Verästelungen ergeben sich einfache und wirkungsvolle Verbindungen zwischen architektonischen Elementen und einer natürlichen Verteilung der Gebäude in der Landschaft. Die Anlage der Straßen basiert ebenfalls auf einem fraktalen Grundmuster, das die Selbstreproduktion bis ins Unendliche mit variablen Dimensionen und die rotierende Achse des Binärbaums beinhaltet. Mit dieser Methode lassen sich die in drei hierarchischen Ebenen aufgeteilten Verkehrswege der Stadt strukturieren. Im Außenraum entsteht ein freier Erschließungsbereich. Die vertikale Entwicklung der Wohngebäude setzt einen Prozess in Gang, der diese vollständig in den umgebenden Raum integriert.

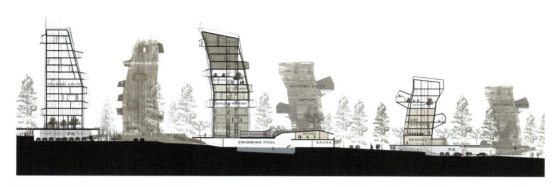

- Tree Plug is a concept for an urban residential complex with highrises in Finland, based on the geometrical structure of the binary tree Y.
- Tree Plug ist der Entwurf für eine urbane Wohnstruktur mit Hochhäusern in Finnland, die auf der fraktalen geometrischen Struktur des Binärbaumes Y basiert.

- LABscape was founded in 2003 by Robert Ivanov and Tecla Tangorra in Milan and Brussels. It is a cooperation of architects, urban planners, landscape architects, designers, artists, and media artists from all over the world. Meanwhile, the firm also has offices in New York and Pisa. LABscape is inspired by culture, technology, social conditions, and by the conviction that good architecture can be a meaningful experience for many people of different persuasion. By forming and redirecting an awareness of architecture, city, and landscape, LABscape creates concepts for complex and extremely contrasting experiences of space, new programmatic relations, and stunningly simple structures of organism, which have a positive effect on the environment.

- LABscape, gegründet 2003 von Robert Ivanov und Tecla Tangorra in Mailand und Brüssel, ist ein Zusammenschluss von Architekten, Stadtplanern, Landschaftsarchitekten, Designern, Künstlern und Medienkünstlern aus aller Welt. Inzwischen hat das Büro auch Zweigstellen in New York und Pisa. Inspiration bezieht LABscape aus Kultur, Technologie, den sozialen Bereichen sowie aus der Überzeugung, dass gute Architektur bedeutungsvolle Erfahrungen für sehr viele und sehr verschiedene Menschen bereithalten kann. Indem LABscape das Bewusstsein für Architektur, Stadt und Landschaft neu formt und ausrichtet, entstehen Konzepte für komplexe und extrem unterschiedliche Raumerfahrungen, neue programmatische Beziehungen und verblüffend einfache Organismusstrukturen mit positivem Einfluss auf die Umwelt.

LUCA D'AMICO LUCA TESIO
TURIN, ITALY

"There is a growing necessity for architectures that can evolve over time, adapting to external inputs. Flexible, dynamic, fast construction and disassembly will be key themes in the future, where buildings will change according to the user's request."

„Eine Architektur mit Entwicklungspotenzial, deren Gebäude auf äußere Anforderungen reagieren, wird zunehmend notwendig. Flexibler, dynamischer, schneller Auf- und Abbau sind entscheidende Themen der Zukunft, in der sich Gebäude nach den Wünschen ihrer Nutzer ändern."

NOMAD SKYSCRAPER, 2011

Finalist eVolo Skyscraper Competition 2011

● ENGLISCH   Globalization has turned quite a large number of city dwellers into nomads – people who settle down in different cities around the world for some weeks, months, or years. Nomad Skyscraper, a container highrise, offers nomadic abodes to this special type of urban population. It consists of an open skeleton frame for standard shipping containers, which have been converted into insertable residential units. The framework offers infrastructure as well as recreational zones, while the individual container can be moved by ship, truck, or train to almost any larger city worldwide, thus offering the urban nomad the feeling of a mobile home. The standardized structure of the building is formed by a tight network of steel pillars. At regular intervals platforms are attached, which add stability to the structure and at the same time serve as an urban microenvironment within the skyscraper – an indoor and an outdoor space for leisure and social activities. The motto is: Think Global, Live Local.

- Nomad Skyscraper is the standardized skeleton of a highrise, where regular residential containers can be inserted and removed again as desired.
- Der Nomad Skyscraper ist ein genormtes Hochhausgerüst, in das standardisierte Wohncontainer variabel eingefügt und wieder entfernt werden können.

- Luca D´Amico and Luca Tesio first met at the polytechnic in Turin. They both work for the firm DEA in Turin, which was founded in 1981 and became famous mostly for its residential projects in Piedmont. They concern themselves with the possibilities offered by architecture and urban planning fit for the future and our modern times.

- Luca D'Amico und Luca Tesio lernten sich während ihres Studiums am Turiner Polytechnikum kennen. Beide arbeiten im Büro DEA in Turin, das 1981 gegründet wurde und vor allem durch seine Wohnhaus-Projekte im Piemont bekannt geworden ist. Die Architekten beschäftigen sich mit zukunftsfähigen Anwendungsmöglichkeiten zeitgemäßer Architektur und Stadtplanung.

● DEUTSCH   Die Globalisierung hat einen beträchtlichen Teil der Stadtbewohner zu modernen Nomaden gemacht – Menschen, die sich für ein paar Wochen, Monate oder Jahre in verschiedenen Städten rund um die Welt niederlassen. Der Nomad Skyscraper schafft als Containerhochhaus für diese speziellen mobilen Stadtbewohner nomadische Behausungen. Er besteht aus einer offenen Skelettkonstruktion für Standard-Frachtcontainer, die zu einsteckbaren Wohneinheiten umfunktioniert werden. Das Rahmenkonstrukt des Skyscrapers bietet eine Infrastruktur sowie Erholungsbereiche, während die Container-Wohneinheiten per Schiff, LKW oder Zug in praktisch jede große Stadt auf der Welt versandt werden und dem modernen Stadtnomaden so ein Gefühl von transportabler Heimat ermöglichen können. Die standardisierte Struktur des Gebäudes setzt sich aus einem dichten Netz von Stahlträgern zusammen. In regelmäßigen Abständen ist eine Plattform angebracht, die die Konstruktion einerseits aussteift und zum anderen ein urbanes Mikroumfeld innerhalb des Wolkenkratzers bildet – einen Innen- und Außenraum zur Erholung und für gesellschaftliche Aktivitäten. Das Motto heißt: Global denken, lokal wohnen!

MASS STUDIES
SEOUL, KOREA

"Good architecture responds to both past and present while simultaneously revealing possibilities for the future. The challenge is to anticipate the increasingly overpopulated, rapidly changing society of the future, and to somehow manage to be sustainable at the same time."

„Gute Architektur reagiert sowohl auf die Vergangenheit als auch auf die Gegenwart und eröffnet zugleich Perspektiven für die Zukunft. Die Herausforderung heißt: Vorhersagen über die zunehmende Überbevölkerung und die sich schnell wandelnde Gesellschaft der Zukunft zu treffen und gleichzeitig nachhaltig zu handeln."

SEOUL COMMUNE 2026, 2005

Seoul, Korea

Gourd Bottle Tower Matrix + Honeycomb Matrix

● ENGLISCH   With their project Seoul Commune 2026 Mass Studies is taking a look at the feasibility of an alternative and sustainable form of settlement for the overpopulated metropolises of the future. Using the Korean city of Seoul in the year of 2026 (which is not so far away) as an example, they explore the urban concept "towers in a park", with the park marking the public, the high-rise towers the private space. However, public and private spaces are linked by a green tent-like membrane that covers the entire structure. The fifteen towers have the function of an architectural basic unit. They are shaped like gourds, their surface having a honeycomb structure (Gourd Bottle Tower Matrix + Honeycomb Matrix), and can be reached by elevators in their center.

The private housing units are relatively small cells of about 30 square meters and consist of a bedroom and a bathroom only. All other rooms like dining room and living room have been removed to the semi-public space of the hotels, thus serving as social meeting places for a constantly mobile nomadic population. Besides the living quarters, the towers also offer spaces for offices, medical facilities, administration, restaurants, and stores. All sixteen towers are connected to one another: in the ground floor there are circular walks for pedestrians only. Motorized traffic and parking structures have been moved below ground. At the second level a tramway takes care of public transportation.

The outer hull of the towers consists of a hexagonal grid, whose openings are filled with energy-efficient photovoltaic glass. The surface of the grid is coated with a geotextile material, which helps the growth of shadegiving creepers like vines and ivy. These integrated green plant structures are equipped with their own irrigation and tempering systems.

● DEUTSCH   Mit dem Projekt Seoul Commune 2026 untersucht Mass Studies die Machbarkeit einer alternativen und nachhaltigen Siedlungsform für die überbevölkerten Metropolen der Zukunft. Am Beispiel der koreanischen Stadt Seoul im Jahr 2026 (also schon bald) wird das urbane Konzept der „Türme im Park" durchgespielt, bei dem der Park den öffentlichen Bereich und die Hochhaustürme das private Terrain markieren. Die alles umspannende grüne Zellmembran verbindet dabei öffentlichen Raum und Privatsphäre auf eine biologisch-natürliche Art und Weise miteinander. Die 15 Türme in Form von Flaschenkürbissen mit Honigwabenstruktur (Gourd Bottle Tower Matrix + Honeycomb Matrix) fungieren als architektonische Grundeinheiten, die über Aufzüge im Zentrum jedes Turmes erschlossen werden.

Die privaten Wohneinheiten sind als relativ kleine Zellen von ca. 30 m² konzipiert und umfassen jeweils nur ein Schlaf- und Badezimmer. Alle weiteren Wohnräume wie Ess- und Wohnzimmer werden in den halböffentlichen Bereich der Hotels ausgelagert und sind somit soziale Treffpunkte für eine ständig mobile, nomadisierte Gesellschaft. Neben den Wohnräumen nehmen die Türme auch Raumkomplexe für Büros, medizinische Einrichtungen, Verwaltung, Restaurants und Geschäfte auf. Verkehrstechnisch sind alle 15 Türme miteinander verbunden: In der Erdgeschosszone gibt es Rundwege, die ausschließlich den Fußgängern vorbehalten sind. Der gesamte Autoverkehr wie auch die Parkhäuser werden unter die Erde verlegt. Auf Höhe der zweiten Ebene verläuft eine Schienenbahn als öffentliches Nahverkehrsmittel.

Die Außenhaut der Türme besteht aus einer sechseckigen Gitterkonstruktion, deren Öffnungen mit energieeffizientem Fotovoltaikglas gefüllt sind. Die Oberfläche der Gitterstruktur ist mit einem Geotextil beschichtet, das das Wachstum von schattenspendenden Rankpflanzen wie Wein oder Efeu fördert. Diese integrierten grünen Pflanzenstrukturen haben ein eigenes Bewässerungs- und Temperierungssystem.

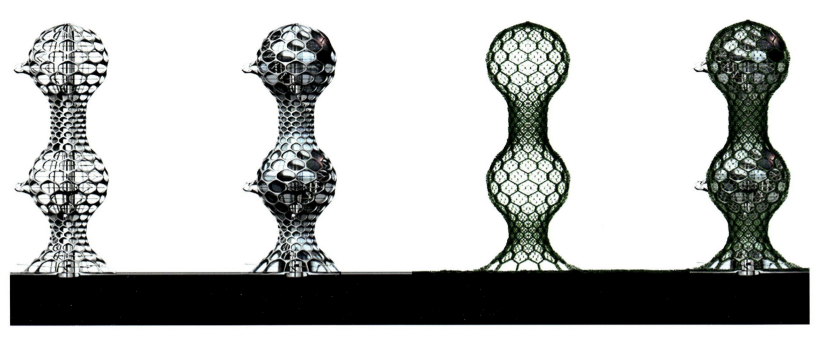

• Models of the highrise-towers shaped like a gourd-matrix with honeycomb-structure
• Schemata der Hochhaustürme in Form einer Flaschenkürbis-Matrix mit Honigwabenstruktur

• The Seoul Commune 2026 provides semi-public outdoor terraces to promote a social life in a green environment.
• In der Seoul Commune 2026 gibt es halböffentliche Außenterrassen, die ein soziales Miteinander in grüner Umgebung ermöglichen.

- Fifteen highrise-towers, having an outer hull formed by plants with an autonomous eco-system are turned into an urban entity by a park, circular paths, and trams on all levels.
- 15 Hochhaustürme, die eine Pflanzenhaut mit eigenständigem Ökosystem besitzen, werden durch einen Park und umlaufende Wege sowie Verkehrsbahnen in allen Geschossen zu einer urbanen Einheit verbunden.

- Mass Studies was founded in Seoul in 2003 by Minsuk Cho, wo had worked for the New York firms Kotalan/Mac Donald Studio and James Stewart Polshek & Partners as well as for OMA in Rotterdam before. As hinted by the name, the architectural firm concerns itself with the problems of overpopulation and mass production in global metropoles, especially in Asia. Cho does not ignore the difficulties an overpopulated mega-city might face in the future, but devises master-plans for a green city, which guarantees sustainability and a high quality of life in spite of its masses of inhabitants.

- Mass Studies wurde 2003 in Seoul von Minsuk Cho gegründet. Vorher arbeitete Cho in den New Yorker Büros Kolatan/Mac Donald Studio und James Stewart Polshek & Partners sowie bei OMA in Rotterdam. Wie der Name Mass Studies bereits andeutet, beschäftigt sich das Architekturbüro mit der Problematik von Überbevölkerung und Massenproduktion in den globalen Metropolen, vor allem Asiens. Cho blendet die zukünftigen Probleme einer überbevölkerten Megacity nicht aus, sondern entwirft Masterpläne für eine grüne Stadt, die trotz Vermassung Nachhaltigkeit und Lebensqualität gewährleistet.

ATMOSPHERE

The idea that architectures and even entire cities can create their own atmospheric systems is not a new one. Richard Buckminster Fuller already in 1950 designed a giant geodetic dome with a diameter of 3.5 kilometers, intended as a climatic cover for Manhattan. Not only since the first moon landing (1969) and the ensuing rise of Space Architecture and Design have space capsules as models for residential units and mobile houses become a common phenomenon. Architects also have learned from nature and its biological processes, like osmosis and climate, when devising atmospheric buildings and spaces.

However, our visionary approach to "world climate" has dramatically changed since the 1960s. While Frei Otto was convinced of the possibility to control the earth´s climate (unfortunately with the help of nuclear energy), in order to found settlements of buildings made from climatic membranes even in hostile environments like deserts and steppes, Philip Rahm´s vision of a metereological architecture, in view of the threat of a climatic catastrophe, is rather more down-to-earth. By now, the human race has learned the painful lesson that it already has strongly influenced the global climate by its behavior, while being unable to control it in a positive way.

In the light of this development, modern models of climatic architectures and spaces always take the environmental and ecological consequences into account. This, of course, does not mean the end of imaginative concepts of ephemeral and flexible units like bubbles, clouds, and pneumatic tubes. Just the opposite is true: architectural visions of spheric spatial continuities probably have never been as pronounced and innovative as they are today.

ATMOSPHÄRE

Die Vorstellung, dass Architekturen und sogar ganze Städte eigene atmosphärische Systeme ausbilden können, ist nicht neu. Richard Buckminster Fuller entwarf bereits 1950 eine riesige geodätische Kuppel mit einem Durchmesser von 3,5 km als Klimahülle für Manhattan. Und spätestens seit der ersten Mondlandung 1969 und dem damit verbundenen Aufkommen von Space-Architektur und -Design sind Raumkapseln als Entwürfe für Wohnungseinheiten und mobile Häuser weit verbreitet. Auch von der Natur und ihren biologischen Prozessen wie beispielsweise Osmose und Klimatisierung haben Architekten für ihre Entwürfe atmosphärischer Bauten und Räume gelernt.

Ein Unterschied zwischen den Zukunftsvisionen zum Thema „Erdklima" besteht jedoch zwischen den 1960er-Jahren und heute. Während Frei Otto noch davon überzeugt war, dass man das Weltklima kontrollieren und regeln könne (fataler Weise mithilfe von Atomenergie), sodass auch in unzugänglichen Gegenden wie Wüsten und Steppen mit Klimamembran-Bauten gesiedelt werden könne, fällt Philippe Rahms Vision einer meteorologischen Architektur in Anbetracht der drohenden Klimakatastrophe wesentlich nüchterner aus. Die Menschheit heute muss teilweise schmerzhaft erfahren, dass sie die globalen klimatischen Verhältnisse zwar bereits durch ihr Verhalten stark beeinflusst hat, sie aber nicht zu ihren Gunsten unter Kontrolle bringen kann.

Vor diesem Hintergrund sind die zeitgemäßen Modelle für Klima-Architekturen und -Räume stets mit der Berücksichtigung umweltökologischer Konsequenzen verbunden. Das schließt jedoch die fantasievolle Gestaltung ephemerer und wandelbarer Gebilde wie Blasen, Wolken und pneumatischer Schläuche in keinster Weise aus. Im Gegenteil, die Architekturvisionen sphärischer Raumkontinua waren wahrscheinlich noch nie so ausgeprägt und innovativ wie heute.

PAUL-ERIC SCHIRR-BONNANS
RENNES, FRANCE

"Future is relative. Future is not absolute. Future is preexisting. Future is just somewhere around us. Future is an invisible treasure just in front of our eyes. Architecture of the future can only emerge from finding new collages of existing components."

„Zukunft ist relativ. Zukunft ist nicht absolut. Zukunft präexistiert. Zukunft ist einfach irgendwo um uns herum. Zukunft ist ein unsichtbarer Schatz direkt vor unseren Augen. Die Architektur der Zukunft kann nur durch neue Kompositionen bestehender Komponenten entstehen."

FLAT TOWER ("TORME" = TOUR-DOME), 2011

Proposal for Rennes, France

2nd place eVolo Skyscraper Competition 2011

- With its energy-efficient surface Flat Tower arches over a large green zone.
- Mit seiner energieeffizienten Oberfläche überwölbt der Flat Tower eine große Grünfläche.

● ENGLISCH   This flat dome, which arches over the French city of Rennes like a bubble, offers the option of creating residential clusters without dominating the city´s silhouette or building on green zones. Flat Tower stretches over a large green area and makes use of sunlight and rainwater, thus being a sustainable solution for major development plans. Due to the density of our present cities, it is almost impossible to construct new buildings without damage to the environment. Still, the demand for residential, commercial, and utility spaces remains rather high and is even expected to grow in the future. Therefore, highrise towers are the most common choice, as they need a minimum amount of space relative to their height. The race for the highest building is still going on, while building standards are continually improved. Paul-Eric Schirr-Bonnans, together with Yohann Mescam and Xavier Schirr-Bonnans, thinks that the time has come for a paradigm shift: cities should not be built higher and higher any longer, but into an "arched width". For this purpose he chose a flat domed structure, arching over a wide area at a low height, while preserving the beauty and functionality of the existing environment by enveloping it. A honeycomb structure with open and closed cells makes it possible to illuminate both the enclosed areas and the ground. This shape is especially suited for the production of renewable energies, as the dome´s large surfaces can collect rainwater and provide space for solar panels.

- Flat Tower is a flat domed structure projected for the city of Rennes.
- Der Flat Tower ist für die französische Stadt Rennes als ein flaches Kuppelgebäude geplant.

● Paul-Eric Schirr-Bonnans founded his firm for architecture, design, and urban planning in March 2010 in Rennes, France. With each of his projects he emphasizes the importance of devising architectural processes that take the respective conditions in regard to environment, landscape, climate, cultural history, and social structure into account.

● Paul-Eric Schirr-Bonnans gründete sein Büro für Architektur, Design und Stadtentwicklung im März 2010 im französischen Rennes. Bei jedem seiner Projekte legt er besonderen Wert auf die Konzeptionierung architektonischer Prozesse, bei denen die jeweiligen Konditionen von Umwelt, Landschaft, Klima, Kulturgeschichte und Sozialstruktur berücksichtigt werden.

● DEUTSCH Der vorgeschlagene flache Kuppelbau, der sich wie eine Blasenhülle über die französische Stadt Rennes wölbt, bietet die Möglichkeit, Wohndichte herzustellen, ohne die Stadtsilhouette zu dominieren oder Grünflächen zu überbauen. Der Flat Tower überfängt einen großen Grünbereich, verwertet Sonnenlicht und Regenwasser und stellt damit eine nachhaltige Lösung für größere Entwicklungsvorhaben dar. Die derzeitige hohe Dichte in Städten erlaubt es kaum noch, neue Gebäude zu errichten, ohne die Umwelt zu zerstören. Dennoch ist aber nach wie vor der Bedarf an Wohnraum sowie an Räumen für Arbeit und Versorgung in den Städten sehr hoch und wird auch in der Zukunft weiter ansteigen. Der für diese Zwecke am häufigsten eingesetzte Baukörper ist das Turmhochhaus, bei dem Höhe und bebaute Fläche in günstigem Verhältnis stehen. Der Wettlauf um das höchste Gebäude hält an, und die allgemein anerkannten Standards werden immer weiter entwickelt. Paul-Eric Schirr-Bonnans, Yohann Mescam und Xavier Schirr-Bonnans meinen, dass es Zeit ist für einen Paradigmenwechsel: In der Stadt sollte nicht mehr in die Höhe, sondern vielmehr in die „überwölbende Breite" gebaut werden. Deshalb wählten sie eine flache Kuppelkonstruktion, die eine weite Fläche überspannt und die Schönheit und Funktionalität der bestehenden Umwelt erhält, indem sie diese einhüllt. Eine Wabenstruktur mit offenen und geschlossenen Zellen ermöglicht die Belichtung der geschlossenen Bereiche und der Bodenflächen. Die Kuppelform eignet sich besonders für die Nutzung erneuerbarer Energien, da die große Oberfläche zum Auffangen von Regenwasser und zur Anbringung von Solaranlagen genutzt werden kann.

WERNER SOBEK
STUTTGART, GERMANY

"The most important task that architects and engineers have to solve is not only to make sure that all relevant norms are observed but to make ecology breathtakingly attractive and exciting."

„Die wichtigste Aufgabe, die Architekten und Ingenieure lösen müssen, ist allerdings nicht, für eine Einhaltung aller relevanten Normen zu sorgen, sondern Ökologie atemberaubend attraktiv und aufregend zu machen."

R 129,
2001–2012

- R 129 is a visionary mobile residential capsule with a light-weight build and can also float on water.
- R 129 ist eine visionäre mobile Wohnkapsel in Leichtbauweise, die auch auf dem Wasser schwimmen könnte.

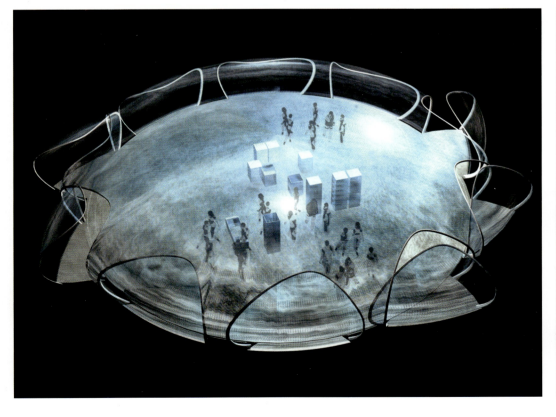

- The transparent and organically shaped surface of R 129 produces energy and provides utilities.
- Die transparente, organisch geformte Haut von R 129 ist eine Energie- und Versorgungshülle.

• ENGLISCH R 129 is the visionary study for a mobile residential capsule and an attempt to explore the options of expanding the limits of transparency and dematerialization in construction. The capsule´s enclosed main body is made of a very light-weight and transparent synthetic material and can be moved freely on land as well as on water due to its domed top and rounded underside. The supporting structure consists of hollow carbon struts, the carbon platform contains two layers that house the heating and technical systems as well as an energy-storing device and outlets for electricity, water, pressurized air, and communications technologies. Inside R 129, the spaces dedicated to the different aspects of living can be flexibly devided. The obligatory sanitary and kitchen appliances are located in a mobile central unit. The top of the structure is equipped with an electrochrome film, which makes it possible to turn the entire surface, or only parts of it, light, dark, transparent, or opaque.

• DEUTSCH R 129 ist eine visionäre Studie für eine mobile Wohnkapsel, bei der ausgelotet wird, wie weit die Grenzen der Transparenz und der Entmaterialisierung im Bauwesen verschoben werden können. Der geschlossene Baukörper der Kapsel besteht aus einem sehr leichten und transparenten Kunststoff und ist mit seiner abgerundeten Ober- und Unterseite frei im Raum und auf dem Wasser beweglich. Das Traggerüst wird aus Karbonhohlträgern gebildet, die Karbonbodenplatte trägt einen Heiz- sowie einen Technikboden, der Speichermöglichkeiten und Anschlüsse für Strom, Wasser, Druckluft und Kommunikationstechnologien bietet. Im Innenbereich der Kapsel R 129 gibt es keine festgelegten Abtrennungen von einzelnen Wohnfunktionsbereichen, in einer verschiebbaren Zentraleinheit sind die notwendigen Sanitär- und Kücheneinrichtungen untergebracht. Die äußere Hülle ist mit einer elektrochromen Folie beschichtet, mit der einzelne Partien oder die gesamte Oberfläche hell, dunkel, transparent oder undurchsichtig geschaltet werden können.

• The architect Werner Sobek enjoys a worldwide reputation as a specialist for engineering, design, and sustainable concepts. His corporation has seats in Stuttgart, Dubai, Frankfurt, Istanbul, Cairo, Moscow, New York, and Sao Paolo. The creations of the firm, founded in 1992, are marked by their designs based on good engineering and complex concepts to cut down the comsumption of energy and material. The focus lies on the building of highrises, the planning of façades, and on special constructions in steel, glass, titanium, fabric, and wood as well as on concepts for sustainable edifices. As the successor of Frei Otto and Jörg Schlaich, Werner Sobek heads the institute of light-weight construction, drafts, and design at the university of Stuttgart. He also holds the Mies van der Rohe professorship at the Illinois Institute of Technology in Chicago.

• Der Architekt Werner Sobek ist weltweit als Experte für Engineering, Design und nachhaltige Konzepte bekannt. Seine Firmengruppe hat Niederlassungen in Stuttgart, Dubai, Frankfurt, Istanbul, Kairo, Moskau, New York und São Paulo. Die Arbeiten des 1992 gegründeten Büros zeichnen sich durch ihre Gestaltung auf der Basis von gutem Ingenieurwesen und ausgeklügelten Konzepten zur Minimierung von Energie- und Materialverbrauch aus. Besondere Schwerpunkte liegen im Hochhausbau, in der Fassadenplanung, in Sonderkonstruktionen aus Stahl, Glas, Titan, Stoff und Holz sowie in der Planung von nachhaltigen Gebäuden. Als Nachfolger von Frei Otto und Jörg Schlaich leitet Werner Sobek das Institut für Leichtbau, Entwerfen und Konstruieren an der Universität Stuttgart. Er hat darüber hinaus die Mies-van-der-Rohe-Professur am Illinois Institute of Technology in Chicago inne.

PHILIPPE RAHM
PARIS, FRANCE

"Climate change is forcing us to rethink architecture radically, to shift our focus away from a purely visual and functional approach towards one that is more sensitive, more attentive to the invisible, climate-related aspects of space."

„Der Klimawandel zwingt uns, radikal neu über Architektur nachzudenken, unseren Fokus von einem rein visuellen und funktionalen Ansatz abzuwenden und sensibler und aufmerksamer für die unsichtbaren klimatischen Raumaspekte zu werden."

DOMESTIC ASTRONOMY, 2009

Shown at the exhibition „Green Architecture for the Future", Louisiana Museum of Modern Art, Humlebæk, Denmark

● ENGLISCH   Philippe Rahm devised the residential concept Domestic Astronomy for an exhibition with the title "Green Architecture for the Future", held in Denmark in 2009. Rahm´s basic idea of future living is founded on the notion that space is inhabited not only in terms of size, but also in regard to the prevailing atmosphere. Accordingly, the usual domestic appliances like furniture and sanitary installations are taken off the ground and moved to higher spheres. They are accessible by stationary ladders, which cut across the rooms. The physical differences in temperature within the room itself are illustrated by light effects. Archimedes´ principle that says that warm air rises, while cold air remains close to the ground, has led to a standardized concept in regard to tempering the different zones of living: 16°C for the bedroom, 18°C for the kitchen, and 22°C for the bathroom. Rahm, however, reverse this system by evenly heating a common room, thus creating a warmer zone in its upper and a cooler one in its lower region. Bed, bathtub, and toilet are installed at different heights, following these temperature zones.

• Lamps and light effects in the atmospheric living space mark the temperature and its fluctuation.
• Lampen und Lichteffekte kennzeichnen im atmosphärischen Wohnraum Temperaturzustände und -schwankungen.

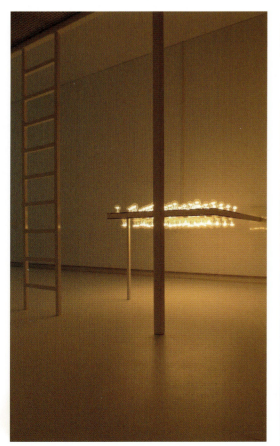

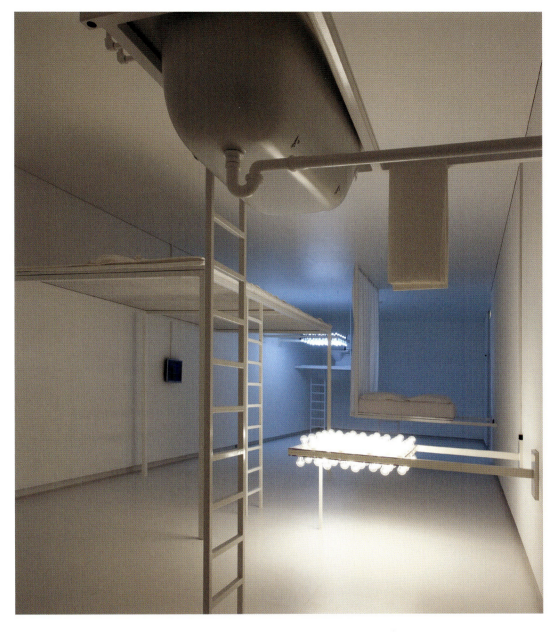

- In a heated room warm air rises, while cooler air remains close to the ground. Therefore, built-in furniture is installed at different levels.
- Im beheizten Wohnraum steigt die warme Luft nach oben, die kühlere hält sich im Bodenbereich. Dementsprechend sind die Einbaumöbel auf unterschiedlichen Raumhöhen angebracht.

- Philippe Rahm is an experimental architect and architectural theorist, based in Paris. In 2008 he was one of the 20 architects invited to the architectual biennial in Venice by Aaron Betsky. In 2009 his book "Architecture météorologique" was published, in which he advocates a future architecture, following climate, atmosphere, and moods. In 2009 he was appointed chairman of the "Symposium on Architecture and Climate: Towards an Atmospheric Architecture" at the Royal Danish Academy, which took place parallel to the UN conference on climate. Currently, Philippe Rahm is involved in a number of visionary, but also realizable projects like designing office buildings in France and Italy.

- Philippe Rahm ist ein experimentell arbeitender Architekt und Architekturtheoretiker, der in Paris arbeitet. 2008 gehörte er zu den 20 Architekten, die Aaron Betsky zur Architektur-Biennale nach Venedig einlud. 2009 erschien sein Buch „Architecture météorologique", in dem er sich für eine zukünftige Architektur des Klimas, der Atmosphäre und der Stimmungen ausspricht. Er wurde 2009 zum Direktor des „Symposium on Architecture and Climate: Towards an Atmospheric Architecture" an der Königlich Dänischen Akademie berufen, das parallel zur UN-Klimakonferenz stattfand. Derzeit arbeitet Philippe Rahm an einer Reihe von visionären, aber dennoch realisierbaren Projekten, wie beispielsweise der Konzeption von Bürogebäuden in Frankreich und Italien.

- DEUTSCH Philippe Rahm entwarf das Wohnkonzept Domestic Astronomy für eine Ausstellung 2009 in Dänemark mit dem Titel „Green Architecture for the Future". Rahms Grundidee für ein zukünftiges Wohnen ist die Vorstellung, dass man im Raum nicht nur die Fläche, sondern vor allem auch die im Raum vorhandene Atmosphäre „bewohnt". Zu diesem Zweck wird die übliche Wohnungsausstattung wie Möbel und sanitäre Einrichtungen vom Boden gelöst und in höheren Raumsphären angebracht. Zu erreichen sind sie über festinstallierte Leitern, die die Raumvolumina durchschneiden. Die physikalischen Unterschiede der Temperaturverteilung im Raum werden durch Lichteffekte sichtbar gemacht. Der archimedische Grundsatz, dass warme Luft nach oben steigt und kalte Luft sich unten am Boden hält, hat für ein Standardkonzept zur empfohlenen Temperierung unterschiedlicher Wohnräume geführt: Der Schlafraum sollte 16°C, die Küche 18°C und das Badezimmer 22°C haben. Rahm kehrt nun diese Systematik um, indem er einen Einheitswohnraum gleichmäßig beheizt und damit wärmere Luft im oberen Bereich und kühlere Luft in der unteren Zone erzeugt. Entsprechend dieser Temperaturzonen im Raum bringt er die Einbauten von Bett, Badewanne und Toilette auf unterschiedlichen Raumhöhen an.

TOWARDS A METEOROLOGICAL ARCHITECTURE

The building industry is one of the main culprits in global warming because the burning of fossil fuels to heat or cool dwellings is the source of nearly 50% of greenhouse gas emissions. Following some resistance and procrastination the whole industry is now mobilised in favour of sustainable development and arguing for improved heat insulation on outside walls, the use of renewable energies, consideration for the whole life cycle of materials and more compact building designs.

It is clear that these steps all have a definite objective, which is to combat global warming by reducing CO_2 emissions. But over and above that goal, beyond such socially responsible and ecological objectives, might not climate be a new architectural language, a language for architecture rethought with meteorology in mind? Might it be possible to imagine climatic phenomena such as convection, conduction or evaporation for example as new tools for architectural composition? Could vapor, heat or light become the new bricks of contemporary construction?

Climate change is forcing us to rethink architecture radically, to shift our focus away from a purely visual and functional approach towards one that is more sensitive, more attentive to the invisible, climate-related aspects of space. Slipping from the solid to the void, from the visible to the invisible, from metric composition to thermal composition, architecture as meteorology opens up additional, more sensual, more variable dimensions in which limits fade away and solids evaporate. The task is no longer to build images and functions but to open up climates and interpretations. At the large scale, meteorological architecture explores the atmospheric and poetic potential of new construction techniques for ventilation, heating, dual-flow air renewal and insulation. At the microscopic level, it plumbs novel domains of perception through skin contact, smell and hormones. Between the infinitely small of the physiological and the infinitely vast of the meteorological, architecture must build sensual exchanges between body and space and invent new aesthetic philosophical approaches capable of making long-term changes to form and to the way we will inhabit buildings tomorrow.

Philippe Rahm

PLÄDOYER FÜR EINE METEOROLOGISCHE ARCHITEKTUR

Die Bauindustrie gehört zu den Hauptschuldigen an der Erderwärmung, da durch die Verbrennung von fossilen Brennstoffen zum Heizen und Kühlen von Wohnungen fast 50% der Treibhausgase entstehen. Nach einigem Widerstand und Zögern ist der gesamte Industriezweig nun sensibilisiert für eine nachhaltige Entwicklung und setzt sich für bessere Wärmedämmung an Außenwänden, den Einsatz erneuerbarer Energien, die Betrachtung des gesamten Lebenszyklus' von Materialien und kompaktere Gebäudeentwürfe ein.

Natürlich haben diese Schritte ein klares Ziel, nämlich die Bekämpfung der Erderwärmung durch Reduktion der CO_2-Emissionen. Aber abgesehen von diesem Ziel, das von gesellschaftlicher und ökologischer Verantwortung geprägt ist, könnte nicht das Klima selbst eine neue Sprache der Architektur werden, eine Sprache für die Architektur, bei der alles mit Blick auf die Meteorologie überdacht wird? Könnte es möglich sein, sich klimatische Phänomene wie etwa Konvektionsströme, Wärmeleitung oder Verdunstung als neue Werkzeuge für den Entwurf in der Architektur vorzustellen? Könnten Dampf, Wärme oder Licht die neuen Bausteine des zeitgenössischen Bauens werden?

Der Klimawandel zwingt uns, radikal neu über Architektur nachzudenken, unseren Fokus von einem rein visuellen und funktionalen Ansatz abzuwenden und sensibler und aufmerksamer für die unsichtbaren klimatischen Raumaspekte zu werden. Indem man sich vom Massiven zum Offenen, vom Sichtbaren zum Unsichtbaren, vom exakten Entwurf zur thermischen Komposition wendet, eröffnet die Architektur als Meteorologie zusätzliche, fühlbarere, variablere Dimensionen, in denen sich Grenzen auflösen und Festes verdampft. Die Aufgabe besteht nicht mehr darin, Bilder und Funktionen zu bauen, sondern Klimasituationen und Interpretationen zu eröffnen. Im Großen ergründet die meteorologische Architektur das atmosphärische und poetische Potenzial der neuen Bautechniken für Belüftung, Heizung, zweiflutigen Luftwechsel und Dämmung. Im Kleinen lotet sie neue Wahrnehmungsmöglichkeiten durch Hautkontakt, Geruch und Hormone aus. Zwischen dem unendlich Kleinen des Physischen und dem unendlich Weiten des Meteorologischen muss Architektur sinnlich erfahrbare Austauschmöglichkeiten zwischen Körper und Raum schaffen und neue ästhetische und philosophische Ansätze erfinden, die in der Lage sind, langfristige Veränderungen an den Formen und der Art und Weise zu erreichen, wie wir morgen unsere Gebäude bewohnen werden.

Philippe Rahm

ARCHITECTURE AND VISION

VITERBO, ITALY
MUNICH, GERMANY

"We envision a world where technology helps to reach a harmony between human beings and nature."

„Wir stellen uns eine Welt vor, in der die Technologie die Harmonie zwischen Mensch und Natur unterstützt."

MOON VILLE, 2009

Client: Cité de l'Espace, Toulouse, France

• Moon Village is supposed to become reality in 2050 as a permanent human settlement on the moon.
• Als dauerhafte menschliche Siedlung auf dem Mond soll Moon Ville im Jahr 2050 Realität werden.

● ENGLISCH   Moon Ville is the computer simulation of a permanent human settlement on the moon, projected for the year 2050. It offers residential and commercial spaces for 100 inhabitants and visitors. Owing to its location at the south pole, infrastructure and the hothouses where air and water are processed and fruit and vegetables are grown can be constantly powered by solar energy. Locally harvested lunar rocks (regolith) produce oxygen that fuels the space shuttles during their return to earth. Space telescopes, installed in lunar craters, open new views into galaxies yet unknown.

● DEUTSCH   Moon Ville ist die Computersimulation einer dauerhaften menschlichen Siedlung auf dem Mond für das Jahr 2050. Sie bietet Wohn- und Arbeitsraum für 100 Einwohner und Besucher. Ihre Lage am Südpol ermöglicht die konstante Nutzung der Sonnenenergie zur Versorgung der technischen Infrastruktur und der Treibhäuser, in denen Luft und Wasser aufbereitet sowie Obst und Gemüse angebaut werden. Mit dem vor Ort abgebauten steinigen Mondboden (Regolith) wird Sauerstoff produziert, der die Raumfähren auf ihrem Rückflug zur Erde antreibt. In Mondkratern installierte Weltraumteleskope eröffnen neue Blicke in heute noch unbekannte Galaxien.

MOON BASE TWO, 2007

NASA and ESA are following programs to develop permanent Moon bases and to land astronauts on the Moon by 2020

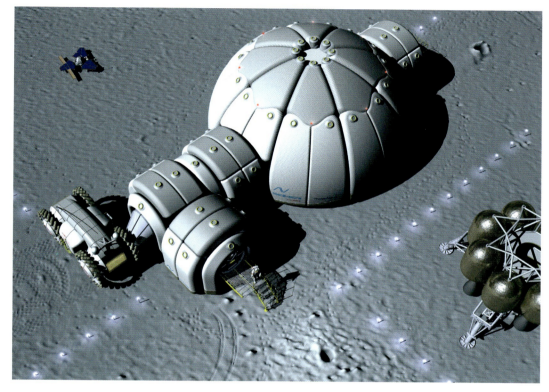

- Moon Base Two is meant to be a lab as well as a supply unit for the next manned moon landing in 2020.
- Moon Base Two ist Forschungsstätte und Versorgungslager, konzipiert für die geplante Mondlandung 2020.

● ENGLISCH   Moon Base Two is the concept of a permanent station on the moon for purposes of research and discovery. It is projected for the planned landing of astronauts from NASA and ESA in 2020 and also serves as a lab for studies that explore the possibility of founding permanent human settlements far away from Earth. The lab was especially designed to be transported into space by the rocket Ares-V. It unfolds after landing and is immediately able to house the first astronauts, which means up to four persons for six months at a time.

● DEUTSCH   Moon Base Two ist der Entwurf für eine Langzeit-Station auf dem Mond, für die Forschung vor Ort und zur Erkundung der Umgebung, konzipiert für die geplante Landung von Astronauten der NASA und ESA auf dem Mond im Jahr 2020. Darüber hinaus dient sie als Forschungsstätte für Studien über mögliche dauerhafte menschliche Siedlungen fernab der Erde. Das Labor wurde dafür ausgelegt, mit der Ares-V-Rakete in den Weltraum transportiert zu werden. Nach der Landung entfaltet sich die Station und kann sofort die ersten Astronauten aufnehmen, und zwar bis zu vier Personen für jeweils sechs Monate.

● Architecture and Vision is an international and interdisciplinary architectural and design studio, founded in 2003. It specializes in innovative solutions and the transfer of the different technologies developed for aviation and space-travel to use on earth. The name "Architecture and Vision" does not only stand for the initials of its two founders, Arturo Vittori and the Swiss Andreas Vogler, but also reflects their conviction that architecture can only make a lasting cultural contribution to its era if it takes a visionary look at the future. Architecture and Vision´s utopias aim at improving the conditions of life for everyone. Therefore, technologies and utilizable resources are meant to be used in a way that leads to a peaceful coexistence of man, technical innovation, and nature.

● Architecture and Vision ist ein 2003 gegründetes internationales und interdisziplinäres Architektur- und Design-Studio, das sich auf die Entwicklung innovativer Lösungen und den Transfer unterschiedlichster Luft- und Raumfahrttechnologien, auch für Anwendungen auf der Erde, spezialisiert hat. Der Name Architecture and Vision leitet sich nicht nur von den Initialen der beiden Gründer, dem Italiener Arturo Vittori und dem Schweizer Andreas Vogler, ab, er spiegelt auch deren Überzeugung wider, dass Architektur in ihrer Zeit nur dann einen dauerhaften kulturellen Beitrag leisten kann, wenn sie eine Vision von der Zukunft hat. Mit seinen utopischen Entwürfen verfolgt Architecture and Vision das Ziel, die Lebensqualität der Menschen zu verbessern. Dafür sollen Technologien und nutzbare Ressourcen so verwendet werden, dass ein harmonisches Miteinander von Mensch, Technik und Natur entstehen kann.

FOSTER + PARTNERS
LONDON, UK

"The architecture of the future will be driven by the global ambition to develop a sustainable way of living and to tackle the challenges we face as the world's urban populations proliferate. Buildings account for around half the energy consumed in the world. We must therefore take into account also the infrastructure of cities – particularly transport, because buildings and the movement of people account for 70% of the energy we consume."

„Die Architektur der Zukunft wird bestimmt sein von dem weltweiten Ziel, einen nachhaltigen Lebensstil zu entwickeln und die Herausforderungen angesichts der ständig wachsenden Bevölkerungszahlen in den Städten zu meistern. Gebäude verbrauchen etwa die Hälfte der weltweit eingesetzten Energie. Aber auch die Infrastruktur der Städte muss in die Planungen einbezogen werden – insbesondere der Verkehr, da Gebäude und die Beförderung der Menschen für 70% der verbrauchten Energie verantwortlich sind."

SPACEPORT, 2006–2011

Roswell, New Mexico, USA

● ENGLISCH   Spaceport, which is located in the desert-like landscape of New Mexico, will be a private airport for space travel and thus the first one of its kind. Norman Foster´s concept reflects the thrill of the imminent possibility of space tourism, while trying to be as environment-friendly as possible. Formally, the projected airport building follows the contours of the future spaceship. Visitors and astronauts enter the building through a groove, cut into the desert. The supporting walls create a room for an exhibition on the history of space-travel, the region, and its inhabitants. The imposing linear axis of the groove is continued into the interior of the building, reaching over a gallery into the super-hangar, which houses the spaceships and a simulation room, and finally into the terminal. The glass wall facing the runway offers a spectacular view of the starting and landing spaceships, which visitors can enjoy from the vantage-point of a platform. The sunken building is lowered into the desert ground to make use of the thermic mass, which protects the building from New Mexico´s extreme climate, while using the westerly winds for ventilation. Skylights allow the daylight to stream in, thus making artificial light largely superfluous. The building will be constructed mainly with the help of local materials and techniques, in order to meet the demands of sustainability and to keep the negative impact on the environment as low as possible.

• The first space-travel airport of its kind will be situated in the desert of New Mexico and be shaped like future spaceships.
• Der erste Weltraumflughafen seiner Art soll in der Wüste von New Mexiko stationiert werden und hat die Form zukünftiger Raumschiffe.

- Visitors and astronauts enter Spaceport by an aisle, cut deep into the desert.
- Über eine tief in den Wüstenboden eingeschnittene Schneise betreten Besucher und Astronauten den Spaceport.

DEUTSCH In der wüstenähnlichen Landschaft von New Mexico gelegen, wird der Spaceport als privater Flughafen für Weltraumflüge das erste Gebäude seiner Art überhaupt sein. Norman Fosters Entwurf gibt dem Nervenkitzel Ausdruck, den der bevorstehende Weltraumtourismus auslösen kann, und soll gleichzeitig möglichst umweltschonend ausfallen. Formal orientiert sich der projektierte Baukörper des Airports an den Dimensionen des Raumschiffs der Zukunft. Besucher und Astronauten betreten das Gebäude durch eine Schneise, die tief in die Wüstenlandschaft eingeschnitten ist. Die Stützwände bilden einen Ausstellungsbereich, der die Geschichte der Raumfahrt sowie der Region und ihrer Siedler dokumentiert. Die mächtige lineare Schneisenachse verlängert sich im Gebäudeinneren über eine Galerieebene hinweg bis zum Super-Hangar, der das Raumschiff und den Simulationsraum beherbergt, und setzt sich bis zur Abfertigungshalle fort. Die Glasfassade zur Startbahn gewährt dem Besucher von einer Plattform aus die begehrte Aussicht auf startende und landende Raumschiffe.

Der Bau ist deshalb tief in die Wüstenlandschaft eingegraben, um die thermische Masse zu nutzen, die das Gebäude vor dem extremen Klima New Mexikos schützt. Gleichzeitig können so die Westwinde für die Belüftung genutzt werden. Oberlichter leiten das Tageslicht optimal in den Bau, sodass tagsüber kaum zusätzliches Kunstlicht nötig ist. Es kommen vorwiegend örtliche Baumaterialien und regionale Bautechniken zum Einsatz, die dem Bemühen um Nachhaltigkeit und geringe Umweltbelastung gerecht werden.

- Foster + Partners is headed by its founder and CEO, Lord Norman Foster. The firm has its headquarters in London and project offices all over the world. Already some time ago, it advocated an approach of sustainability in architecture and urban planning reflected in its projects, which range from giant masterplans to product design. Among the more famous projects of Foster + Partners are the world's largest airport terminal in Beijing, the headquarters of Swiss Re in London, the Millau viaduct in France, the dome of the Reichstag in Berlin, the Great Court of the British Museum in London, and the headquarters of the HSBC Bank in Hong Kong and London.

- Foster + Partners wird von seinem Gründer und Vorsitzenden Lord Norman Foster geleitet. Das Büro mit Hauptsitz in London unterhält Projektbüros in aller Welt und setzte bereits früh auf einen nachhaltigen Ansatz bei seinen Architektur- und Stadtplanungen, die vom gigantischen Masterplan bis zum Produktdesign reichen. Zu den bekannteren Projekten von Foster + Partners gehören der weltgrößte Flughafenterminal in Peking, die Hauptverwaltung der Swiss Re in London, das Millau Viadukt in Frankreich, die Reichstagskuppel in Berlin, der Great Court im Londoner British Museum und die Hauptverwaltungen der HSBC-Bank in Hongkong und London.

CARLORATTI-ASSOCIATI
TURIN, ITALY

"Digital civilization seeks and will find its architectural expression!"
[APOLOGIES TO LE CORBUSIER]

„Die digitale Gesellschaft sucht ihren architektonischen Ausdruck und wird ihn sicher finden!"
[ENTSCHULDIGUNG AN LE CORBUSIER]

THE CLOUD, 2009

London, UK

Competition proposal
Public structure – symbol for the London 2012 Olympics

Design team: Walter Nicolino and Carlo Ratti, with Alex Haw; Consultants: schlaich bergermann und partner, Arup, Agence Ter, GMJ, Studio FM Milano, Tomas Saraceno

- The Cloud is the concept for a viewing platform surrounded by oversize air-bubbles with integrated digital networks for the 2012 Olympics in London.
- The Cloud ist der Entwurf für eine Aussichtsplattform für die Olympiade 2012 in London, die von riesigen Luftblasen mit digitalen Netzwerksystemen umwölkt wird.

● ENGLISCH Buildings constructed for Olympic games and world fairs often are marked by a massive and monolithic heavy-handedness, while also occupying lots of space, in Carlo Ratti´s eyes an obsolete approach. Therefore, his project The Cloud seems to be as light as air and is a homage to the digital era, characterized by bits and atoms, leaving the confines of traditional materials like steel and glass. The construction is meant to symbolize the social networks of a peaceful global community, an image that is the motor of the Olympic games, to be hosted by London in 2012. The Cloud is a concept for a visitors´ platform for those who came to watch this global athletic event. The viewing platform soars, amid bubbles, over a tower structure, which has an elevator in its core and is surrounded by a spiral ramp. From here, visitors have not only a view of the whole of London and the Olympic grounds, but also of the whole world via digital networks and monitors installed in the bubbles. Thus, the observers are standing in the middle of a cloud system that broadcasts live data and images from the city and around the globe. The Cloud, during the 2012 Olympics, will unite people from all over the world. The viewing tower also saves and stores energy, as the elevators´ electrodynamic brakes, for example, will feed the energy they produce back into the system.

PAGE/SEITE 126/127
- The spheres will be supported by thin, metal frames, making it possible for people to inhabit them.
- Die Blasenkörper werden durch dünne Metallrahmen verstärkt, sodass Menschen sich darin aufhalten können.

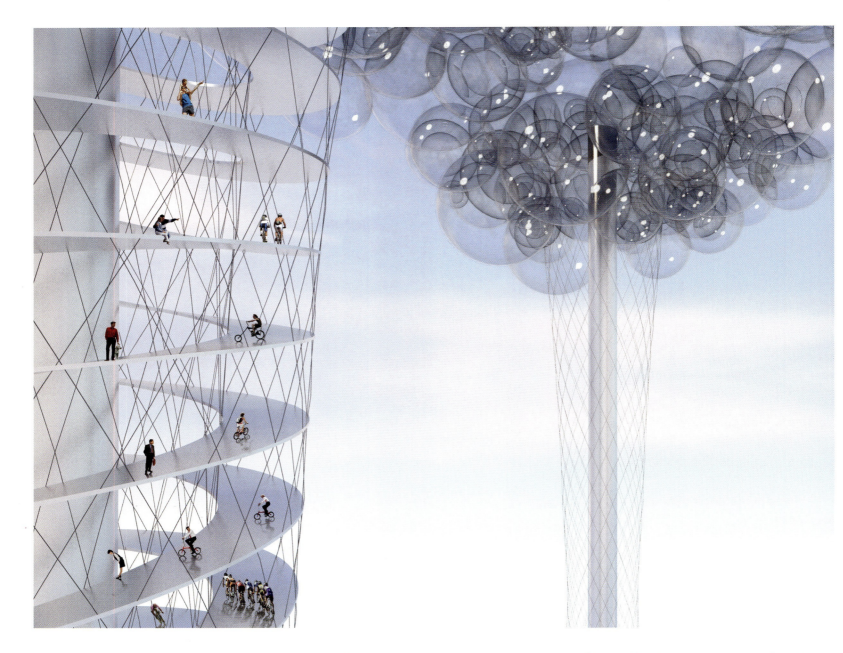

● DEUTSCH   Bauten für Olympische Spiele und Weltausstellungen zeichnen sich häufig durch massive Volumina, schwerfällige Monumentalität und einen hohen Platzbedarf aus. Dies ist für Carlo Ratti nicht mehr zeitgemäß. Deshalb erscheint sein Projekt The Cloud so leicht wie die Luft – eine Hommage an das digitale Zeitalter geprägt von Bits und Atomen, jenseits der alten Baustoffe Stahl und Glas. Es ist eine Konstruktion, die symbolisch für die sozialen Netzwerke einer friedlichen Weltgemeinschaft steht. Und dieses Bild ist Antriebskraft für die Olympischen Spiele, deren Gastgeber die Stadt London 2012 sein wird. The Cloud ist der Entwurf für eine Besucherplattform dieses globalen Sportevents. Über einer Turmkonstruktion mit Aufzugkern und umlaufender Spiralrampe erhebt sich das Aussichtsplateau, das von Blasenkörpern umwölkt wird. Von hier oben hat man nicht nur einen Blick über ganz London und seine olympischen Spielstätten, sondern auch in die ganze Welt über die digitalen Netzwerke und Bildschirme, die in den Blasenkörpern installiert sind. Der Besucher steht also in einem Wolkensystem, das live Daten und Bilder aus der Stadt und vom gesamten Globus überträgt: The Cloud vereinigt die Menschen aus aller Welt bei der Olympiade 2012. Der Aussichtsturm wird auch dazu dienen, Energie zu sparen und zu speichern; so können beispielsweise die elektrodynamischen Nutzbremsen der Aufzuganlage die beim Fahren frei werdende Energie wieder einspeisen.

• The ensemble of glowing speres are anchored by lightweight, transparent towers.
• Die leuchtenden Blasenkörper werden an leichtgewichtigen, transparenten Türmen verankert.

- The towers serve as access points to the hovering spheres and are themselves accessed by a spiral ramp.
- Die Türme dienen als Zugang zu den schwebenden Blasenkörpern und werden über eine Spiralrampe erschlossen.

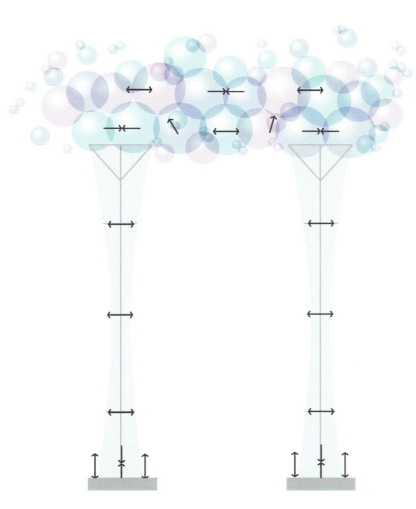

- carlorattiassociati is a fast growing architectural firm, founded in Turin by Walter Nicolino and Carlo Ratti in 2002. Thanks to Carlo Ratti´s experiences during the conception of the urban research lab "Senseable City Lab" at the MIT in Cambridge, USA, the firm currently is involved in many projects in Europe, the United States, and Asia. carlorattiassociati aims at creating an architecture which merges urban and digital structures. It is meant to guarantee social, economic, and ecologic sustainability on all levels of future planning.

- carlorattiassociati ist ein rasch wachsendes Architekturbüro, das 2002 von Walter Nicolino und Carlo Ratti in Turin gegründet wurde. Auf den Erfahrungen von Carlo Ratti bei der Konzeption des urbanen Forschungslabors „Senseable City Lab" am MIT in Cambridge, USA, aufbauend, ist das Büro zurzeit an vielen Projekten in Europa, den Vereinigten Staaten und Asien beteiligt. carlorattiassociati möchte eine Architektur schaffen, in der urbane und digitale Strukturen zusammengeführt werden. Zuden soll sie auf allen Ebenen zukünftiger Planung die soziale, wirtschaftliche und ökologische Nachhaltigkeit gewährleisteten.

STUDIO MASSAUD
PARIS, FRANCE

"Whether architecture or design, innovation can only be human, i.e. cultural and behavioral."

„Ob Architektur oder Design, Innovation kann nur menschlicher Natur sein, im Sinne von Kultur und Verhalten."

MANNED CLOUD, 2005–2008

Cruise Airship
Capacity: 55 persons
Volume: 520,000 m³
Dimensions: L 210 m x W 82 m x H 52 m
Range: 5,000 km / 72 h
Maximum speed: 170 km / h
Scientific partnership and project development: ONERA (Office National d'Études et de Recherche Aérospatiale)

- Manned Cloud is an airship, serving as a "flying hotel", that floats over the landscape in an environment-friendly way and as light as a cloud.
- Manned Cloud ist ein Luftschiff, das als „fliegendes Hotel" dient und umweltfreundlich und leicht wie eine Wolke über die Landschaft gleitet.

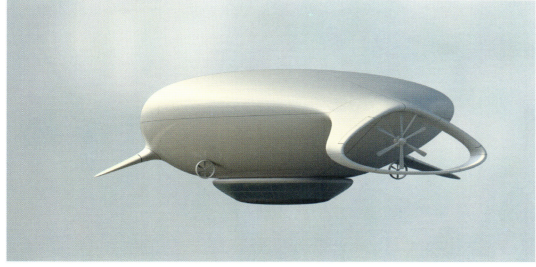

- Jean-Marie Massaud graduated from École Nationale Supérieure de Création Industrielle (ENSCI) in Paris in 1990 and then worked as a product designer. In 2000 he founded the Studio Massaud in Paris, expanding his sphere of interest to architecture and the developing of brands. Massaud rejects fashionable trends and prefers to cast the foundations of the status quo into question, to create progressive concepts, and to find answers to current questions. Jean Marie Massaud strives for the ideal of a symbiosis of man, his creations, and his natural environment – as a catalyst of innovations, as an economic model, and as a project of life.

- Jean-Marie Massaud hat 1990 seinen Abschluss an der École Nationale Supérieure de Création Industrielle (ENSCI) in Paris gemacht und arbeitete danach zunächst als Produktdesigner. 2000 gründete er das Studio Massaud in Paris und dehnte sein Schaffen auf Architektur und Markenentwicklung aus. Trends und Moden lehnt Massaud ab; er zieht es vor, die Grundlagen des Bestehenden zu hinterfragen, an Fortschrittskonzepten zu arbeiten und Antworten auf aktuelle Fragen zu liefern. Massaud strebt das Ideal einer Symbiose zwischen dem Menschen, seinen Kreationen und seiner natürlichen Umwelt an – als ein Katalysator für Innovationen, als ökonomisches Modell und als Lebensprojekt.

- ENGLISCH Manned Cloud is the concept of a manned airship, whose shape and color resemble those of a cloud floating in the sky. This airborne vehicle functions like an airship and is meant to serve as a "flying hotel". The idea behind this concept is Massaud's plans for a gentle tourism, which does not put additional pressure on the already overstrained infrastructures of roads, trains, and passenger airlines. Jean-Marie Massaud's vision is that of people exploring and traveling the world in a comfortable way, but without playing havoc with the environment.

- DEUTSCH Manned Cloud ist ein Projekt für ein bemanntes Luftschiff, das in Form und Farbe an eine am Himmel schwebende Wolke erinnert. Dieses Luftvehikel funktioniert wie ein Zeppelin und soll in der Zukunft als „fliegendes Hotel" durch die Luft gleiten. Hinter dieser Planung steht die Idee Massauds für neue Möglichkeiten eines sanften Tourismus ohne weitere Belastung der bereits überfrachteten Infrastrukturen von Straße, Bahn und Linienflugverkehr. Jean-Marie Massaud hat die Vision, der Mensch könne zukünftig die Welt auf komfortable Art und Weise entdecken und bereisen, ohne eine umweltzerstörende Spur zu hinterlassen.

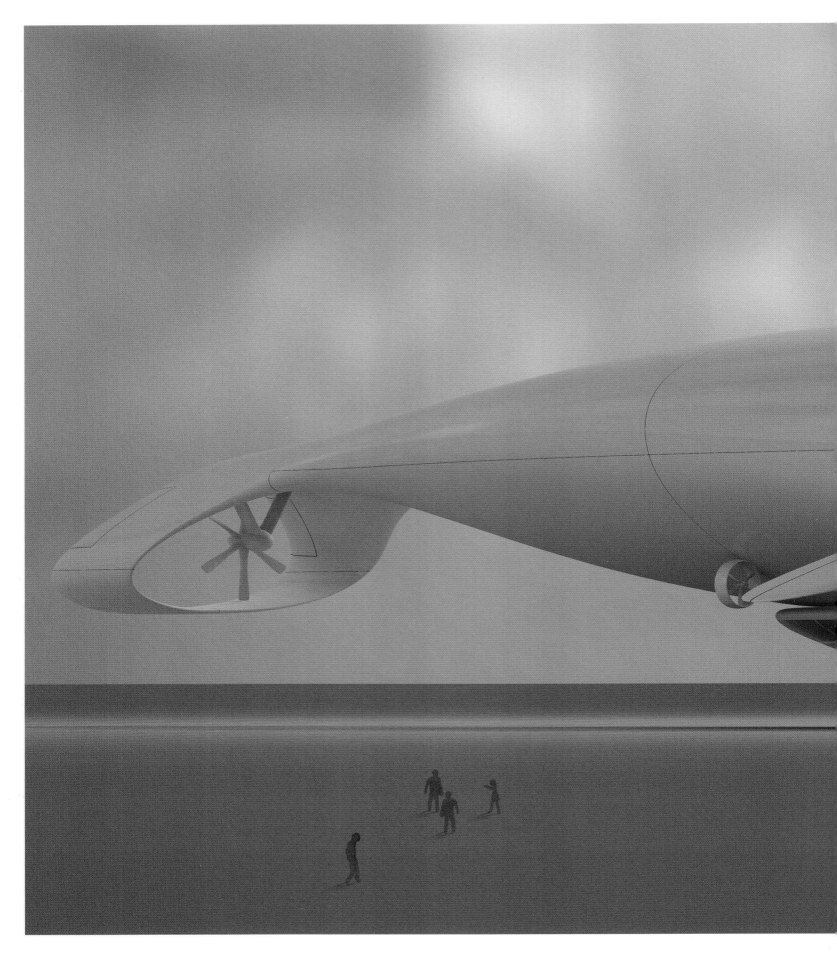

GREEN

Admittedly, the expression "green architecture" sounds quite vague and today is often replaced by the trendy word "sustainability". But what does sustainability really mean when applied to architecture and urban planning? Sustainable development usually stands for the approach that ecological aspects have to enjoy the same priority as social and economical criteria with the aim to guarantee comfortable living conditions in the future. In the context of planning and construction we are thinking of a low consumption of resources and an energy-efficient use of technology and materials.

It can be said that there are two schools of green architecture, which are also reflected in the visionary concepts presented here by different architectural firms. First, there is the notion that sustainable urban und structural scenarios can be created by high-tech solutions. One example is a city whose buildings are equipped with solar panels or windmills, thus becoming their own power plants. Another idea would be digitally controlled transportation systems with driverless electric vehicles, making gas-guzzling automobiles and air pollution a thing of the past. The second approach to green architecture follows a low-tech strategy that aims at returning to the environment-friendly building methods in practice either in the past or in other regions of the world, using simple techniques, local materials and structural concepts that take climatic conditions into consideration. The traditional Arab city, the old town of Damascus for instance, illustrates this way of thinking very well: a tight maze of narrow alleys and dead ends keeps the heat out of the city, while wide arteries leading from east to west, where the wind comes from for the most part, provide ventilation.

However, high-tech or low-tech does not really make a difference, because the architecture of the future cannot afford to ignore sustainable designs and green thinking. That ecological construction has its aesthetic merits, too, is very impressively shown by various green designs.

GRÜN

Der Begriff „grüne Architektur" ist zugegebenermaßen recht vage und wird inzwischen gerne durch das Trendwort „Nachhaltigkeit" ersetzt. Doch was bedeutet eigentlich Nachhaltigkeit im Zusammenhang mit Architektur und Städtebau? Nachhaltige Entwicklung definiert sich allgemein dadurch, dass ökologische Gesichtspunkte die gleiche Priorität wie soziale und wirtschaftlichen Aspekte haben müssen, um eine zukünftige lebenswerte Welt gewährleisten zu können. Für das Planen und Bauen heißt das in erster Linie Ressourcen schonender und energieeffizienter Einsatz von Technologien und Baumaterialien.

Generell sind bei diesem Idealmodell einer grünen, postfossilen Architektur zwei unterschiedliche Ansätze anzutreffen, die sich auch in den visionären Entwürfen der Architekturbüros wiederfinden: Der erste geht von der Vorstellung aus, dass man mit der Weiterentwicklung hochtechnisierter Konzepte nachhaltige Stadt- und Architekturszenarien entwerfen kann, indem beispielsweise das Wohngebäude in der Stadt mit Solar- und Windkraftanlagen ausgestattet wird und so zum eigenen Kraftwerk firmiert; oder dadurch, dass digitalisierte Straßenverkehrssysteme mit fahrerlosen Elektromobilen zum Einsatz kommen, die Benzin fressenden Pkw-Verkehr und Luftverschmutzung zu einer Sache der Vergangenheit machen. Der zweite Ansatz einer zukünftigen grünen Architektur orientiert sich an Lowtech-Konzepten, bei denen durch die Rückbesinnung auf umweltschonendes Bauen der Vergangenheit und in anderen Weltregionen einfache handwerkliche Konstruktionsmethoden, ortsbezogene Baumaterialien und klimagerechte Raum- und Bauformen eingesetzt werden. Ein städtebauliches Beispiel in diesem Zusammenhang stellt das Gefüge der traditionellen arabischen Stadt dar, wie es beispielsweise in der Altstadt von Damaskus anzutreffen ist. Hier wird durch das engmaschig konzipierte System von Gassen und Sackgassen die Hitze aus der Stadt herausgehalten, während breitere durchgängige Straßen in der regionalen Hauptwindrichtung Ost-West für Durchlüftung sorgen.

Egal, ob Hightech oder Lowtech, die Architektur der Zukunft muss nachhaltiges Planen und grünes Denken berücksichtigen. Und dass ökologisches Bauen auch gestalterische Qualitäten besitzt, präsentieren die grünen Entwurfsvisionen sehr überzeugend.

CDMB ARCHITECTS
BERLIN, GERMANY

"Futuristic evokes envisioning and crafting the unimagined forms of life."

„Das Futuristische regt dazu an, sich bisher ungedachte Lebensformen auszumalen und sie zu gestalten."

VARDØ'S ARKS, 2009

Vardo, Norway

"EUROPAN 10" competition
with Michael Seitz & Carlos Lara

● ENGLISCH   The project was developed for the Norwegian island of Vardo (location: peninsula of Varanger, Barents Sea) in view of the dangers of global warming and the effects of the greenhouse factor in the world´s northern regions. The plan is to rebuild the current urban structures along Vardo´s coastline and turn them into small floating arks with outside areas. These ark clusters can be arranged to form a flexible village or town with waterways connecting the individual houseboats. In the worst-case scenario, that is an extreme flood in the area, it is possible to join these ark-modules to form a mother-ship, the Vardo Ark.

● DEUTSCH   Das Projekt bezieht sich auf die zukünftige Entwicklung der norwegischen Insel Vardø (Lage: Varanger-Halbinsel, Barentssee) im Kontext der globalen Erwärmung und der Auswirkungen des Treibhauseffekts auf die nördlichen Regionen der Erde. Die momentanen urbanen Strukturen entlang der bestehenden Küstenlinie Vardøs würden wiederhergestellt und in kleine, auf dem Wasser treibende Archen mit außen liegenden Wohnbereichen umgewandelt werden. Diese Archen können flexible Dorf- oder Stadtgefüge bilden, in denen Wasserstraßen die einzlnen Hausboote verbinden. Im schlimmsten Katastrophenfall, also einer meterhohen Überflutung der Region, könnten die einzelnen Arche-Module zu einem „Mutterschiff", der Vardø-Arche, zusammengefügt werden.

• Vardo Arks float on the water as housing units, forming village or city structures as needed.

• Die Vardø-Archen treiben als Wohneinheiten auf dem Wasser und bilden je nach Bedarf Dorf- oder Stadtstrukturen aus.

GREEN DESERT MINE, 2007

Megacities in Subtropical Regions

● ENGLISCH   When looking at the ruinous exploitation of resources that takes place in and around our mega-cities two types of devastating effects can be observed: first the destruction of fertile soil and second the subsequent migration of the local population. More than two million people worldwide are affected by this phenomenon: they are living in arid regions.

The Green Desert Mine project is based on the vision of turning hostile deserts into fertile regions rich in biodiversity that allows for contemporary lifestyles. A number of thermal chimneys absorb the rays of the sun and efficiently utilize the heat given off by machines, human bodies, and the environment. The bases of these chimneys form the sites of a new economic and urban landscape when human settlements are founded around the towers in a mixture of cultivated fields and urban clusters. The minimal energetic load will prevent the desert from spreading thanks to a garden, protected by a double membrane that collects solar energy and transports the heat into the chimneys' turbines. The garden's natural biological filter system collects and purifies the city's sewage and feeds it back into a system of cisterns.

All the facilities for the city's infrastructure are housed in the utility zones of the chimney structures. The inhabitants of this city would be able to work close to home. As the system would be autonomous, energy, water, produce, and financial and technological services could be exported. A maglev railway close to the ground ensures fast travel between the regional and urban centers.

● DEUTSCH   Vor dem Hintergrund des Raubbaus an den inneren und äußeren Zonen der Megacitys lassen sich zwei Arten von „Verwüstung" feststellen: erstens die Zerstörung des fruchtbaren Landes und zweitens die nachfolgende Abwanderung der dortigen Bevölkerung. Mehr als zwei Milliarden Menschen auf der Welt sind inzwischen von dieser Situation betroffen: Sie leben in ariden Regionen.

Das Projekt Green Desert Mine entwirft die Vision der Umwandlung lebensfeindlicher Wüstenregionen in fruchtbare Gebiete, die reich an Biodiversität sind und zeitgemäße Lebensstile erlauben. Eine Serie von Thermalschornsteinen fängt die Sonneneinstrahlung auf und verwertet die Hitze energieeffizient, die von Maschinen, menschlichen Körpern und der Umwelt ausgeht. Im unteren Bereich dieser Schornsteine entsteht eine neue wirtschaftliche und urbane Landschaft, in der rund um die Türme Menschen angesiedelt und Nutzflächen für die verdichtete Stadt geschaffen werden. Dank der minimalen energetischen Gesamtbelastung kann das umliegende Land vor der Wüstenbildung geschützt werden: mit einem Garten, der von einer doppelten Membran überfangen wird. Durch diese lässt sich Sonnenenergie gewinnen und Wärmeenergie in die Turbinen der Schornsteine übertragen. Die Abwässer der Stadt können über ein natürliches biologisches Filtersystem des Gartens gereinigt, gesammelt und wieder dem Zisternensystem zugeführt werden.

Alle die Infrastruktur der Stadt betreffenden Einrichtungen sind in den Wirtschaftszonen der Schornstein-Konstruktionen platziert. Das ermöglicht den Stadtbewohnern ein Arbeiten in der Nähe des eigenen Wohnsitzes. Durch die Autonomie des Systems können Energie, Wasser, landwirtschaftliche Erzeugnisse und finanzielle oder technische Dienstleistungen exportiert werden. Eine erdbodennahe Magnetschwebebahn sorgt für schnelle Verbindungen zwischen den regionalen und städtischen Zentren.

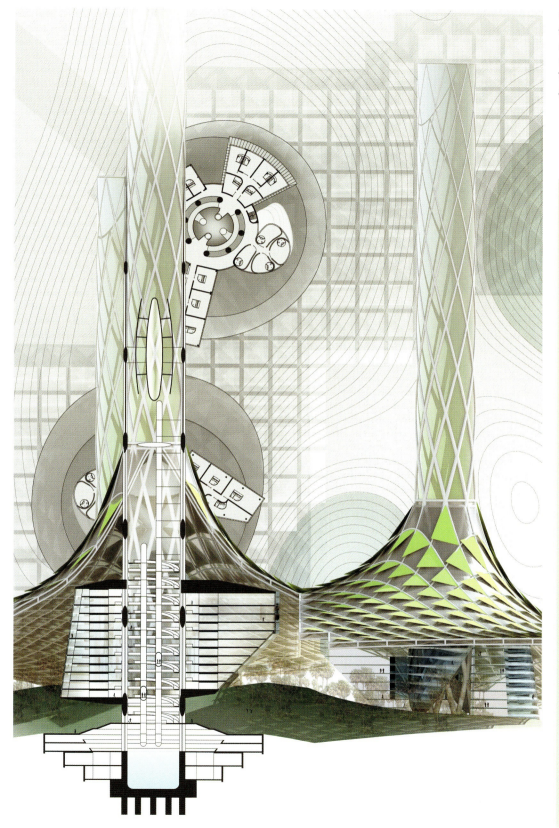

- The thermal chimneys with their membrane tents in the deserts serve as power plants, water purifying system, living quarters, and garden in one.
- Die Thermalschornsteine mit Membranzelten in der Wüste sind Energieerzeuger, Wasseraufbereitungsanlage, Wohnstätte und Gartenanlage in einem.

- The award-winning studio CDMB from Berlin has a pioneer role when it comes to the devising and realization of ecological and efficient architectural projects. The firm was founded in 2003 by Christophe DM Barlieb to work on aesthetic and structural solutions together with artists, designers, architects, and various institutions, as well as to promote socially and ecologically acceptable forms of architecture. CDMB wants its concepts to be seen in a context with nature: "This architecture celebrates nature."

- Das preisgekrönte Studio CDMB aus Berlin ist ein Vorreiter auf dem Gebiet der Planung und Ausführung ökologiebewusster und leistungsfähiger Architekturprojekte. Christophe DM Barlieb gründete 2003 das Büro, um an der Lösung von gestalterischen und baulichen Aufgaben mit Künstlern, Designern, Architekten und entsprechenden Institutionen zusammen zu arbeiten sowie die Entwicklung sozial und ökologisch vertretbarer Architekturen voranzutreiben. CDMB will seine Architekturentwürfe im Bezug auf die Natur verstanden wissen: „Diese Architektur zelebriert die Natur."

• An extensive biodiversity is introduced to intensify the oasis.
• Die Einführung einer extensiven Biodiversität soll dazu dienen, den Oasencharakter zu unterstützen.

MARCOSANDMARJAN
LONDON, UK

"The future is: augmented, bio-technological, convoluted, digital, experiential, figural, gelatinous, hybrid, inlucent, jelly-like, kaleidoskopic, latent, mutant, neoplasmatic, ornamental, poetic, quirky, robotic, soft, threeandahalf-dimensional, unpredictable, voluptuous, whimsical, x-uberant, yippee, zealous…"

„Die Zukunft ist: gesteigert, bio-technologisch, verwickelt, digital, erfahrungsbezogen, figürlich, gallertartig, hybrid, intransparent, geleeartig, kaleidoskopisch, verborgen, mutierend, neoplasmatisch, dekorativ, poetisch, gerissen, roboterhaft, weich, dreieinhalbdimensional, unvorhersehbar, sinnlich, skurril, überschwänglich, eifrig …"

KHATABA (AL JADIDA), AGROPOLIS, 2009

Self-Sufficient City, Egypt

• The agropolis Khataba (Al Jadida) is supposed to be urban metropolis and agricultural village in one; the circular fields are either cultivated or equipped with solar panels.
• Die Agropolis Khataba (Al Jadida) in Ägypten soll eine Mischung aus Stadtmetropole und Bauerndorf mit Agrarwirtschaft darstellen; die kreisrunden Felder dienen als landwirtschaftliche Flächen und zur Solarenergiegewinnung.

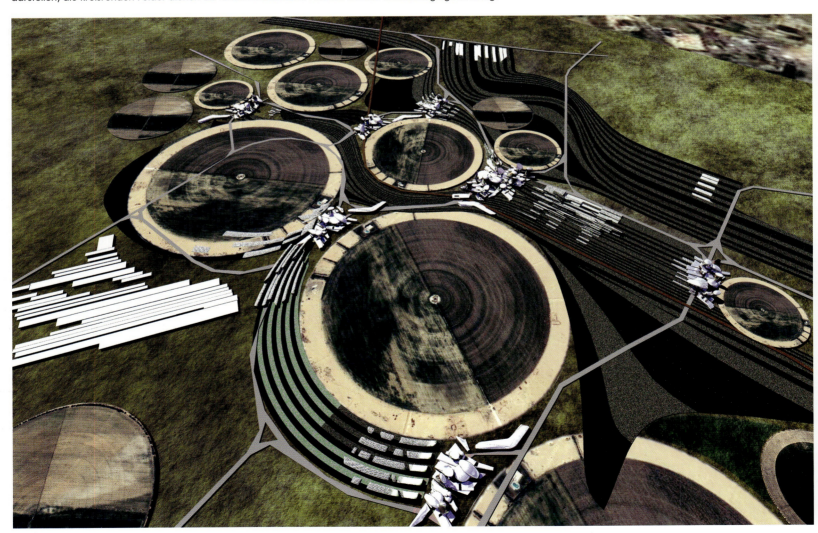

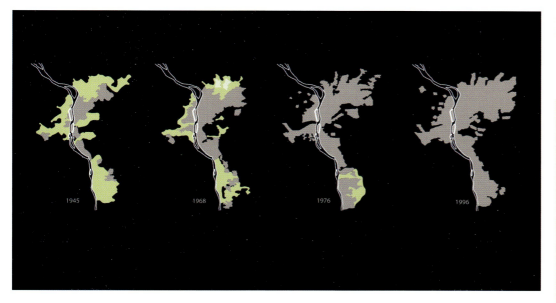

- Settlement Khataba (Al Jadida), Egypt
- Siedlung Khataba (Al Jadida) in Ägypten

● ENGLISH   Marcosandmarjan's concept is the answer to the uncontrolled urban spread surrounding the Egyptian cities of Cairo and Alexandria, a tendency that is intended to be remedied by founding agro-urban settlements in the Nile delta in cooperation with local agriculture. Khataba (Al Jadida) is the first of these autonomous future settlements that will be half urban, half agricultural – an agropolis. The morphology of this agropolis and its successors will be marked by linear and circular agricultural patterns. A matrix of complementary enmeshed centers will develop in the agricultural area, especially in the spaces between the grid of fields and the irrigation circles. Instead of pursuing a strategy of monoculture and zoning as has been the tendency since the 1950s, this agropolis relies on ecologically balanced and diversified agricultural production, providing plenty of food for its inhabitants in a sustainable and environment-friendly way. Furthermore, Khataba (Al-Jadida) is planned as a CO_2 free urban settlement, where the different types of waste like sewage and houshold garbage will be recycled. Liquid waste is processed and used to support the necessary irrigation of the surrounding fields. Electricity is produced almost solely by solar collectors on roofs, walls and some of the circular plots of land.

● DEUTSCH   Der Entwurf von Marcosandmarjan ist die Antwort auf die unkontrollierte Zersiedelung rund um die ägyptischen Städte Kairo und Alexandria, der mit neuen agro-urbanen Gründungen am Nildelta begegnet werden soll. Khataba (Al Jadida) ist die erste dieser geplanten autarken Siedlungen, die zur einen Hälfte städtisch und zur anderen landwirtschaftlich geprägt sein sollen – eine Agropolis. Lineare und zirkulare agrarische Muster legen die morphologische Struktur der Agropolis und weiterer Gründungen fest. Eine Matrix von komplementären, miteinander vernetzten Kernen soll sich auf dem Agrarland entwickeln, vor allem in den Räumen zwischen dem Raster der Felder und den großen Bewässerungskreisen. Statt eine Strategie der Monokultur und der Zonierung zu verfolgen, wie es in der Stadtentwicklung ab der Mitte des 20. Jahrhunderts in hohem Maße geschehen ist, soll bei der Agropolis auf eine ökologisch ausgeglichene und diversifizierte landwirtschaftliche Produktion gesetzt werden. Diese könnte die Bevölkerung auf nachhaltige und umweltfreundliche Weise mit genügend Nahrungsmitteln versorgen. Darüber hinaus ist Khataba (Al Jadida) als CO_2-freies Ballungsgebiet geplant. Die verschiedenen Abfallstoffe wie Abwasser und Hausmüll sollen wiederverwertet werden. Flüssige Stoffe werden aufbereitet und für die Bewässerung des umliegenden Ackerlandes genutzt. Strom soll fast vollständig aus Solarenergie gewonnen werden, durch Sonnenkollektoren auf Dächern, Fassaden und auf einigen der kreisförmig angelegten Landwirtschaftsflächen.

● Marcosandmarjan is an experimental architectural firm, founded by Marjan Colletti and Marcos Cruz in London in 2000. Marjan Colletti studied architecture in Innsbruck and Graz and then worked for the firm of Archigram-founder Peter Cook, before writing his PhD thesis on "Digital Poetics" at the Bartlett School of Architecture, UCL, in 1999. Marcos Cruz is director of the Bartlett School of Architecture, walking the line between architecture and design. In 2000 he was a member of the team of designers involved in the Grazer Kunsthaus, which was devised by Peter Cook and Colin Fournier as spectacular "blob-architecture". Marcos Cruz also promotes neoplasmatic architecture, which emphasizes haptic and material aspects as opposed to the digitally produced draft. In this context the questions raised by a biotechnical and ecologically motivated architecture of the future are also discussed.

● Marcosandmarjan ist ein experimentell arbeitendes Architekturbüro, das im Jahr 2000 von Marcos Cruz und Marjan Colletti in London gegründet wurde. Marjan Colletti studierte Architektur in Innsbruck und Graz und arbeitete danach im Büro von Archigram-Gründer Peter Cook in London. 1999 absolvierte er an der Bartlett School of Architecture des University College London (UCL) seinen PhD, Doktor der Philosophie, über „Digital Poetics". Marcos Cruz ist Direktor der Bartlett School of Architecture, UCL, und arbeitet an der Schnittstelle zwischen Design und Architektur. 2000 war er Mitglied im Designteam für das Grazer Kunsthaus, das von Peter Cook und Colin Fournier als spektakuläre „Blob-Architektur" konzipiert wurde. Cruz beschäftigt sich u.a. mit der Thematik einer Neoplasmatischen Architektur, die im Unterschied zum digital erzeugten Entwurf wieder mehr das Haptische und Materielle in den Vordergrund stellt. In diesem Kontext werden auch Fragestellungen bezüglich einer biotechnisch und ökologisch motivierten Architektur der Zukunft diskutiert.

MVRDV
ROTTERDAM, THE NETHERLANDS

"We continue to pursue our fascination with density using a method of shaping space through complex amounts of data to create outspoken buildings and exemplary urban plans that help to conceive a better future. This futurology is also what The Why Factory is about: providing arguments for architecture and urbanism by envisioning the cities of the future."

„Wir lassen uns weiterhin vom Reiz der Dichte begeistern und formen Raum, indem wir komplexe Datenmengen verwenden, um klare Gebäude und beispielhafte städtebauliche Planungen für eine bessere Zukunft zu schaffen. Um diese Zukunftsforschung geht es auch bei The Why Factory: Sie soll durch einen Blick auf die Städte der Zukunft der Architektur und Stadtplanung Argumente an die Hand geben."

GWANGGYO POWER CENTRE, 2007–2011

Kyunggido, Seoul, Korea

● ENGLISCH Since the beginning of the new millennium Korean urban planning has been marked by local and highly concentrated clusters and a mixed architecture. This strategy called "Power Centre" is based on a concept of urban living-and-business towers whose ground floors offer room for shopping facilities. How can this situation be adapted to modern times and the changes in our environment? Is it possible to make it more sustainable and greener? The Gwanggyo Power Centre close to Seoul belongs to an area where a new city consisting of different functional sections will be founded. 200,000 square meters of living space, 48,000 square meters of office space, and 200,000 square meters of land to build cultural, educational, and leisure facilities as well as 200,000 square meters for parks have been set aside.

During the last decades most new Korean cities have been built in valleys with a negative effect on natural ventilation and the cooling of the air. MVRDV´s masterplan for Gwanggyo involves an urban structure marked by high towers soaring from the ground in a circle. They are equipped with terraces where green plants grow. The water-absorbing plants that cover the façades of the towers will make for a a pleasant biosphere. On the outskirts of the city green parks and a lake will be created. Thus, the city´s silhouette will not be the classic one marked by box-like skyscrapers but resemble an urban cone-shaped hillscape.

• The silhouette of the new green city Gwanggyo looks like a cone-shaped hillscape.
• Die Silhouette der neuen grünen Stadt Gwanggyo ähnelt einer kegelförmigen Hügellandschaft.

• DEUTSCH Seit dem Beginn des neuen Jahrtausends nutzt man in der koreanischen Stadtplanung lokale Knotenpunkte mit hoher Konzentrationsdichte und einem gemischten Bauprogramm. Diese Strategie des „Power Centre" basiert auf dem Konzept der städtischen Wohn- und Geschäftstürme mit Einkaufsmöglichkeiten im Erdgeschossbereich. Wie lässt sich diese Typologie aktualisieren und den veränderten Umweltbedingungen anpassen? Kann sie nachhaltiger und grüner werden? Das Gwanggyo Power Centre in der Nähe von Seoul ist Teil eines Entwicklungsgebietes für eine neue Stadt mit unterschiedlichen Funktionsbereichen. Es sollen insgesamt 200.000 m² Wohnflächen, 48.000 m² Büroflächen, 200.000 m² Bauflächen für Kultur, Bildung und Freizeit sowie 200.000 m² Parkflächen zur Verfügung gestellt werden.

In den letzten Jahrzehnten wurden in Korea die meisten Stadtentwicklungsmaßnahmen in Tälern realisiert. Das hat sich nachteilig auf den natürlichen Luftaustausch und die natürliche Kühlungsfunktion der Luft in den Städten ausgewirkt. Der Masterplan für Gwanggyo von MVRDV sieht nun eine Stadtstruktur aus hohen Türmen vor, die kegelförmig emporwachsen und mit begrünten Terrassen versehen sind. Durch die Bepflanzung der gesamten Außenhaut der Türme wird Wasser gebunden und eine angenehme Biosphäre erzeugt. Auch der Außenbereiche der Stadt sollen mit Parkanlagen und einem See ausgestattet werden. Die städtische Silhouette wandelt sich vom klassischen Bild der eckigen Skyscraper zur Anmutung einer urbanen, kegelförmigen Hügellandschaft.

• MVRDV was founded in 1993 in Rotterdam by Winy Maas, Jacob van Rijs, and Nathalie de Vries. The globally operating architectural firm has a wealth of experience in regard to creative solutions for urban challenges. Projects like the headquarters of the Dutch public radio station VPRO and the retirement-home project WoZoCo in Amsterdam have met with international recognition. MVRDV´s Dutch pavilion at the Expo 2000 in Hanover, too, was noticed worldwide. Projects are developed by a staff of sixty in an interdisciplinary design process that thrives due to a close cooperation while applying the highest technical standards and strict criteria of sustainability. Together with the technical university of Delft MVRDV heads the "Think Tank" and the research facility The Why Factory (t?f). See p. 24.

• MVRDV wurde 1993 von Winy Maas, Jacob van Rijs und Nathalie de Vries in Rotterdam gegründet und ist ein global operierendes Architekturbüro mit großem Erfahrungsschatz an kreativen Lösungen für urbane Aufgabenstellungen. Frühe Projekte wie die Zentrale des niederländischen öffentlich-rechtlichen Rundfunksenders VPRO und das Altenheim-Projekt WoZoCo in Amsterdam fanden internationale Anerkennung. Auch der Niederländische Pavillon von MVRDV auf der Expo 2000 in Hannover erregte weltweit Interesse. 60 Büromitarbeiter konzipieren die Projekte fachübergreifend in einem Designprozess, der von der engen Zusammenarbeit lebt und bei dem höchste technische Standards und strenge Nachhaltigkeitskriterien Anwendung finden. MVRDV leitet zusammen mit der Technischen Universität Delft den Thinktank und die Forschungseinrichtung The Why Factory (t?f). Vgl. S. 25.

• Plants also grow on the paths, squares, and terraces of the ecological towers of Gwanggyo.
• Auch die Wege, Plätze und Terrassen im Außenbereich der ökologisch konzipierten Türme von Gwanggyo sind mit Pflanzen bewachsen.

VINCENT CALLEBAUT

LA LOUVIÈRE, BELGIUM
PARIS, FRANCE

"The Ecopolis of tomorrow will promote its own sustainable developement through the possibility of a fusion between science and technology."

„Die Ökopolis von morgen wird sich durch die Möglichkeit der Verschmelzung von Naturwissenschaften und Technologie dauerhaft selbst entwickeln."

HYDROGENASE, 2010

Shanghai, China

Algae farm to recycle CO_2 for biohydrogen airship

● ENGLISCH For this project Vincent Callebaut has invented a new generation of hybrid airships, powered by a biofuel made from seaweed. Their design imitates nature, as they are autonomous biochemical miniature power plants that absorb CO_2, while producing utilizable energy. Hydrogenase keeps seas and oceans clean by scooping out, processing, and destroying the floating debris left behind by the world's energy-consuming population. These mobile vertical airships also are inhabitable.

● DEUTSCH Vincent Callebaut entwarf für dieses Projekt eine neue Generation hybrider Luftschiffe, die durch einen Biokraftstoff aus Seetang angetrieben werden. Ihre Gestaltung ahmt die Natur nach; sie sind eigenständige biochemische Minikraftwerke, die CO_2 aufnehmen und nutzbare Energie abgeben können. Die Hydrogenase reinigen Meere und Ozeane, indem sie die schwimmenden Abfälle der energieverzehrenden Weltbevölkerung abschöpfen, verarbeiten und zerstören. Die mobilen, vertikal ausgerichteten Luftschiffe sind bewohnbar.

PAGE/SEITE 155
• The airships Hydrogenase, purifying air and water in Shanghai in 2020
• Die Luftschiffe Hydrogenase als Luft- und Wasserreiniger in Schanghai 2020

• These seaweed-powered airships are inhabitable and able to dock in to floating terminals and organic farms.
• Die durch Seetang betriebenen Luftschiffe sind bewohnbar und können an schwimmenden Terminals und Biofarmen andocken.

PAGE/SEITE 157
• View of the interior of an airship with membrane-like fuselage
• Blick in das transparente Innere eines Luftschiffes mit membranartiger Außenhaut

THE PERFUMED JUNGLE, 2007

Hong Kong, China

PAGE/SEITE 160–161
• With their roots deeply anchored in the South China Sea, the techno-organic towers shoot from the water into the sky.
• Die Wurzeln tief im Südchinesischen Meer verankert, schießen die techno-organischen Türme aus dem Wasser in den Himmel.

● ENGLISCH Hong Kong with its 30,000 inhabitants per square kilometer is one of the most densely populated cities of the world, afflicted with the usual problems like daily traffic congestions and above all smog. To remedy this situation, Vincent Callebaut, together with Arnaud Martinez and Maguy Delrieu, developed a masterplan for Hong Kong´s Seaside, which includes an urban jungle. The idea is to install an artificial island with highrises off the present shore. The buildings will be overgrown with plants, thus creating a jungle in front of Hong Kong´s skyline, whose photosynthetic processes would dramatically improve the air in the city. The jungle also would serve as a green natural resort for people to enjoy.

● DEUTSCH Hongkong ist mit 30.000 Einwohnern pro km² eine der am dichtesten besiedelten Städte dieser Welt. Damit verbunden sind die allseits bekannten Komplikationen wie tagtägliche Verkehrsstaus und vor allem Smog. Um dem entgegenzuwirken, entwarf Vincent Callebaut zusammen mit Arnaud Martinez und Maguy Delrieu einen Masterplan für die Küste von Hongkong mit integriertem städtischen Dschungel. Vor die bestehende Küstenfront wird eine künstliche Insel mit zahlreichen wild-wuchernden Grünflächen und begrünten Hochhäusern gesetzt. Dieser Dschungel vor der Skyline Hongkongs könnte durch fotosynthetische Prozesse die Luftatmosphäre in der Stadt wesentlich verbessern und würde darüber hinaus den Stadtbewohnern zusätzliche Grünzonen zur Erholung bieten.

• The jungle zone off Hong Kong offers green recreational zones.
• Die Dschungelzone vor der Küste Hongkongs bietet grüne Erholungsgebiete.

LILYPAD, 2008

• Lilypad off the coast of Monaco
• Lilypad vor der Küste von Monaco

- Lilypad is an autonomous floating city, providing room for up to 50,000 people.
- Lilypad ist eine autarke schwimmende Stadt, die bis zu 50.000 Einwohner aufnehmen kann.

● ENGLISCH Lilypad is a floating autonomous city, a visionary answer to the fact that the sea level is expected to rise due to global warming. Callebaut´s reasoning makes sense: if an increase in sea level takes away our space, the people affected will have to resort to living on the water. Lilypad is the prototype of an "amphibian ecopolis", belonging to both the aquatic and the terrestrial spheres. The floating city will be able to travel on all oceans from the equator to the polar regions and can house up to 50,000 people. Lilypad´s residential quarters are arranged around a central freshwater lagoon, which also serves as a rainwater reservoir. The multi-functional floor plan consists of three harbors and three hills with spaces for work, production, and entertainment. The landscape of Lilypad is marked by residential buildings and gardens. The structure itself has been inspired by nature: the leaf of the giant water lily, an autonomous unit which takes care of its own water and oxygen supply, while offering room for ecological niches, aquatic cultures, and natural habitats.

● DEUTSCH Lilypad ist eine schwimmende, autonome Stadt, die visionäre Antwort auf den wahrscheinlich bevorstehenden Anstieg des Meeresspiegels infolge der Erderwärmung. Callebauts Folgerung ist einleuchtend: Wenn der steigende Meeresspiegel Lebensraum eliminiert, müssen die davon betroffenen Menschen aufs Wasser umgesiedelt werden. Lilypad ist der Prototyp einer „amphibischen Ecopolis" – sie ist dem Wasser wie dem Land zugehörig. Die Stadt ist für 50.000 Einwohner ausgelegt und soll auf den Ozeanen vom Äquator bis zu den Polen schwimmen können. Der bewohnbare Raum ist um eine zentrale Süßwasserlagune angelegt, die auch der Regenwassergewinnung dient. Das multifunktionale Bauprogramm umfasst drei Häfen und drei Hügel mit Räumen für Arbeit, Gewerbe und Unterhaltung. Das landschaftliche Erscheinungsbild wird von Wohnhäusern und Gärten bestimmt. Als Vorbild diente die Natur, genauer gesagt das Blatt der Riesenseerose. Sie kann als autarke Einheit den eigenen Bedarf an Sauerstoff und Energie decken und bietet darüber hinaus innerhalb ihres eigenen Ökosystems umweltfreundliche Nischen, Aquakulturen und naturnahe Lebensräume für andere Organismen.

● The Belgian architect, Vincent Callebaut, born in 1977, owns firms in France and Belgium, excelling in concepts for a future-oriented and environment-friendly architecture. Since 2005 Callebaut has been involved in developing a sustainable concept for a new "ecopolis" that uses "parasitical" strategies to merge biological and IT technologies. With his projects he creates imaginative eco-systems, constructed as dynamic complexes, while interacting with all natural cybernetic data of the respective location.

● Der 1977 geborene, belgische Architekt Vincent Callebaut betreibt in Frankreich und Belgien Büros, die sich vor allem mit Entwürfen für eine zukunftsorientierte, ökologisch vertretbare Architektur auseinandersetzen. Seit 2005 spricht sich Callebaut für die nachhaltige Entwicklung einer neuen „Ecopolis" aus, bei der mithilfe „parasitärer" Strategien biologische und informationstechnische Technologien miteinander verbunden werden. Mit seinen Projekten kreiert er fantasievolle Ökosysteme, die als dynamische Komplexe aufgebaut sind und mit allen natürlichen und kybernetischen Daten des Standortes interagieren.

IWAMOTOSCOTT
SAN FRANCISCO, USA

"While the role of an architect is to imagine the future, it is exciting to be able to think of it in a more synthetic sense. For us, this suggests researching bleeding edge materials and technologies that are being developed now in other industries. How these can be applied in design for the future that will increasingly be asked to solve more and more problems is both fascinating and a challenge."

„Es ist die Aufgabe eines Architekten, sich die Zukunft auszumalen. Spannend wird es, wenn man dies in einem umfassenden Sinn tut. Für uns bedeutet das, dass wir uns mit den allerneuesten Materialien und Verfahren auseinandersetzen, die gerade in anderen Bereichen entwickelt werden. Wie diese in der Stadtplanung der Zukunft eingesetzt werden können, um die stetig wachsenden Probleme zu lösen, ist Faszination und Herausforderung zugleich."

HYDRO-NET, 2008

Proposal for San Francisco, USA

Grand Prize Winner of History Channel's competition City of the Future 2008

● ENGLISCH This urban project is based on the assumption that future cities will have to be more closely linked and more autonomous at the same time. In the Bay Area around San Francisco, California, the population is expected to have doubled by the year 2108. If the region wants to meet the challenge of housing this additional number of people without risking a spread of the urban sprawl, a new infrastructural network is called for to autonomously organize the production and distribution of water, energy, fuel, and food as well as the transport and mobility of locals and tourists alike. Hydro-Net is a symbiotic construction, functioning in different dimensions, a walk-in infrastructure that takes over the city´s most important transactions. An underground pipe serves as the main artery for hydrogen-powered hovercraft which takes pressure off the streets above. On the coast and at various intersections within the residential areas Hydro-Net emerges from the ground to collect, store, and distribute fresh water and geothermal energy. If the sea level really does rise up by one and a half meters as a result of climatic changes, lakes with algae would form again in San Francisco Bay. From these zones of aquaculture new residential clusters would grow like a forest of organic highrise towers.

● DEUTSCH Dieses urbane Projekt geht von der Annahme aus, dass die Städte der Zukunft besser vernetzt und gleichzeitig autarker sein müssen. Für die Bucht von San Francisco in Kalifornien wird bis 2108 mit einer Verdoppelung der Bevölkerung gerechnet. Es wird eine große Herausforderung sein, zusätzlichen Wohnraum für alle diese Menschen zu schaffen. Will man keine weitere Zersiedlung des Umlandes riskieren, so benötigt die Region ein neues infrastrukturelles Netzwerk. Dieses sollte die Gewinnung und Verteilung von Wasser, Energie, Brennstoffen und Lebensmitteln eigenständig organisieren können und den Transport sowie die Mobilität von Bewohnern und Touristen gewährleisten. Als symbiotische Konstruktion, die in verschiedenen Größenordnungen funktioniert, ist Hydro-Net eine begehbare Infrastruktur, die wichtige Ströme der Stadt aufnimmt. Eine unterirdische Röhre dient als Hauptschlagader für wasserstoffbetriebene Hovercraft-Fahrzeuge und entlastet so die oberirdischen Straßen. An der Küste und an diversen Knotenpunkten in den Wohngebieten wird Hydro-Net an der Oberfläche sichtbar, wo es Trinkwasser, Erdwärme und Wasserstoff sammelt, speichert und verteilt. Aufgrund des Klimawandels, der zu einem Anstieg des Meeresspiegels bis zu 1,5 m führen kann, würde es in der Bucht von San Francisco wieder Algenseen geben. In dieser Zone der Aquakultur würde sich das neue, stark verdichtete Wohnen als eine Art „Wald" aus organischen Wohntürmen darstellen.

• Map of San Francisco Bay, showing the infrastructure of Hydro-Net
• Lageplan der Bucht von San Francisco mit Einzeichnung der Infrastruktur von Hydro-Net

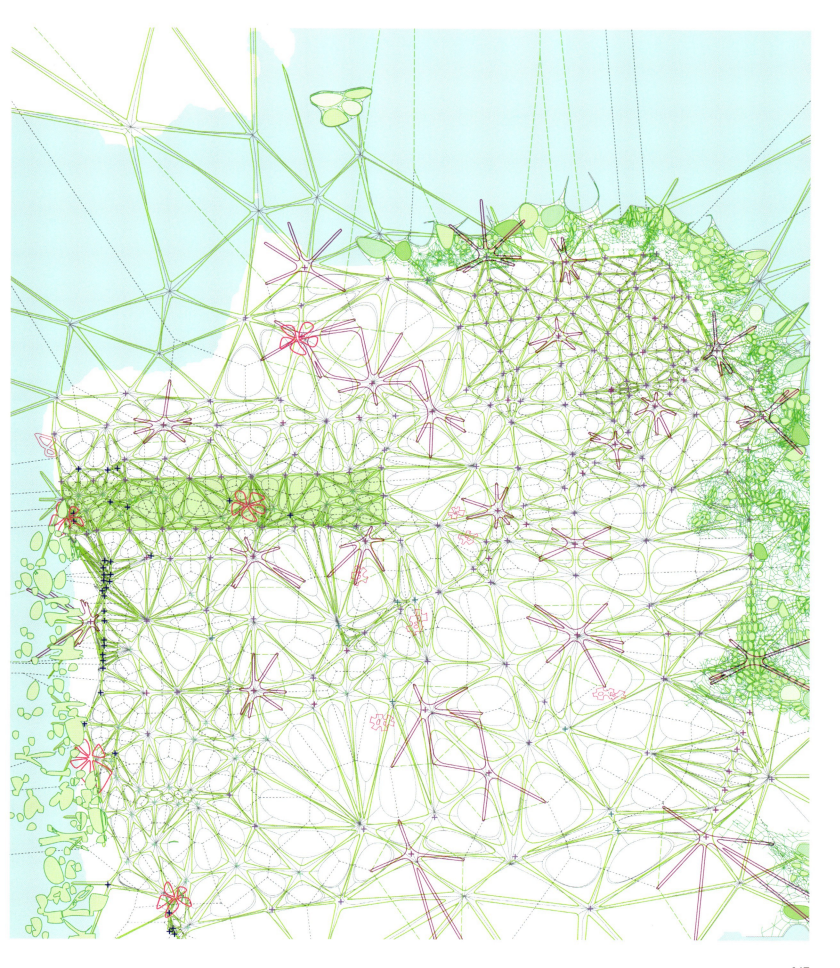

- San Francisco Bay with the surfacing end-pieces of Hydro-Net, which supplies the city with water, energy, and fuel.
- Die Bucht von San Francisco mit den oberirdischen Ausläufern des Hydro-Net, das die Stadt mit Wasser, Energie und Brennstoffen versorgt.

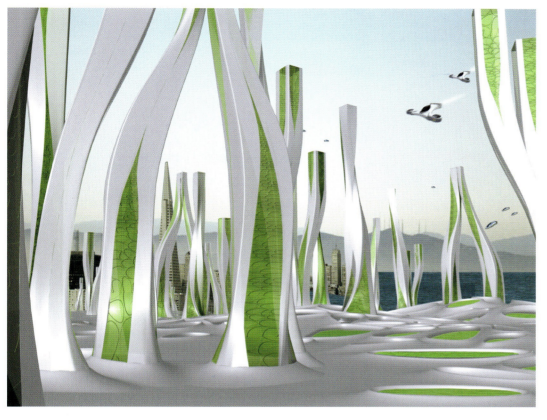

- The new organic residential towers on the coast of San Francisco
- Die neuen organischen Wohntürme an der Küste San Franciscos

- View of San Francisco and the partly underground structure of Hydro-Net
- Blick auf San Francisco mit der teilweise unterirdischen Struktur des Hydro-Net

- IwamotoScott is an architectural and design firm based in San Francisco. It is headed by Lisa Iwamoto and Craig Scott. IwamotoScott wants its architectural projects to be seen as applied research in design, and works with design concepts of different dimensions and in various contexts. Their creative process focuses on honing the perception of architecture, to bring about a direct connection with environment and location, to try out new materials and technologies, and to create innovative spaces.

- IwamotoScott ist ein Büro für Architektur und Gestaltung mit Sitz in San Francisco. Geführt wird es von Lisa Iwamoto und Craig Scott. IwamotoScott versteht seine Architekturprojekte auch als angewandte Design-Forschung und arbeitet an gestalterischen Konzepten unterschiedlicher Größe und in verschiedenen Kontexten. Kern ihres Schaffens ist es, die Wahrnehmung von Architektur zu schärfen, jeweils einen direkten Umwelt- und Ortsbezug herzustellen, neue Materialien und Technologien zu erproben und innovative Raumgestaltungen umzusetzen.

VERTICAL FARM

By the year 2050, nearly 80% of the earth's population will live in urban centers. The human population will increase by about 3 billion people during the interim. An estimated 10^9 hectares of new land (more than the size of Brazil) will be needed to grow enough food to feed them, if traditional farming practices continue as they are practiced today. Vertical farming could be a potential solution to avoid this impending disaster. It challenges how we produce food and the way we consume it in the city. It responds to the need to reduce the dependence on food grown and transported long distances before delivered to urban consumers, due to decreasing farmland and increasing population within urban area. It suggests producing food vertically as a holistic approach to urban living, by creating a new civic space as social and cultural infrastructure tied in with food production and water recycling systems; a center for urban sustainable living.

An entirely new approach to indoor farming must be invented, employing cutting-edge technologies. The Vertical Farms must be efficient, cheap to construct and safe to operate. Many stories high, they will be situated in the heart of the world's urban centers. If successfully implemented, they offer the promise of urban renewal, sustainable production of a safe and varied food supply, and the eventual repair of ecosystems that have been sacrificed for horizontal farming. It took humans 10,000 years to learn how to grow most of the crops we now take for granted. Today, over 800 million hectares is committed to soil-based agriculture, or about 38% of the total land surface of the earth. It has re-arranged the landscape in favor of cultivated fields at the expense of natural ecosystems, reducing most natural areas to fragmented, semi-functional units, while completely eliminating many others.

We have evolved into an urban species, in which 60% of the human population now lives vertically in cities. Due to a rapidly changing climate, massive floods, protracted droughts, hurricanes, and severe monsoons take their toll each year, destroying millions of tons of valuable crops. Don't our harvestable plants deserve the same level of comfort and protection that we now enjoy? The time is at hand for us to learn how to safely grow our food inside environmentally controlled multi-story buildings within urban centers. If we do not, then in just another 50 years, the next 3 billion people will surely go hungry, and the world will become a much more unpleasant place in which to live.

Dickson Despommier

VERTIKALE FARMEN

Im Jahr 2050 werden fast 80% der Weltbevölkerung in städtischen Zentren leben. Bis zu diesem Zeitpunkt wird die Menschheit um ungefähr 3 Milliarden Menschen wachsen. Schätzungsweise 10^9 Hektar neues Land (mehr als die Größe von Brasilien) werden benötigt werden, um ausreichend Nahrungsmittel für diesen Zuwachs an Menschen anzubauen, sofern die bestehenden Techniken des Ackerbaus weitergeführt werden. Vertical Farming, ein Konzept, dass den Anbau von Nahrungsmittel in der Stadt und deren Konsum vor Ort revolutionieren würde, könnte ein Lösungsansatz sein, um das drohende Disaster zu verhindern. Mit ihm ließe sich die Abhängigkeit von Nahrungsmitteln reduzieren, die – aufgrund abnehmender Ackerbauflächen in urbanen Zonen bei gleichzeitigem Anstieg der Bevölkerung – in weit entfernten Regionen angebaut und von dort zu den städtischen Verbrauchern transportiert werden müssen. Der vertikale Anbau von Nahrungsmitteln ermöglicht im Sinne eines holistischen Konzepts urbanen Lebens das Entstehen von neuen öffentlichen Räumen, in denen die soziale und kulturelle Infrastruktur mit der Nahrungsmittelproduktion und mit Wasserrecyclingsystemen verknüpft werden kann. Auf diese Weise bilden sich Zentren nachhaltigen städtischen Lebens.

Die Realisierung solcher Konzepte erfordert den Einsatz modernster Technologien und völlig neue Ansätze bei der Treibhauszucht. Vertikale Farmen müssen effizient, preiswert zu errichten und sicher zu betreiben sein. Die vielstöckigen Gebäude werden in den Kernzonen der großen urbanen Zentren stehen. Wenn sich eine derartige Technologie erfolgreich implementieren lässt, kann sie zu einer Form der Stadterneuerung werden, die die nachhaltige Herstellung von gesunden Lebensmitteln in großer Vielfalt garantieren und vielleicht sogar die Regenerierung von Ökosystemen ermöglichen könnte, die dem traditionellen Ackerbau geopfert wurden. Der Mensch hat 10.000 Jahre gebraucht, um den Anbau der Kulturpflanzen zu erlernen, die für uns heute selbstverständlich sind. 800 Millionen Hektar Land werden heutzutage für herkömmliche Landwirtschaft genutzt, ungefähr 38% der gesamten Landmasse der Erde. Die daraus resultierende Umgestaltung der Erdoberfläche ist auf Kosten natürlicher Ökosysteme gegangen: Sie hat Naturräume entweder in kleine, nur halb lebensfähige Teilstücke zerschnitten oder sie völlig vernichtet.

Die Menschheit ist zu einer urbanen Spezies geworden, 60% der Weltbevölkerung wohnen in vertikalen Bauten in der Stadt. Angesichts eines rapiden Klimawandels werden massive Überflutungen, lang anhaltende Dürreperioden und schwere Orkane und Monsune Jahr für Jahr Opfer fordern und Millionen Tonnen wertvoller Feldfrüchte zerstören. Die Pflanzen, die der Mensch erntet, haben jedoch ebenso Pflege und Schutz verdient wie der Mensch selbst. Es ist an der Zeit zu lernen, wie man Feldfrüchte in Hochhäusern in urbanen Zentren anbaut, in denen sie unter klimatisch sicheren Bedingungen wachsen können. Ohne diese Alternative werden in nur 50 Jahren weitere 3 Milliarden Menschen hungern und die Welt wird ein sehr viel unwirtlicherer Ort als heute sein.

Dickson Despommier

• Urban Farm, Urban Epicenter by Jungmin Nam (JNStudio) is a social vision in response to the increasing concern for sustainable urban farming.
• Urban Farm, Urban Epicenter von Jungmin Nam (JNStudio) ist eine soziale Vision als Antwort auf die Sorge um eine nachhaltige städtische Landwirtschaft.

LUC SCHUITEN
BRUSSELS, BELGIUM

"We already know that we cannot build a future that retains continuity with our present, because the planet's resources are dwindling much faster than the time we allow them to regenerate."

„Wir wissen bereits, dass wir keine Zukunft gestalten können, in der sich unsere Gegenwart fortsetzt, weil die Ressourcen des Planeten deutlich schneller schwinden als die Zeit, die wir ihnen zur Regeneration geben."

VEGETAL CITY, 2008
THE CITY OF THE WAVES, 2003

● ENGLISCH   Luc Schuiten is worried about the future of our planet and therefore feels committed to an ecological approach. He is convinced that the human race will only survive if it develops a closer relation to natural processes. This not only means increased efforts to protect the environment, but also the invention of new technologies, which will be geared to natural materials and processes and take care of their own energy-supply without producing pollutants any longer. With his bionic project Vegetal City he has created the concept of "archiborescence", a principle of construction and growth that is a symbiosis of architectural construction and the growth of trees. Luc Schuiten´s idea is to gradually turn our present cities into nature-like entities and cycles by following this principle. It is important to Schuiten that his urban visions, even though they are rather detailed, should not be seen as monolithic, but as some of the many possible alternatives for a cityscape. His scenarios for the future raise the question of whether the human race really is ready for a radical change of lifestyle.

In the City of Waves constant renewal takes place at the shores of a lake, where people use the trees´ rhythm of life as the structuring element and follow it by migration. This city works like a giant self-regulating organism – with homeostasis and its own metabolism.

• Vegetal City

• The City of the Waves

● DEUTSCH   Luc Schuiten fühlt sich aus Sorge um die Zukunft des Planeten bei seinen Entwürfen einem ökologischen Ansatz verpflichtet. Er ist davon überzeugt, dass die Zukunft der Menschheit nur in stärkerem Einklang mit den Prozessen der Natur möglich ist. Dies schlägt sich nicht nur in einem umfassenden Schutz der Natur, sondern auch in der Entwicklung neuer Technologien nieder, die sich stärker an natürlichen Materialien und Prozessen orientieren, ihre Energieversorgung selbst sichern und keine Schadstoffe mehr produzieren. Mit seinem bionischen Ansatz der Vegetal City hat Schuiten das Konzept der „Archiboreszenz" entwickelt, ein Bau- und Wachstumsprinzip, das eine Symbiose zwischen Architekturkonstruktion und Baumwachstum darstellt. Nach seinen Vorstellungen könnten mit diesem Prinzip die bisher bestehenden Städte allmählich zu naturähnlichen Gebilden und Kreisläufen umgestaltet werden. Schuiten ist es wichtig, dass seine Stadtvisionen bei allem Detailreichtum keine festgelegten Bilder liefern, sondern er entwickelt vielmehr mehrere mögliche Stadtbild-Alternativen. Seine Zukunftsszenarien werfen die Frage auf, inwieweit die Menschheit tatsächlich ihren Lebensstil umfassend ändern kann.

In der City of the Waves findet eine beständige Erneuerung rund um einen See statt; die Zu- und Abwanderung der Bewohner richtet sich nach dem Lebensrhythmus der Bäume als strukturgebendem Element der Stadt. Diese Stadt funktioniert wie ein riesiger Organismus, der sich selbst reguliert – mit Homöostase und einem eigenen Stoffwechsel.

URBACANYON, 2009
THE HOLLOW CITY, 2009

● ENGLISCH   Urbacanyon consists of housing clusters made of a new silicate concrete, which is poured into molds that make them look like rocks. This material is produced by copying the process of biomineralization that forms the shells of mollusks.

● DEUTSCH   Im Urbacanyon entstehen Wohncluster, die wie Felsen aussehen, indem neuartiger Silikatbeton in entsprechende Formen gegossen wird. Bei der Herstellung des Materials wird die Biomineralisierung der Schalenbildung von Mollusken kopiert.

• Urbacanyon

• The Hollow City is constructed entirely around a tramway loop and an underground service ring road.
• Die Hollow City ist ganz um einen Straßenbahnring und eine unterirdische Versorgungsringstraße gebaut.

● Luc Schuiten from Belgium is a visionary architect. In addition to his work with high-grade ecological buildings, he devotes part of his time to science fiction. Worried both about the exploitation of the earth's resources and about future living conditions for people in a time of climate change, he uses fantastical drawings and models to develop proposals for re-designing important parts of the city and its surroundings in harmony with nature. His visionary architectural projects are based on poetic utopias in which the harmonious relationship with nature plays a dominant role.

● Der Belgier Luc Schuiten ist ein visionärer Architekt. Neben der Beschäftigung mit hochwertigem ökologischen Bauen widmet er einen Teil seiner Arbeit der Science-Fiction. Besorgt um die zukünftigen Lebensbedingungen der Menschen in Zeiten des Klimawandels und der Ausbeutung der Erde, entwickelt er in fantasievollen Zeichnungen und Modellen Vorschläge, wie sich wichtige Teile der Stadt und ihrer Umgebung neu und im Einklang mit der Natur gestalten lassen. Seine visionären Architekturprojekte basieren auf poetischen Utopien, bei denen das harmonische Verhältnis zur Natur eine vorherrschende Rolle spielt.

● ENGLISCH The Hollow City is neither a compact entity nor a city consisting of scattered individual buildings. Instead, different residential areas are lined up around a large green hollow space. The city can grow like a piece of knitting by adding further "rows of stitches". Energy is produced by windmills.

● DEUTSCH Die Hollow City ist weder ein kompaktes Gefüge noch besteht die Stadt aus verstreuten Einzelhäusern. Es reihen sich vielmehr unterschiedliche Wohnbezirke in Streifen um große grüne Bodensenken. Diese Stadt kann wie eine Strickarbeit durch Hinzufügen „neuer Maschen" wachsen. Sie versorgt sich selbst mit Energie, gewonnen aus Windkraft.

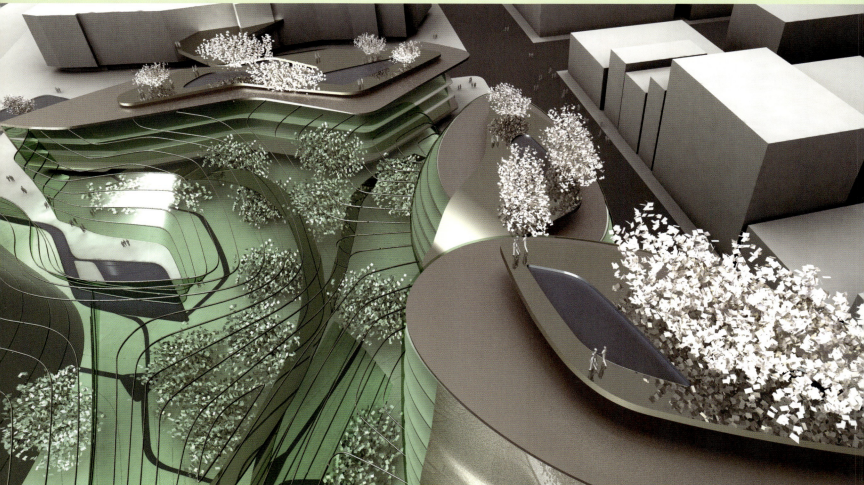

ANTOINE DAMERY
MELBOURNE, AUSTRALIA

"The main challenge for the future of Architecture will be in its ability to become pliable and adaptable to environmental evolutions. The exemplary blueprints of a new living system paradigm should be implemented to inspire people in improving their living interaction within the biome."

„Die größte Herausforderung für die zukünftige Architektur liegt in der Fähigkeit, sich an die veränderte Umwelt anzupassen. Die Blaupause für ein neues Wohnmodell sollte gefunden werden, das die Menschen dazu anregt, stärker im Austausch mit unserem Ökosystem zu leben."

BIOSPACE, 2009

Eco City, Melbourne, Australia

• Biospace is the ecological city of the future with the "Cycle of Life" as its heart and a downtown rainforest.
• Biospace ist eine Ökostadt der Zukunft mit dem „Cycle of Life" als Schaltzentrale und einem innerstädtischen Regenwald.

● ENGLISCH Melbourne, Australia's second largest city, expects to be the home of another million people by 2030, which will lead to a number of environmental changes. The water-supply, in particular, presents a problem, as water is scarce in this region even today. Antoine Damery, together with the Melbourne firm Peddle Thorp Architects, has developed a concept of urban construction and architecture called Biospace for the Australian ecological city of the future.

The "Cycle of Life", located above a train station, is the city's ecological heart. It consists of five blocks of buildings, connected by a rainforest atrium. On the communications level pedestrians are able to move about freely, while crossing rocky plateaus, canyons, or valleys. Perfect ventilation and spatial harmony, the recycling of rainwater, artificial creeks and roof gardens, integrated low-noise windmills, and solar modules, together with the natural climate, create something like a tropical rainforest. This model is the expression of a number of natural metaphors, for instance motion and evolution, thus reminding us of the natural biological cycle of life. The analogy to natural shapes is also demonstrated by the curved organic contours of the individual buildings. Biospace does not aim for a disparate package of technological innovations, but wants to develop a holistic urban concept, whose ecological solutions in combination with the buildings' design are able to imitate a natural environment.

• Architecture and rainforest will enter into a symbiosis that guarantees the natural circulation of water and air.
• Architektur und Regenwald gehen eine Symbiose ein, die natürliche Wasser- und Luftkreisläufe hervorbringt.

● Antoine Damery is an interdisciplinary designer, based in Melbourne. Together with the Australian firm Peddle Thorp Architects, he developed the urban vision Biospace in 2009. Damery adapts his concept to the scale of the project in question. His work includes industrial design, architecture, and automobile design as well as graphic design and art. His comprehensive approach enables him to find solutions on the micro and macro levels. Owing to the wide range of his projects, he considers the creative process a chance to transport ideas, forms, and technologies from one sphere of interest to the other.

● Antoine Damery ist ein interdisziplinär arbeitender Designer in Melbourne. Zusammen mit dem australischen Architekturbüro Peddle Thorp Architects entwickelte er 2009 die Stadtvisionen zu Biospace. Je nach Größe und Anforderung reicht Damerys Konzeptualisierung vom Industriedesign über Architektur und Automobildesign bis hin zur Grafik und Kunst. Sein umfassender Ansatz ermöglicht es ihm, Konzepte und Designlösungen auf der Mikro- wie auf der Makro-Ebene zu entwickeln. Aufgrund der Bandbreite seiner Projekte sieht er im Gestaltungsprozess die Möglichkeit, Ideen, Formen und Technologien von einem Gebiet auf ein anderes zu übertragen.

● DEUTSCH   Melbourne, die zweitgrößte Stadt Australiens, bereitet sich darauf vor, bis zum Jahr 2030 über eine Million Einwohner mehr aufzunehmen. Damit ist eine Vielzahl von veränderten Umweltbedingungen verbunden. Eine besondere Problematik stellt die Wasserversorgung dar – denn Wasser ist bereits heute in dieser Region knapp. Antoine Damery hat zusammen mit dem Melbourner Architekturbüro Peddle Thorp Architects das städtebauliche und architektonische Konzept der Biospace entwickelt, für eine australische Ökostadt der Zukunft.

Der über einem Bahnhof thronende „Cycle of Life" ist die ökologische Schaltzentrale der Stadt. Sie besteht aus fünf Baublöcken, die durch ein Regenwald-Atrium verbunden werden. Auf der Kommunikationsebene können sich Fußgänger frei bewegen und dabei Felsplateaus, Schluchten oder Täler durchqueren. Optimale Luftzirkulation und räumliche Harmonie, Recycling von Regenwasser, künstlich angelegte Wasserläufe und Dachgärten, integrierte, nahezu lautlose Windräder und Solarmodule sorgen gemeinsam mit dem natürlichen Klima dafür, dass in der Biospace City eine Art tropischer Regenwald entsteht. Das Modell verleiht verschiedenen Naturmetaphern Ausdruck, beispielsweise Bewegung und Evolution, und erinnert dadurch an den natürlichen biologischen Kreislauf des Lebens. Eine Analogie zu Naturformen wird auch an den organisch geschwungenen Konturen der diversen Einzelgebäude sichtbar. Das Ziel von Biospace ist nicht, ein disparates Paket innovativer technischer Errungenschaften für ein urbanes Konzept zusammenzustellen. Vielmehr geht es darum, ein umfassendes ganzheitliches Stadtmodell zu entwickeln, dessen umwelttechnische Lösungen zusammen mit dem Gebäudedesign die Umgebung der Natur zu imitieren vermögen.

BIG – BJARKE INGELS GROUP
COPENHAGEN, DENMARK

"The general perception of sustainability is this idea of: How much of our existing quality of life are we prepared to sacrifice to afford being sustainable? At BIG we look at how sustainable cities and buildings can increase the quality of life by designing cities and buildings as double ecosystems that are both ecologically but also economically profitable."

„Im Allgemeinen wird beim Thema Nachhaltigkeit gefragt: Wie viel unserer bestehenden Lebensqualität sind wir bereit zu opfern, um uns Nachhaltigkeit leisten zu können? Bei BIG betrachten wir die Frage, wie nachhaltige Städte und Gebäude die Lebensqualität steigern können, indem wir Städte und Gebäude als doppelte Ökosysteme gestalten, bei denen sowohl die Ökologie als auch die Ökonomie stimmen."

ZIRA ISLAND, 2008

Zira Island, Azerbaijan

With Ramboll Ongoin

- Inspired by the seven mountains marking the landscape, the "Seven Mountains" on the island of Zira are planned as zero-energy building complexes.
- Auf der Insel Zira in Aserbaidschan sollen analog zu den die Landschaft prägenden sieben Bergen die „Sieben Gipfel" als Null-Energie-Baukomplexe entstehen.

● ENGLISCH   "The Seven Summits of Azerbaijan" is a masterplan for a zero-ernergy holiday and entertainment resort on the island of Zira in the Caspian Sea. The concept is meant to be a model for a sustainable urban development and includes an iconic skyline, which will be visible from the shore of the capital Baku. The "Seven Summits" are a group of building complexes, whose geometric silhouettes are shaped like the seven famous mountains of Azerbaijan. Each individual building complex combines public and private spaces. Together, the highrise structures form an organic skyline, blending in with the island´s natural topography. A centrally located public "valley" links a densely built-up lively downtown area with golf courses, beaches, and a number of private residential and holiday villages. An uninterrupted public hiking path connects the "mountains" with one another, beckoning visitors to climb all seven summits. For Azerbaijan as a young post-Soviet democracy recovering national identity plays a major role. The masterplan´s architectural landscape mimics its natural counterpart. Besides having an iconic function, the "Seven Summits" are supposed to set an example for sustainable urban development with each mountain being a complete and self-contained eco-system. The vision sees the island of Zira as an autonomous entity, absolutely independent of external resources.

● DEUTSCH „Die Sieben Gipfel von Aserbaidschan" ist ein Masterplan für ein Null-Energie-Urlaubs- und Vergnügungsresort auf der Insel Zira im Kaspischen Meer. Der Entwurf versteht sich als Modell für eine nachhaltige Stadtentwicklung und sieht eine ikonische Skyline vor, die vom Ufer der Haupstadt Baku aus sichtbar sein soll. Die „Sieben Gipfel" sind eine Ansammlung von Gebäudekomplexen, deren geometrische Gestalt jeweils einem der sieben berühmten Berge von Aserbaidschan nachempfunden ist. Jeder Baukomplex stellt für sich genommen eine Mischung aus privaten und öffentlichen Bereichen dar. In ihrer Gesamtheit bilden die Hochhäuser eine organische Skyline, die mit der natürlichen Topografie der Insel verschmilzt. Eine dicht bebaute, pulsierende städtische Zone ist über ein zentral gelegenes öffentliches „Tal" mit Golfplätzen und Stränden an diverse private Wohn- und Feriendörfer angebunden. Ein durchgehender öffentlicher Wanderweg verbindet die „Berge" untereinander und animiert die Besucher, die Gipfel aller sieben Berge zu erklimmen. Als junge post-sowjetische Demokratie spielt die Wiederentdeckung der nationalen Identität für Aserbaidschan eine wichtige Rolle. Die architektonische Landschaft des Masterplans nimmt auf die natürliche Landschaft Bezug. Jenseits ihrer ikonischen Funktion sollen die „Sieben Gipfel" zu einem Musterbeispiel für nachhaltige Stadtentwicklung werden: Jeder Berg stellt ein komplettes, in sich geschlossenes Ökosystem dar. Die Vision der Planer zeigt die Insel Zira als ein autarkes Gebilde, das von externen Ressourcen vollständig unabhängig ist.

• The mountain Savalan is conceived as a network of different programs from the hotel at the center, branching out into apartments, row houses and finally inversing into a dense street grid with shops, bars and cafés.
• Der Savalan-Gipfel ist als Netzwerk konzipiert. Ausgehend von einem Hotel im Zentrum, verzweigt er sich in Appartements, Reihenhäuser und schließlich in ein dichtes Straßennetz mit Shops, Bars und Cafés.

AMAGERFORBRÆNDING, 2008

Copenhagen, Denmark

A New Waste Treatment Plant

● ENGLISCH   Situated in an industrial estate near the center of Copenhagen, this new facility for the thermic utilization of waste will not only be a shining example of how to turn refuse into energy, but also a new landmark in Copenhagen´s cityscape. The project will replace the 40-year-old incinerating plant nearby and be equipped with the latest technologies in order to utilize waste in an environment-friendly way. Instead of treating Amagerforbrænding as an isolated archtectural project, Bjarke Ingels Group made use of the chance to create an attraction for visitors that is worth taking a look at, in order to point out the ecological aspects that will mark our future lives. The roof, for instance, the roof will offer 31,000 square meters worth of skiing slopes to the inhabitants of Copenhagen. From a distance the entire building gives the impression of being covered with a green blanket. The façade consists of planters, stacked like bricks, that make the building look like a mountain. With each ton of fossil CO_2 emitted, smoke rings float from the building´s 30-meter-high chimney. At night, laser beams turn these smoke rings into little ephemeral works of art.

● DEUTSCH   In einem Industriegebiet nahe des Stadtkerns von Kopenhagen gelegen, wird diese neue Anlage zur thermischen Reststoffverwertung nicht nur zu einem Vorzeigemodell in puncto Abfallverwertung und Energiegewinnung werden, sondern auch zu einem neuen Wahrzeichen der Kopenhagener Stadtlandschaft. Der Neubau ersetzt die nahe gelegene, 40 Jahre alte Müllverbrennungsanlage und nutzt neueste umweltfreundliche Technologien der Abfallverwertung. Anstatt Amagerforbrænding als isoliertes Architekturprojekt zu entwickeln, hat die Bjarke Ingels Group das Gebäude zum Anlass genommen, ein sehenswertes Besucher- und Ausflugsziel zu schaffen, um auf den zukunftsweisenden ökologischen Aspekt aufmerksam zu machen. Das Dach der Anlage wird beispielsweise im Winter zur 31.000 m² großen Skipiste für die Einwohner Kopenhagens. Aus der Entfernung betrachtet, erscheint das gesamte Gebäude wie in eine grüne Hülle eingepackt. Die Fassade besteht aus Pflanzmodulen, die wie Ziegelsteine gestapelt sind und das Gebäude von Weitem gesehen in einen Berg zu verwandeln scheinen. Mit jeder freigegebenen Tonne fossilen CO_2 steigen Rauchkringel aus dem Schornstein des Gebäudes in 30 m Höhe. Bei Nacht verwandeln farbige Laserstrahlen diese Rauchkringel in kleine ephemere Kunstwerke.

• The planned new incinerating plant in Copenhagen also serves as a recreational facility with skiing slopes on its roof.
• Die geplante neue Müllverwertungsanlage in Kopenhagen dient, mit einer Skipiste auf dem Dach, gleichzeitig als städtisches Freizeitzentrum.

(DRIVER)LESS IS MORE, 2010

Proposal for the Audi Urban Future Award 2010 competition ran by the Audi Urban Future Initiative. The initiative aims to establish a dialog on the synergy of mobility, architecture and urban development by means of a view into the future and is curated by Stylepark AG.

• ENGLISCH   The driverless vehicle could become the next revolutionary change in the world of urban traffic: downtown areas that are not carless, but driverless. Vehicles steering themselves, while moving in coordinated harmony with others, take up only a quarter of the room than cars with human beings behind the wheel. Soundless and clean electric cars would mean the end of separate spheres for traffic, pedestrians, and cyclists, thus creating an elastic urban space, a "shared space", which is able to expand or contract as needed, thus making it possible to use a park or a square for traffic purposes only temporarily. The urban pavement becomes a programmable digital surface. A network of sensors coordinates traffic by communicating with the fleet of driverless cars, while collecting solar energy as well as the piezoelectric energy produced by walking humans. This energy then is transferred to the electric cars by wireless electromagnetic induction. The streets' digital surfaces will inform pedestrians of the imminent arrival of a driverless vehicle, enabling them to react in time. This way, within the same day, the function of a street can switch back and forth from pedestrian, vehicular, or recreational use.

• DEUTSCH   Das fahrerlose Auto könnte die nächste Revolution im urbanen Verkehrsraum sein: nicht autofreie, sondern einfach „fahrerlose" Innenstädte. Wenn sich selbstfahrende Autos in koordinierter Harmonie mit all den anderen Pendlerfahrzeugen bewegen, nehmen sie nur ein Viertel des Raumes der von Menschen gelenkten Autos ein. Geräuschlose und saubere Elektroautos würden das Ende der Trennung von Bereichen für Autos, Fußgänger und Radfahrer bedeuten. Ein elastischer urbaner Raum entsteht, ein „shared space", der sich nach Bedarf ausdehnt oder zusammenzieht, und es ermöglicht, dass ein Park oder ein Platz nur temporär vom Autoverkehr beansprucht wird. Das städtische Pflaster wird zu einer programmierbaren digitalen Oberfläche. Ein Sensoren-Netzwerk koordiniert die Verkehrsflüsse durch Kommunikation mit dem Strom der fahrerlosen Autos und sammelt gleichzeitig Sonnenenergie sowie die durch die menschliche Fortbewegung erzeugte piezoelektrische Energie. Diese könnte dann durch elektromagnetische Induktion drahtlos an Elektroautos übertragen werden. Die digitale Straßenoberfläche wird mehrere Sekunden im Voraus durch Lichtpunktsignale die aktuellen Bewegungen von fahrerlosen Fahrzeugen anzeigen, sodass Fußgänger frühzeitig darauf reagieren können. Innerhalb eines Tages könnte so die Funktion der Straße mehrfach zwischen Fußgänger-, Fahrzeug- und Erholungsnutzung wechseln.

• The city streets' digital surface with their changing signal fields make space-saving driverless vehicles and the multi-functional use of urban space possible.
• Die digitale Straßenoberfläche der Stadt mit wechselnden Signalfeldern ermöglicht den platzsparenden Einsatz von fahrerlosen Autos sowie die energieeffiziente multifunktionale Nutzung des Stadtraums.

- Bjarke Ingels Group (BIG) is a group of architects, designers, and scientists based in Copenhagen and not only involved in archtitecture and urban development, but also in the fields of research and development planning. BIG enjoys the reputation of constructing buildings which are innovative in regard to technology and design as well as low-cost and resource-efficient. The firm´s focus lies on the specific demands raised by building context and specific use. According to BIG, contemporary architecture has gotten stuck in either one of two problematic approaches: it is naively utopian or frozen in pragmatism. Instead of choosing one of the two sides, BIG walks the progressive line between these contrasting views, opting for a utopian pragmatism and following the practical aim of creating residential and commercial spaces, perfectly adapted to the respective social, economic, and ecologic conditions.

- Die Bjarke Ingels Group (BIG) ist eine in Kopenhagen ansässige Gruppe von Architekten, Designern und Wissenschaftlern, die sich über Architektur und Städtebau hinaus auch in den Bereichen Forschungs- und Entwicklungsplanung engagiert. BIG hat eine Reputation für die Errichtung von Gebäuden, die ebenso technisch und im Programm innovativ wie kosten- und ressourceneffizient sind. Das Büro legt besonderes Augenmerk auf die spezifischen Anforderungen von baulichem Kontext und Nutzungsprogramm. Nach der Auffassung von BIG steckt die zeitgenössische Architektur in zwei unfruchtbaren Ansätzen fest: Entweder ist sie naiv utopisch oder sie erstarrt im Pragmatismus. Statt die eine Seite der anderen vorzuziehen, bewegt sich BIG im progressiven Schnittfeld dieser gegenläufigen Ansichten: Sie ist pragmatisch utopisch; ihr praktisches Ziel ist die Schaffung von Lebens- und Arbeitsräumen, die perfekt an ihre jeweiligen sozialen, ökonomischen und ökologischen Bedingungen angepasst sind.

WATER

Due to our densely populated cities and urban sprawls, building on the shore and living with or on the water today are more topical and attractive than ever. Coastal and harbor towns, buildings on islands or bridges, and hotels and private homes directly at the seaside are water architectures that have always held a lot of fascination. Meanwhile, threatening environmental scenarios have been added to these romantic and idyllic notions, as climatic changes might call for for people to live on or below the water on a permanent basis. Global warming and the ensuing raising of the sea level could lead to cities and entire regions being flooded. Countries like the Netherlands, where 25% of the territory is located below sea level, as well as atolls like the Maldives are already affected.

Modern architectural visions that concern themselves with water fall back on scenarios taken from science-fiction novels and films like Jules Verne´s "Twenty Thousand Leagues Under the Sea" or Kevin Kostner´s "Waterworld". Entire cities are conceived as giant floating islands or clusters of underwater capsules. The oceans, which up to now have been blank spaces on the map, are increasingly being discovered as new locations by architects and designers. As utopian as many of these concepts may look – they always take the ecology of the interface between architecture and water into account. The projects use water power as an important source of energy, often in combination with the power of the wind, which is blowing over the oceans. New biotechnical systems and constructions process salt water, thus turning it into vital fresh water. The oceanic cities of the future have their own metabolism and a functioning bio system, which make them independent of the mainland.

WASSER

In unserer heutigen Zeit der Stadtverdichtung und Flächenzersiedlung fällt dem Bauen am Wasser und Leben mit sowie auf dem Wasser eine aktuelle und nicht unattraktive Bedeutung zu. Küsten- und Hafenstädte, bebaute Inseln oder Brücken, Hotels und Wohnhäuser direkt am Meer strahlten schon immer eine große Faszination aus. Nun kommen neben den romantisch-verklärenden Kriterien bedrohliche Umweltszenarien hinzu, die ein zukünftiges Wohnen des Menschen auf und im Wasser als langfristige Konsequenz des Klimawandels nach sich ziehen könnte. Die Erderwärmung und der damit verbundene Anstieg der Meeresspiegel können zu einer Überflutung von Städten und ganzen Regionen führen. Länder wie die Niederlande mit 25% der Fläche unter Meeresspiegelhöhe oder auch Atolle wie die Malediven sind beispielsweise schon jetzt akut betroffen.

Heutige Architekturvisionen zum Thema Wasser greifen durchaus auf fiktive Szenarien von Science-fiction-Romanen und Filmen wie Jules Vernes „20.000 Meilen unter den Meeren" oder Kevin Costners „Waterworld" zurück. Ganze Stadtkomplexe werden als riesige schwimmende Inseln oder als clusterförmige Unterseekapseln entworfen. Waren die Ozeane bisher eher Leerstellen auf der Landkarte, so werden sie zunehmend von Architekten und Designern als neu zu bebauender und zu gestaltender Lebensraum entdeckt. So utopisch viele dieser Konzepte auch ausfallen mögen – sie nehmen immer Bezug auf die ökologischen Bedingungen, die mit dieser Schnittstelle zwischen Architektur und Wasser verbunden sind. Die Wasserkraft wird bei diesen Projekten als wichtige Energiequelle eingesetzt, häufig auch in Verbindung mit der Kraft des Windes, der über die Meere weht. Neue biotechnische Systeme und Konstruktionen sorgen dafür, dass Salzwasser zu lebenswichtigem Süßwasser aufbereitet werden kann. Die ozeanischen Städte der Zukunft haben einen eigenen Stoffwechselkreislauf und ein funktionierendes Biosystem, das sie autark und unabhängig vom Festland macht.

ARUP
SYDNEY, AUSTRALIA

"We aim for a future of biomimetic cityscapes nestled into a range of natural ecosystems. They integrate by using re-interpreted ecological attributes from the surrounding environment. The resulting symbiosis supports a sustainable human civilization."

„Wir streben eine Zukunft an, in der es biomimetische Stadtlandschaften gibt, die sich harmonisch in die sie umgebenden Ökosysteme einfügen. Dazu interpretieren sie ökologische Attribute ihrer Umwelt neu. Die daraus resultierende Symbiose kann eine nachhaltig lebende Zivilisation tragen."

OCEAN CITY, 2010

Proposal for Sydney, Australia

Shown at the Australian Pavilion,
12th International Architecture Exhibition,
La Biennale di Venezia 2010

- The underwater city of the future consists of individual capsules, whose shape and motions resemble those of jellyfish and multi-celled oceanic denizens.
- Die Unterwasserstadt der Zukunft besteht aus einzelnen Kapseln, die sich in ihrer Form und Fortbewegung an Quallen und mehrzelligen Meereslebewesen orientieren.

• The capsules of Ocean City can float by themselves in the deep seas or form clusters on the surface.
• Die Kapseln der Ocean City können allein in der Meerestiefe schwimmen oder sich zu Clusterformationen unter der Meeresoberfläche zusammenschließen.

● ENGLISH   As utopian as this project may look, for Australia Ocean City could become a real urban option within the near future (40 years?), due to climatic changes. Siph City is the draft for an eastward expansion of Sydney into the ocean, which offers a reasonably stable living space, as it is not threatened by high waters, floods, or tsunamis. The individual elements of the underwater city consist of capsules resembling jellyfish and other multi-celled ocean denizens. The joining of these capsules creates functional clusters, which can dive as well as float. On quiet days the city floats on the surface, storing solar energy for the photosynthesis needed to grow produce. Currents, waves, tides, wind, and sun all contain giant amounts of natural energy, only waiting to be tapped by the ocean. Fresh water is produced with a minimal use of energy by imitating osmosis, which is the way natural cells process liquids. The nutrients for the growing of produce are generated by hydrocultures and taken directly from the ocean. Thus, the ocean, the origin of all life, becomes a new living space for the human race.

● DEUTSCH   So utopisch dieser Entwurf heute noch erscheinen mag, für Australien zumindest könnte Ocean City in nicht allzu weiter Zukunft (in 40 Jahren?) infolge des Klimawandels zu einer realen urbanen Option werden. Die Siph City ist der Entwurf für die Expansion Sydneys ostwärts in den Ozean hinein. Das Meer bietet für die Menschen einen relativ stabilen Lebensraum, der nicht durch Hochwasser, Überschwemmung und Tsunamis bedroht ist. Die einzelnen Elemente der Unterwasserstadt bestehen aus Kapseln, die in ihrer Formgebung Analogien zu Quallen und mehrzelligen Meeresbewohnern aufweisen. Der Zusammenschluss dieser Einzelkapseln führt zu funktionalen Clustern, die in die Meerestiefe abtauchen, aber auch unter der Meeresoberfläche schwimmen können. An ruhigeren Tagen schwebt die Stadt an die Oberfläche und tankt Sonnenenergie für die Fotosynthese der Nahrungsmittelproduktion. Strömungen, Wellen, Gezeiten, Wind und Sonne enthalten allesamt riesige Mengen natürlicher Energie, die nur darauf warten, vom Meer aus angezapft zu werden. Durch die Nachahmung der Osmose lebendiger Zellen zur Flüssigkeitsaufbereitung wird frisches Trinkwasser unter minimalem Energieaufwand produziert. Auch die Nährstoffe für die Nahrungsmittelproduktion auf der Basis von Hydrokulturen stammen direkt aus dem Meer. Der Ozean könnte so zu einem neuen Lebensraum des Menschen werden, dort, wo alles Leben auf der Erde seinen Ursprung nahm.

● Arup is an international firm of consultants working in the areas of construction, planning, and building design, infrastructural projects, urban planning, and project management. The firm employs about 10,000 people in 70 branches, located in more than 40 countries. The Sydney office offers a wide range of services in the field of planning and design, like urban planning, building technology, and the analysis of sustainability. Arup believes in feasible visions of a better world, which the designers want to be part of. They trust in the collective ability of the human race to meet the challenges of climatic changes and shortage of resources. However, people will have to come to terms with the consequences of their current behavior, if they want to do so successfully. The time has come to consciously choose what this future is to look like. Photo: Alanna Howe and Alexander Hespe.

● Arup ist ein international tätiges Beratungsunternehmen im Bereich Bau, Planung und Gestaltung von Gebäuden, Infrastrukturmaßnahmen sowie Stadtplanung und Projektmanagement. Das Unternehmen beschäftigt etwa 10.000 Mitarbeiter in 70 Niederlassungen, die über 40 Länder verteilt sind. Die Niederlassung in Sydney bietet eine breite Palette an Dienstleistungen im Bereich Planung und Gestaltung, darunter Stadtplanung, Gebäudetechnik und Nachhaltigkeitsanalysen. Arup glaubt an realisierbare Visionen einer besseren Welt, an der sie als Gestalter mitwirken wollen. Sie vertrauen auf die kollektive Fähigkeit des Menschen, die Herausforderungen des Klimawandels und der Resourcenknappheit zu meistern. Um sich diesen großen Herausforderungen zu stellen, müssen sich die Menschen jedoch damit befassen, welche Konsequenzen ihr Handeln von heute in der Zukunft haben wird. Und sie müssen bereits jetzt bewusst entscheiden, auf was für eine Zukunft sie hinarbeiten wollen. Foto: Alanna Howe und Alexander Hespe.

JACQUES ROUGERIE

PARIS, FRANCE

"A re-conquest of the original surroundings is part of our civilizations' future. Living underwater is a true wish that takes place on the same level as mankind's great steps along its evolution."

„Eine Rückeroberung der ursprünglichen Umgebungen ist Teil unserer zukünftigen Zivilisationen. Unter Wasser zu leben, ist ein ernsthafter Wunsch, der auf der gleichen Stufe wie die großen Evolutionsschritte der Menschheit anzusiedeln ist."

SEAORBITER, 1999–2013

● ENGLISCH   SeaOrbiter is a projected French sealab "underwater architect" Jacques Rougerie has been working on since 1999. The launch is planned for 2013. The vertical vehicle is 51 meters high, with 30 meters of its bulk being submerged. The 10 decks offer room for 18 people. As opposed to other underwater vehicles and submarines, SeaOrbiter will float with the currents and not emit any noise.

Behind this project is the idea to send new high-sea explorer ships across the oceans, thus following the tradition of the great expeditions of the past, as many areas of the world´s oceans are still unchartered. SeaOrbiter allows people to move about in the hearts of the oceans, drifting with their powerful current, while conducting studies and enjoying the advantages of a direct and permanent access to living spaces on and under water. In this respect, SeaOrbiter is a unique way to communicate, open one´s eyes, and learn more about the secret ocean world.

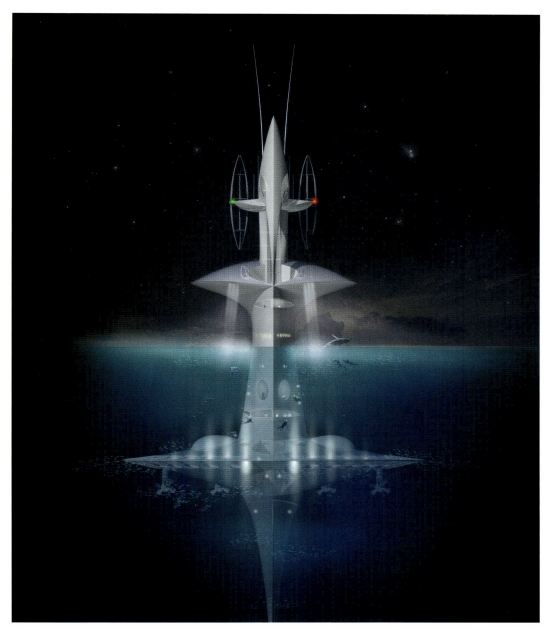

- SeaOrbiter, a sea lab, will drift over the oceans of the world with the current to uncover new scientific knowledge about the cycles and creatures of the ocean.
- Der SeaOrbiter soll als Forschungsstation mit den Strömungen durch die Ozeane dieser Welt gleiten und neue wissenschaftliche Erkenntnisse über Kreisläufe und Lebewesen im Meer liefern.

- Already in the 1970s the architect Jacques Rougerie designed futuristic settlements on the ocean floor and imaginative submarines. His firm based in Paris is mostly involved in projects that have something to do with water or the vicinity to the ocean, like the plans for an underwater museum of archeology in Alexandria, Egypt, or a therapy-sea-center in Okinawa, Japan. The current work on SeaOrbiter is conducted in cooperation with NASA. The first launch is planned for 2013 in the Mediterranean.

- Der Architekt Jacques Rougerie entwarf bereits in den 1970er-Jahren futuristische Siedlungen auf dem Meeresgrund und fantasievolle U-Boote. Sein in Paris angesiedeltes Büro befasst sich vorrangig mit Bauprojekten, die in irgendeiner Form mit Wasser und der Nähe zum Meer zu tun haben, so u. a. die Planungen für ein Unterwasser-Archäologie-Museum im ägyptischen Alexandria oder ein Therapie-Sea-Centre im japanischen Okinawa. Die aktuellen Planungen zum SeaOrbiter erfolgen in Zusammenarbeit mit der NASA, ein erster Stapellauf der Forschungsstation ist für 2013 im Mittelmeer vorgesehen.

- DEUTSCH Der SeaOrbiter ist eine geplante französische Seeforschungsstation, die der auf Unterwasserprojekte spezialisierte Architekt Jacques Rougerie seit 1999 konzipiert und deren Stapellauf für 2013 vorgesehen ist. Das Gefährt ist vertikal orientiert und hat eine Gesamthöhe von 51 m, von denen sich 30 m unter der Wasseroberfläche befinden sollen. Auf den insgesamt 10 Decks können sich maximal 18 Personen aufhalten. Der SeaOrbiter soll im Unterschied zu anderen Tiefseefahrzeugen oder U-Booten mit der Meeresströmung treiben, ohne laute Motorengeräusche.

Das Projekt basiert auf der Idee, neue Hochsee-Forschungsschiffe über die Meere zu senden, und steht damit in der Tradition der großen Erkundungsfahrten vergangener Jahrhunderte. Denn die Ozeane der Erde sind nach wie vor in vielen Bereichen noch unerforscht. Der SeaOrbiter erlaubt es der Menschheit, sich im Herzen der Ozeane fortzubewegen, sich mit den großen Meeresströmungen treiben zu lassen, Beobachtungsstudien durchzuführen und die Vorteile eines direkten und dauerhaften Zugangs zu Lebensräumen im und unter Wasser auszuschöpfen. So gesehen bietet SeaOrbiter die einzigartige Chance, über die geheimnisvolle Welt der Ozeane zu kommunizieren, zu forschen und zu lernen.

UNDERWATER CITY

If climate changes cause sea-level rise, coastal cities worldwide will be particularly threatened. Given the rising likelihood of such scenarios, designing floating or underwater cities is becoming increasingly considered as an important task for the future. 71% of the Earth's surface is covered with water, which is likely to increase to up to 80% in future through ground losses. According to the alarming forecasts of international scientists, the ocean level is expected to rise about 1 m due to unmitigated emissions. Global sea-level is likely to increase at least twice as much as projected in 2007 by the IPCC (Intergovernmental Panel on Climate Change) Fourth Assessment Report that predicted a growth from 18–59 cm during the 21st century versus 10–20 cm in the 20th century. Only since the early 1990s, Satellites show great global average sea-level rise of 3.4 mm/year over the past 15 years. This acceleration is consistent with a doubling in contribution from melting of glaciers and the Greenland and West- Antarctic ice-sheets. Several meters of sea level changes must be expected over the next few centuries. The scientific advisory board of the German Federal Government (WBGU) for example, forecasts an increase of even 2.5–5.1 m up to 2300. Vast coastal areas will be submerged in water. At the same time 45% of the world population live in coastal areas, where 75% of all megacities are situated. We have to deal with the disappearance of coastal regions, to think about long-term responses to inundation risk, salinization of the ground water, immense dam construction strains and, finally, less inhabitable area. The retreat to cramped, limited areas is the only option for many coastal inhabitants. We have to face up the question of how many means for dams and other flooding preventive measures can be still justified if there could be less expensive solutions. Some countries do not have enough space for further resettlement in the hinterlands or in higher situated regions, or are already located mainly below sea level. Do we migrate to the interior, competing for scarce resources, or do we develop technologies to sustain ourselves in a life aquatic? One possibility would be to view the sea itself as a human habitat yet to be discovered. One day self-sufficient floating cities or artificial islands might drift across the oceans. Already above the ocean surface, offshore platforms bustle with activity, extracting precious hydrocarbons. Why then should an underwater version be overlooked, considering that valuable resources do exist underwater? In an effort to extend the range of habitable spaces for humans, many architects have started to venture beyond our shores and elaborate different ideas of water-bound settlements that could possibly lead to the world's first permanent Aquapolis.

Caroline Klein

UNTERWASSER-STADT

Mit dem durch Klimaveränderungen verursachten Ansteigen der Meeresspiegel, das weltweit die Küstenstädte bedroht, wächst die Notwendigkeit nach auf oder unter Wasser schwimmenden Städten. 71% der Erdoberfläche sind heute mit Wasser bedeckt, eine Zahl, die voraussichtlich in einigen Gebieten aufgrund von weiteren Landverlusten auf 80% steigen wird. Laut der beunruhigenden Vorhersagen von internationalen Wissenschaftlern wird sich der Meeresspiegel im 21. Jahrhundert bei unverminderten Treibhausgas-Emissionen etwa um 1 m erhöhen. Voraussichtlich also mindestens doppelt so stark wie im vierten Sachstandbericht des Weltklimarates (Intergovernmental Panel on Climate Change, IPCC) aus dem Jahr 2007 angenommen wurde (18–59 cm gegenüber 10–20 cm im 20. Jahrhundert). Die erst seit Anfang der 1990er-Jahre durchgeführten Satellitenmessungen belegen, dass der Meeresspiegel in den letzten 15 Jahren um 3,4 mm pro Jahr gestiegen ist. Diese Wachstumsbeschleunigung ist konsistent mit einer Verdoppelung des Beitrags schmelzender Gebirgsgletscher sowie der Eismassen in den Polarregionen. Man rechnet mit einem weiteren Anstieg um mehrere Meter in den kommenden Jahrhunderten. So prognostiziert zum Beispiel der wissenschaftliche Beirat der deutschen Bundesregierung (WBGU) eine Meeresspiegelerhöhung von 2,5–5,1 m bis zum Jahr 2300. Riesige Küstengebiete werden von Wasser bedeckt sein. Zugleich leben 45% der Menschheit in Küstenzonen und 75% aller Megastädte befinden sich genau dort. Man muss sich also dringend mit dem Problem des Verschwindens von Küstenregionen auseinandersetzen und Langzeitlösungen für zunehmende Überschwemmungen, die Versalzung des Grundwassers, gewaltige Dammbau-Anstrengungen und schließlich immer weniger bewohnbare Flächen finden. Der Rückzug ins Landesinnere ist die einzige Option für viele Küstenbewohner. Es stellt sich dabei jedoch die Frage, wie viel Mittel für Dämme und andere Überflutungsschutz-Maßnahmen noch zu rechtfertigen sind, wenn es preiswertere Lösungen geben könnte. Manche Länder haben für die Umsiedlung ins Landesinnere oder in höher gelegene Regionen nicht den Platz, beziehungsweise befinden sie sich heute schon größtenteils unter dem Meeresspiegel. Ist die Lösung also eine Verlagerung ins Innere der Kontinente bei verschärftem Wettbewerb um knappe Ressourcen oder die Entwicklung von Technologien, die dem Menschen das Überleben im und auf dem Wasser ermöglichen? Man könnte das Meer als neu zu entdeckenden Lebensraum begreifen. Schwebende, sich selbst versorgende Städte und schwimmende Inseln könnten eines Tages über die Weltmeere treiben. Auf dem Wasser gibt es bereits heute zahlreiche, den Küsten vorgelagerte Plattformen, auf denen Menschen wohnen und arbeiten und wertvolle Kohlenwasserstoffe fördern. Weshalb sollte auf Unterwasservarianten solcher Bauten verzichtet werden, wo doch bekanntermaßen im Wasser wie im Meeresboden begehrte Ressourcen lagern? In dem Bemühen, neue Regionen der Erde für menschliches Leben bewohnbar zu machen, wagen immer mehr Architekten den Schritt, das feste Land hinter sich zu lassen und Entwürfe für Siedlungsformen im Wasser zu entwickeln. Eines Tages könnte aus diesen Ideen die erste dauerhafte Aquapolis der Welt geboren werden.

Caroline Klein

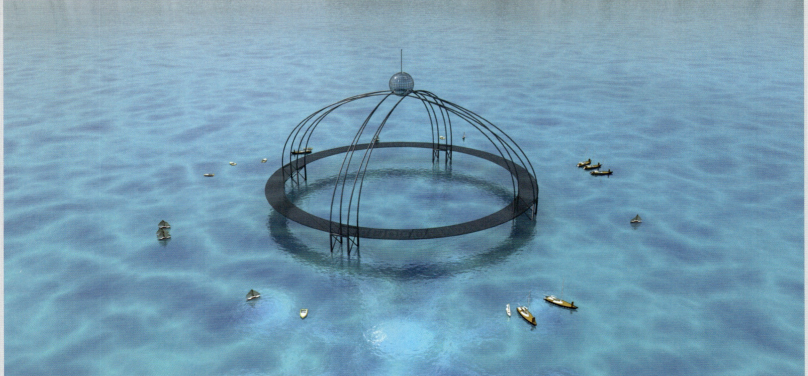

• Sub-Biosphere 2: a self-sustaining marine environment for human, animal and plant life by Phil Pauley, a London-based concept designer
• Sub-Biosphere 2: eine autarke Lebenswelt im Meer für Menschen, Tiere und Pflanzen, entworfen vom Londoner Konzeptdesigner Phil Pauley

KOKKUGIA EMERGENT

NEW YORK, USA
LOS ANGELES, USA

"The future of architecture is dependent on biological thinking. In biology, there is no separation between systems, no reductivism, only drive and excess. Ecologies relentlessly organize matter and reward cooperation. It is long overdue in the crusty practice of architecture that we re-envision a built world inherently composite and coherent."

„Die Zukunft der Architektur ist abhängig von biologischem Denken. In der Biologie gibt es keine Systemtrennung, keinen Reduktivismus, nur Antrieb und Exzess. Ökologien organisieren ununterbrochen Materie und belohnen Kooperation. In der verkrusteten architektonischen Praxis ist eine neue Vision einer gebauten, in sich stimmigen und kohärenten Welt lange überfällig."

Emergent

OCEANIC PAVILION, 2010

Yeosu, Korea

● ENGLISCH This concept for a pavilion floating on the ocean will be presented at the Expo 2012 in Yeosu, Korea, and is the result of a cooperation of the design team EMERGENT and the architectural firm KOKKUGIA. The formal design of the pavilion, which resembles organic structures (like a human heart with two chambers and supporting muscles and blood vessels) is meant to represent a space which wants to be seen as part of the living ocean. At the exhibition, the building will be set up at the interface of oceanic eco-system and human culture. The structure´s surface is marked by a combination of soft membrane bubbles and hard sections made from sea shells. Both systems have their specific textures and qualities: the domed membranes, consisting of the synthetic foil ETFE, are stabilized by a permanent air stream; the sea shells, a layer of pleated compound fibers, lend stability to the structure. The conspicuous color is meant to symbolize the organic cycles and simulated processes of growth inside and outside the pavilion. The inflatable clear bubbles let plenty of natural daylight in. In spite of its seemingly complex general concept, Oceanic Pavilion is a relatively simple light-weight structure and can be quickly dismantled after the Expo.

PAGE/SEITE 205
- Inflatable membrane bubbles and stiffening fibers made from sea shells will be the materials for the light-weight structure of Oceanic Pavilion.
- Aufblasbare Membranen und versteifende Fasermaterialien aus Muschelschalen sind als Materialien für die Leichtbaukonstruktion des Oceanic Pavilion vorgesehen.

• The floating pavilion for the Expo 2012 in Yeosu, Korea, resembles a throbbing organ, a mediator between the oceanic realm and the world of humans.
• Der auf dem Meer schwimmende Pavillon für die Expo 2012 im koreanischen Yeosu wirkt wie ein pulsierendes Organ, das zwischen dem Reich der Ozeane und der Welt der Menschen vermittelt.

• KOKKUGIA (derived from the Greek "nephelokokkygiá", the Cloud-Cuckoo-Land in Aristophanes´s play "The Birds") is a young and experimental firm for architecture and urban planning, headed by Roland Snooks and Robert Stuart-Smith. It explores methods of generative design along the lines of the complex and autonomous types of behavior of biological, social, and material systems.

• EMERGENT was founded by Tom Wiscombe in 1999. The design firm develops state-of-the-art concepts of digital design, inspired by biological models and the natural cyclic processes of mutation and selection. The projects of EMERGENT are marked by a creative synthesis of shape, texture, color, and technology.

• KOKKUGIA (abgeleitet aus dem Griechischen „nephelokokkygiá", dem „Wolkenkuckucksheim" in Aristophanes Drama „Die Vögel") ist ein junges experimentierfreudiges Architektur- und Stadtplanungsbüro unter der Leitung von Roland Snooks und Robert Stuart-Smith, das die Methoden generativen Designs erkundet, orientiert an komplexen, selbstorganisierenden Verhaltensweisen biologischer, sozialer und materieller Systeme.

• EMERGENT wurde 1999 von Tom Wiscombe gegründet. Das Designbüro arbeitet an neuesten Konzepten des digitalen Entwurfs, inspiriert von Modellen aus der Biologie und zyklischen Prozessen der Mutation und Selektion, wie sie in der Natur vorkommen. Die Arbeit von EMERGENT zeichnet sich durch die gestalterische Synthese von Form, Textur, Farbe und Technologie aus.

• DEUTSCH   Dieser Entwurf für einen auf dem Meer schwimmenden Pavillon für die Expo 2012 im koreanischen Yeosu ist das Ergebnis einer Zusammenarbeit zwischen dem Designteam EMERGENT und dem Architekturbüro KOKKUGIA. Die formale Gestaltung des Pavillons, die an Organstrukturen erinnert (z. B. an ein menschliches Herz mit zwei Kammern sowie versorgenden Muskeln und Blutadern), will einen Raum darstellen, der als Bestandteil des lebendigen Ozeans verstanden werden kann. Der Ausstellungsbau soll an der Schnittstelle zwischen dem Ökosystem des Meeres und der menschlichen Kulturwelt angesiedelt sein.

Die Struktur des Pavillongebäudes setzt sich aus einer Verbindung von weichen Membranblasen mit harten Partien aus Muschelschalen zusammen. Beide Materialien haben ihre spezifischen Oberflächenstrukturen und Eigenschaften: Die gewölbten Membranen aus der Kunststofffolie ETFE werden durch permanente Luftströme stabilisiert, die Muschelschalen aus einer gekräuselten Verbundfaserhülle sorgen für die Steifheit des Gebildes. Die auffällige Farbgebung soll die organischen Kreisläufe und simulierten Wachstumsprozesse im und am Pavillon symbolisieren. Durch die aufblasbaren transparenten Membranen kann hinreichend natürliches Tageslicht in den Ausstellungsbereich gelangen. Trotz der sehr aufwändig anmutenden Gesamtkonzeption ist der Oceanic Pavilion eine relativ einfache Leichtbaukonstruktion, die sich in kurzer Zeit nach dem Ende der Expo wieder abbauen lässt.

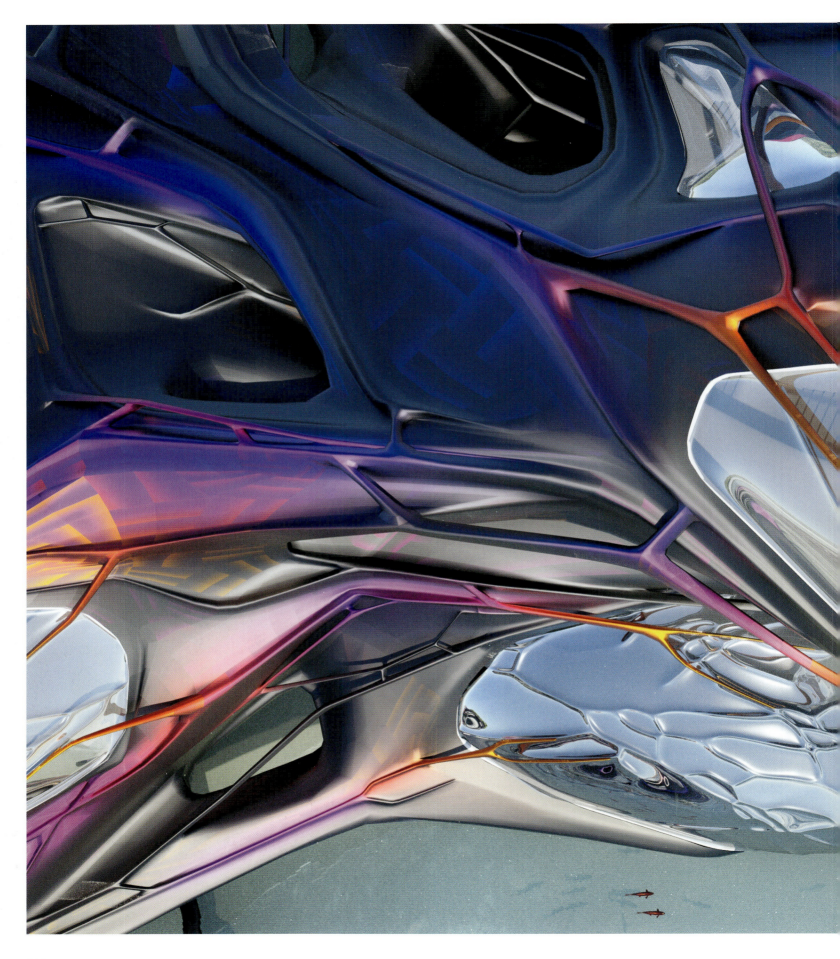

PHU HOANG OFFICE
NEW YORK, USA

"We believe that overlooked intersections between political crisis and rapid ecological change can provide architects with opportunities for architectural innovation."

„Wir glauben, dass nicht wahrgenommene Überschneidungen zwischen politischen Krisenerscheinungen und rasantem ökologischen Wandel den Architekten baukünstlerische Innovationen ermöglichen können."

NO MAN'S LAND, 2007

Dead Sea, Israel/Jordan

PAGE/SEITE 212–213
• The islands of No Man´s Land are equipped with funnel-shaped buildings to provide services to visitors and generate energy.
• Die Inseln von No Man's Land sind mit trichterförmigen Gebäuden bestückt, die sowohl dem Tourismus dienen als auch der Energiegewinnung.

- Artificial islands, serving as ecological holiday resorts and producing energy, will be placed in the no man´s land between Israel, the Palestinian autonomous territories, and Jordan.
- Im Niemandsland des Grenzgebietes zwischen Israel, den Palästinensischen Autonomiegebieten und Jordanien sollen künstliche Inseln als ökologische Touristenanlagen und zur Energiegewinnung platziert werden.

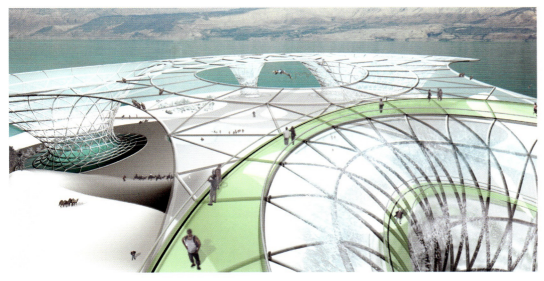

● ENGLISCH This project, meant for a "no man´s land", a narrow unclaimed strip of the Dead Sea, promises help in times of an ecological crisis, while also being considered a contribution to the solution of an ongoing conflict. Many political activities in this region are aimed at gaining control over resources, with water being one of the most conflict-ridden issues. Phu Hoang´s project draws attention to the Dead Sea, whose level has been going down for years, with dramatic consequences for the environment. His concept moves the currently endangered local holiday resorts to a network of artificial islands. The area is intended to be a territory unclaimed by any state, as the borders of the body of water will differ from the political ones. The archipelago will offer all amenities to tourists, while producing ecological energy and processing drinking-water.

● DEUTSCH Dieses im „Niemandsland", einem schmalen, unbeanspruchten Gewässerstreifen des Toten Meeres, angesiedelte Projekt verspricht Hilfe in ökologischen Krisenzeiten und gilt gleichzeitig als Beitrag zur Lösung eines langjährigen Konflikts. Viele der politischen Manöver in der Region zielen darauf ab, Ressourcen zu kontrollieren. Eine der umkämpftesten Ressourcen ist Wasser. Phu Hoangs Projekt lenkt die Aufmerksamkeit auf das Tote Meer, dessen Wasserspiegel seit Jahren sinkt, was erhebliche Umweltschäden verursacht. Der Entwurf verlegt die dort akut gefährdeten Urlaubsanlagen auf ein Netzwerk künstlicher Inseln. Dieses Gebiet soll ein von Staaten unbeanspruchtes Terrain werden, da die Gewässergrenzen nicht mehr mit den politischen Grenzen übereinstimmen. Der Archipel würde alle Annehmlichkeiten für Touristen bieten sowie für ökologische Energiegewinnung und die Aufbereitung von Trinkwasser sorgen.

● Since its opening in New York City in 2007, the architectural firm Phu Hoang Office has been awarded a number of prizes. The firm´s creative processes always begin with taking into account the interplay of the activities inside a building and the environmental conditions outside. Phu Hoang´s mission is to cast into question the difficulties resulting from restrictions and constraints like building regulations and climatic conditions and to solve them with the help of innovative designs.

● Seit seiner Gründung in New York City 2007 hat das Architekturbüro Phu Hoang Office bereits einige Preise gewonnen. Die kreative Arbeit des Büros beginnt bei den Überlegungen zum Zusammenspiel zwischen den Aktivitäten, die in einem Gebäude stattfinden und den entsprechenden äußeren Umweltbedingungen. Der Anspruch von Phu Hoang besteht darin, Probleme, die durch Zwänge und Beschränkungen wie Bauvorschriften und klimatische Gegebenheiten entstehen, zu hinterfragen und durch vollständig neue Designentwürfe zu lösen.

• The islands of No Man´s Land are equipped with funnel-shaped buildings to provide services to visitors and generate energy.
• Die Inseln von No Man's Land sind mit trichterartigen Gebäuden bestückt, die die unterschiedlichen Funktionen des Tourismus sowie der Energiegewinnung beherbergen.

BIOTHING
LONDON, UK

"One of the possible futures for achitecture is the computation of complex design ecologies through the synthesis of a large quantity of data and the integration of non-human factors. Increased-resolution architectural structures of this kind can operate within complex conditions, binding different agencies into a resilient poly-scalar continuum."

„Eine mögliche Zukunftsperspektive ist die Berechnung komplexer Ökosysteme durch die Zusammenfassung einer Vielzahl von Informationen und die Einbeziehung von transhumanen Handlungsträgern. Eine solch höher aufgelöste Architekturstruktur kann sich selbst sogar in kurzlebigen Ökosystemen realisieren, indem sie unterschiedliche Handlungsträger in ein polyskalares stabiles Kontinuum bindet."

FISSUREPORT, 2010

Kaohsiung, Taiwan

● ENGLISCH   Biothing devised the concept of FissurePort for a harbor terminal in Kaohsiung, Taiwan. The building's architecture resembles the structures and vertical fissures of cliff formations and is based on the fractal calculations of natural coastlines with their different degrees of coarseness and ramifications. The architectonic fabric of the terminal is highly heterogeneous and marked by sudden changes in spatial concepts and the modeling of surfaces. Instead of the seamless topological continuity, which is typical for passenger terminals, travelers are exposed to a number of very different spatial experiences, mostly caused by the deep vertical fissures in the building's body. The resulting narrow "canyons" are sources of light and shade at the same time, creating a stream of light within the building, while preventing overheating as well. The proportions of the extremely long and high rooms with their canyon-like coated surfaces make for a rich multi-dimensional spatial experience. Quality and character of the different fissures gradually change between road and sea side: from the dim, semi-opaque façade of an "office fissure" to a very thinly coated glass front with a crystal-clear structure that faces the ocean, offering a panoramic view. LED lights and directional signal systems can be integrated into the complex arrangement of tectonic elements, in order to help passengers to find their way around the terminal.

• FissurePort, a harbor terminal in Taiwan, with its fissured surface and spatial concept is meant to resemble natural rock formations and maritime cliffs.
• Der FissurePort als Hafenterminal in Taiwan orientiert sich mit seiner zerklüfteten Oberfläche und der Raumkonzeption an natürlichen Felsformationen und Meeresklippen.

• The proportions of extremely long space with "canyon-like" glazed surfacing produces very rich poly-dimensional experience.
• Die Proportionen des extrem lang gezogenen Raumes mit seiner zerklüfteten Außenhaut lassen den Eindruck von Mehrdimensionalität entstehen.

● DEUTSCH Für einen Hafenterminal in Kaohsiung, Taiwan, hat Biothing den Entwurf des FissurePort (Klufthafen) vorgelegt, der die Strukturen und senkrechten Klüfte von Klippenformationen aufnimmt. Auch die Texturen von Fraktalberechnungen natürlicher Küstenlinien mit ihren unterschiedlichen „Rauheitsgraden" und Verästelungen haben als Entwurfsgrundlage gedient. Die Architektur des Terminals ist hochgradig heterogen und geprägt durch jähe Wechsel in Raumkonzepten und Oberflächengestaltungen. Statt einem nahtlosen topologischen Kontinuum, wie es für Passagierterminals üblich ist, wird der Reisende hier einer Serie unterschiedlichster Raumerfahrungen ausgesetzt, besonders hervorgerufen durch die starken Vertikalrisse im Baugefüge. Die dadurch entstehenden hohen, engen „Schluchten" sind Lichtquellen und gleichzeitig Verschattungselemente, die im Gebäude eine Lichtflut erzeugen und doch eine Überhitzung vermeiden. Die Proportionen extrem langer und hoher Räume mit schluchtartigen beschichteten Oberflächen ermöglichen ein reichhaltiges, vieldimensionales Raumerlebnis. Wesen und Eigenart der unterschiedlichen Zerklüftungen verändern sich von der Straße zur Meerseite hin: von sehr trüben über halb-durchsichtige „Bürokluft-Fassaden" bis hin zu sehr leicht beschichteten Fensterfronten zum Meer hin, die durch ihre kristalline Glasstruktur weite Ausblicke bieten. In die tektonischen Elemente können LED-Licht- und Leitsysteme mit Signalen integriert werden, die für die Passagiere eine bessere Orientierung gewährleisten.

● The architectural and design firm Biothing was established by Alisa Andrasek and Jose Sanchez in 2001. FissurePort is the work of a team, consisting of Knut Brunier, Gabriel Morales, and Denis Lacej. Biothing focuses on the texture and spatial structure of its architectural projects and develops them with the help of algorithmic infrastructures, often derived from natural shapes and processes.

● Das Architektur- und Designbüro Biothing existiert seit 2001 und geht auf die Gründer Alisa Andrasek und Jose Sanchez zurück. Für die Gestaltung des FissurePort war das Designteam Knut Brunier, Gabriel Morales und Denis Lacej zuständig. Biothing legt besonderen Wert auf die Textur und Raumstruktur ihrer architektonischen Projekte und entwickelt diese im Zusammenhang mit algorithmischen Infrastrukturen, häufig abgeleitet von Formen und Prozessen aus der Natur.

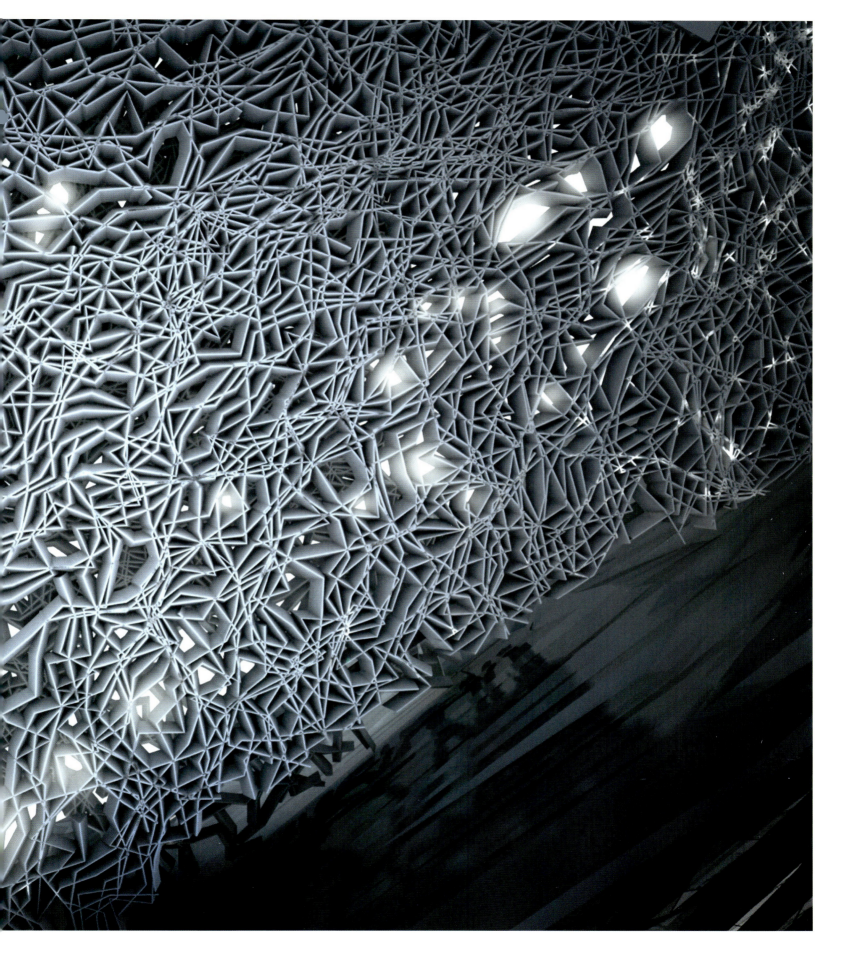

SCOTT LLOYD
ROOM 11
KATRINA STOLL

BEIJING, CHINA / ZURICH, SWITZERLAND
VICTORIA, AUSTRALIA / USA

"Architecture can be differentiated from a purely supporting mechanism when evidence of cultural intent is discovered. Approaching infrastructure with a similar intent allows for new spatial and experiential typologies to arise."

„Sobald Architektur kulturelle Ziele verfolgt, geht sie über eine rein unterstützende Funktion hinaus. Mit einer solchen Sichtweise auch an Infrastrukturen heranzugehen, kann neue räumliche Typologien und Raumerfahrungen erzeugen."

THE ISLAND PROPOSITION 2100, 2010

Shown at the Australian Pavilion,
12th International Architecture Exhibition,
La Biennale di Venezia 2010.

• The Island Proposition 2100 shows an infrastructural main artery, which stretches over land and water as a large bridge structure.
• Die Island Proposition 2100 zeigt eine riesige Brückenarchitektur, die als infrastrukturelle Lebensader über Land und Wasser verläuft.

● ENGLISCH The project proposes a hybrid infrastructure connecting various regions into a sustainable metabolistic system, leading to a symbiotic relationship between urban centers and the surrounding rural areas which supply them with the stocks of urban subsistence – a once neglected relationship. The structure will be a highway for real and virtual transactions of all kinds, distribute goods, alter processes, and determine the future development of the cities. New urban residential, industrial, and commercial spaces will be created, while curtailing urban sprawl and demarcating existing spatial reserves. The main artery adapts its formal configuration to its respective function and context. Thus the infrastructure will harvest energy from solar, wind, and hydro power-stations, use integrated artificial wetlands to clean grey-water, and also serve to collect rainwater. The proposition suggests a mechanism to align urban systems with the critical behavior and adaptability of natural systems, and thus sustain an inclusive and dynamic non-equilibrium.

● DEUTSCH Das Projekt ist der Entwurf für eine hybride Infrastruktur, die verschiedene Gebiete zu einem nachhaltigen metabolischen Netzwerk verbindet. Das Ergebnis ist eine symbiotische Beziehung zwischen urbanen Zentren und den umliegenden ländlichen Gebieten, welche die Versorgung der Stadt mit Nahrungsmitteln sicherstellen – ein lange vernachlässigter Zusammenhang. Das Bauwerk dient als Transportweg für tatsächliche und virtuelle Transaktionen aller Art, verteilt Waren, verändert Abläufe und beeinflusst so die zukünftige Stadtentwicklung. Neue urbane Wohn-, Industrie- und Geschäftszonen entstehen, während der Zersiedlung Einhalt geboten wird und bereits existierende unbebaute Flächen erhalten bleiben. Die Hauptverkehrsader passt sich in ihrem formalen Aufbau der jeweiligen Funktion und dem Kontext an. So gewinnt die Infrastruktur mithilfe von Solar-, Windkraft- und Wasserkraftanlagen Energie, nutzt integrierte Feuchtreservoirs zur Reinigung von Brauchwasser und dient auch dem Sammeln von Regenwasser. Der Entwurf projektiert einen Mechanismus, um urbane Systeme auf die empfindlichen Abläufe und die Anpassungsfähigkeit natürlicher Systeme einzustellen und auf diese Weise ein umfassendes und dynamisches Nicht-Gleichgewicht zu erhalten.

- The masterplan Island Proposition 2100 aims at linking rural and urban regions by a megastructure, a main artery, in a sustainable and energy-efficient way.
- Bei dem Masterplan Island Proposition 2100 soll eine Megastruktur in Form einer Brücke Land- und Stadtregionen wie eine Lebensader nachhaltig und energieeffizient miteinander verbinden.

- The idea behind the cooperation of Scott Lloyd, Katrina Stoll, and Room 11 was to explore the metabolisms of cities and urban architecture. The team founded a platform to consult with different experts, especially from the field of infrastructure. Scott Lloyd works as an architect and curator of exhibitions in Switzerland and China, sometimes together with Room 11. Currently, he is getting his Master of Science degree at the ETH Zurich. Room 11 is an architectual firm, based in Australia, that is involved in projects of various dimensions and from different spheres of interest. Katrina Stoll is an architect, urban planner, and assistant professor for the history of architecture at Syracuse University, the ETH Zurich, and North Carolina State University. She has been cooperating with the firm Studio Gang Architects since 2011.

- Ziel der Zusammenarbeit von Scott Lloyd, Katrina Stoll und Room 11 bei dem vorgestellten Projekt war es, den Metabolismus (Stoffwechsel) der Städte und urbaner Architektur zu untersuchen. Das Team bildete eine Plattform, zu der diverse Experten, vor allem aus dem Bereich der Infrastruktur, eingeladen wurden. Scott Lloyd arbeitet als Architekt und Ausstellungskurator in der Schweiz und China, teilweise gemeinsam mit Room 11. Zur Zeit beendet er seinen Master of Science an der ETH Zürich. Room 11 ist ein Architekturbüro mit Sitz in Australien, das in vielen Größenordnungen und Kategorien arbeitet. Katrina Stoll ist Architektin, Städteplanerin und Dozentin für Architekturgeschichte an der Syracuse University, der ETH Zürich und der North Carolina State University. Seit 2011 arbeitet sie mit dem Büro Studio Gang Architects zusammen.

OFF ARCHITECTURE
PARIS, FRANCE

"The future has been cancelled. We need to re-think it first! Architects often believe their projects are the future, and hope that it will be captured within them. In order to tell how the future will be, we will have to reveal our future projects!"

„Die Zukunft ist abgesagt. Wir müssen sie erst noch einmal überdenken! Architekten glauben oft, ihre Projekte seien die Zukunft, und hoffen, dass sie diese abbilden. Um sagen zu können, wie die Zukunft sein wird, werden wir unsere zukünftigen Projekte offenlegen müssen!"

BERING STRAIT, 2009

The Bering Strait

• Perspective view of Peace Park footbridge from one of the Diomedes Islands
• Ansicht von einer der Diomedes Inseln zur Peace-Park-Fußgängerbrücke

• The Bering Strait is an underwater tunnel, which can also be used by pedestrians, enabling them to experience the underwater world.
• Die Beringstraße ist ein Unterwassertunnel, der auch für Fußgänger begehbar sein soll und ihnen die Unterwasserwelt näherbringt.

• There are plans for a "vertical city" on the Diomedes Islands, which will be connected by a pedestrian bridge.
• Auf den Diomedes-Inseln, die durch eine Fußgängerbrücke verbunden werden sollen, ist eine „vertikale Stadt" geplant.

PAGE/SEITE 228–229
• The Peace Park footbridge consists of a series of 10 by 10 meter cubic modules with a reflective metal facing, which float on the surface of the water.
• Die Peace Park Fußgängerbrücke besteht aus 10 x 10 m großen Würfelmodulen mit einer reflektierenden Metall-Oberfläche, die auf dem Wasser schwimmen.

● ENGLISCH The Bering Strait separates America from Asia. Plans for a bridge, connecting the two continents have been hatched since the 19th century, however, were never realized due to the extreme weather conditions in this region. But as the temperatures rise and the ice is melting as a result of climatic changes, a fundamental change in weather patterns is to be expected. Therefore, a competition of ideas was held in 2009, which again inspired the discussion on a bridge over the Bering Strait. The most radical suggestion was made by the French architectural firm OFF. It does not stop at a commercial route for cars or trains, but projects an underwater tunnel for pedestrians that is in parts inhabitable. The route leads through the Bering Strait´s eco-system like a nature trail, where the underwater world can be watched through perforations in the tunnel. Instead of being ushered past unawares, people are meant to consciously experience nature. Therefore, the project also includes research facilities and maritime museums. The surface of this new Bering passage will offer a protected habitat for different fish, mollusks, and corals. The pack-ice, typical for this region, has inspired the design of the pedestrian bridge, a connection between the Diomedes Islands, where a "vertical city" will be built.

● DEUTSCH Die Beringstraße trennt als Meeresarm Amerika und Asien voneinander. Bereits seit dem 19. Jahrhundert existieren Pläne für eine Verbindung beider Kontinente durch eine Brücke oder einen Tunnel. Sie wurden jedoch aufgrund der extremen Wetterbedingungen in diesem Gebiet bislang nicht realisiert. Mit Klimawandel, schmelzenden Eisflächen und steigenden Temperaturen ist dort jedoch ein grundlegender meteorologischer Wandel absehbar. Ein Ideenwettbewerb 2009 hat die Diskussionen um eine Überbrückung der Beringstraße vorangetrieben. Der weitreichendste Vorschlag kam vom Architekturbüro OFF. Er beschränkt sich nicht auf die Konstruktion einer kommerziellen Auto- oder Eisenbahnverbindung, sondern sieht einen Unterwassertunnel vor, der auch für Fußgänger zu passieren wäre und stellenweise bewohnt werden könnte. Die Route führt wie ein Lehrpfad durch das Ökosystem der Beringstraße; durch Öffnungen im Tunnel kann man die Unterwasserwelt beobachten. Der Mensch soll nicht achtlos an der Natur vorbeigelotst, sondern sich ihrer bewusst werden. Deswegen ist auch die Integration von Forschungseinrichtungen und Meeresmuseen geplant. Die Oberfläche dieser neuen Beringpassage soll Fisch-, Muschel- und Korallenarten einen geschützten Lebensraum bieten. Das für die Gegend typische Packeis war Vorbild für die Gestaltung der Fußgängerbrücke, die die Diomedes-Inseln miteinander verbinden soll. Auf diesen Inseln ist die Errichtung einer „vertikalen Stadt" geplant.

● OFF Architecture is an architectural firm, founded by Manal Rachdi and Tanguy Vermet in Paris in 2004. It operates internationally and in cooperation with renowned architects like Jean Nouvel (masterplan for Slussen, Stockholm). OFF believes that an architectural project cannot be defined without collecting and taking into account all existing information first. Technical considerations do not have priority. The team OFF sees an architectural concept not as an isolated act, but as the accumulation of abilities and an exchange of knowledge. They prefer the method of associative and experimental planning.

● OFF Architecture ist ein von Manal Rachdi und Tanguy Vermet 2004 in Paris gegründetes Architekturbüro, das international und in Zusammenarbeit mit renommierten Architekten wie Jean Nouvel (Masterplan für Slussen in Stockholm) agiert. Für die Architekten ist die Frage der Artikulierung eines Bauprojekts immer an die Aufnahme und Berücksichtigung aller vorliegenden Informationen gekoppelt, technische Überlegungen stehen dabei nicht im Vordergrund. Das Team OFF versteht den Architekturentwurf nicht als isolierte Handlung, sondern als Akkumulierung von Fähigkeiten und als einen Austausch von Wissen. Es präferiert eine Methode assoziativen und experimentellen Entwerfens.

MGS / BILD ARCHITECTURE / DYSKORS / MATERIAL THINKING

MELBOURNE, AUSTRALIA

"Australian cities expand on a diet of forsaken farmland and tenuous infrastructure. The use of rising sea-level as the catalyst to explore the future represents radical re-negotiations of critical issues such as unsustainable sprawl, urban preservation, adaptive re-use and coastal interface."

„Australiens Städte wachsen durch eine Brachland-Diät und eine heikle Infrastruktur: Das Ansteigen des Meeresspiegels zur Erkundung der Zukunft zu nutzen, bedeutet kritische Themen wie nicht nachhaltiges Ausufern, städtischen Denkmalschutz, angepasste Neunutzung und die Küste als Nahtstelle neu zu verhandeln."

SATURATION CITY, 2010

Visionary Concept for the City of Melbourne 2051, Australia

Shown at the Australian Pavilion, 12th International Architecture Exhibition, La Biennale di Venezia 2010.

● ENGLISCH   Saturation City is a visionary concept for the city of Melbourne and was a joint venture between architectural and design practices MGS, Bild Architecture, Dyskors and Material Thinking for the Australian Pavilion at the 2010 Venice Architecture Biennale. The worst-case scenario for the rise of sea-level and the subsequent inundation that Melbourne would be confronted with was taken as an architectural provocation. In Saturation City, new urban islands and rocks emerge as housing, natural landscapes, urban constructs and public spaces. What at first appears to be a city destroyed by global warming turns out to be an opportunity to suggest a future, site-specific, Australian urban condition.

● DEUTSCH   Das visionäre Konzept Saturation City war eine Gemeinschaftsarbeit der Architektur- und Designbüros MGS, Bild Architecture, Dyskors und Material Thinking für den australischen Pavillon auf der Architektur-Biennale in Venedig 2010. Als architektonische Provokation wurde das Worst-Case-Szenario eines Meeresspiegelanstiegs und die daraus folgende Überschwemmung für die Küstenstadt Melbourne angenommen. In Saturation City erscheinen neue urbane Inseln und Felsen, die als Wohngebäude, Naturlandschaften, Städtebauten und öffentliche Räume konzipiert sind. Was zunächst als eine durch die Klimaerwärmung zerstörte Stadt erscheint, entpuppt sich letztendlich als Chance zur Gestaltung einer standortbezogenen Zukunft urbaner Bedingungen in Australien.

• Saturation City, Melbourne in the year 2051: the sea level has risen by 20 meters; new living towers, fit for a coastal region, grow from the flooded city.
• Saturation City, Melbourne im Jahr 2051: Der Meeresspiegel ist um 20 m gestiegen; aus der überfluteten Stadt erwachsen neue, küstentaugliche Wohntürme.

• The four Melbourne architectural and design firms, MGS (McGauran Giannini Soon), Bild Architecture, Dyskors and Material Thinking, believe in collaboration as a critical strategy for innovation in developing concepts and major projects. They consider team-work a stimulating and productive way to promote critical and interdisciplinary design with projects benefitting from the different approaches of everyone involved. Only by this type of joint venture can propositions for an urban future like Saturation City be conceived.
From left: Eli Giannini, Jocelyn Chiew and Catherine Ranger/MGS; Ben Milbourne/Bild Architecture; Edmund Carter/Dyskors; Paul Carter/Material Thinking.

• Die vier Melbourner Architektur- und Designbüros MGS (McGauran Giannini Soon), Bild Architecture, Dyskors und Material Thinking sehen in der Zusammenarbeit eine entscheidende Strategie für Innovationen bei der Entwicklung von Konzepten und Großprojekten. Für sie ist Teamwork ein ebenso anregender wie produktiver Weg, um kritisches, interdisziplinäres Design zu fördern und von den unterschiedlichen Vorgehensweisen aller Beteiligten zu profitieren. Nur diese Gemeinschaftsarbeit erlaubt die Planung urbaner Zukunftsfantasien wie die Saturation City.
Von links: Eli Giannini, Jocelyn Chiew and Catherine Ranger/MGS; Ben Milbourne/Bild Architecture; Edmund Carter/Dyskors; Paul Carter/Material Thinking

BIONIC

Nature and its creations as well as processes of growth in flora and fauna supply architecture with a broad range of morphological and constructive models. From adopting these analogies between biological and architectural structures the science and technology of construction bionics have emerged. Central issues are the environment-friendly air conditioning of buildings and the use of natural materials like wood, mud, or bamboo as well as of light-weight techniques and supporting structures that can be found in bones, corals, spider webs, or the leaves of water-lilies. Another aspect is the arrangement of spatial, constructional, and urban units along bio-ecological guidelines.

When architecture imitates biological construction techniques, it often leads to an adaptation of shapes. The result are buildings that do not follow the classic pattern of metric tectonics and proportions any longer, but are zoomorphic or biomorphic in appearance. One example is the concert hall Parco della Musica in Rome, which was designed by Renzo Piano to resemble a beetle´s giant chitin shield – and also follows its structural scheme. An example of the inspiration by flora is the roof structure of the Venezuelan pavilion by Fruto Vivas and Frei Otto at the Expo 2000 in Hannover, whose kinetic elements opened and closed at dawn and dusk.

Besides these bio-technological and bio-mimetic approaches in contemporary and futuristic architecture, there is the relatively new field of construction botanics, which plays an important role in visionary concepts. Construction botanics is "living archtitecture", growing like a plant and creating inhabitable biologic structures. This model of a self-renewing architecture made from 100% natural materials, however, is still in its early stages, even if the first steps in this direction have already been taken.

BIONIK

Die Natur und ihre Gebilde sowie Wachstumsprozesse aus dem Pflanzen- und Tierreich bieten ein vielfältiges Angebot an morphologischen und konstruktiven Vorbildern für die Architektur. Aus der Nutzbarmachung dieser Analogien zwischen Baustrukturen der Biologie und der Architektur hat sich die Wissenschaft und Technologie der Bau-Bionik etabliert. Zentrale Themenbereiche sind hier die umweltfreundliche Klimatisierung von Bauten und entsprechende natürliche Baumaterialien wie Holz, Lehm oder Bambus, Leichtbauweise und -Tragwerke, wie sie beispielsweise bei Knochen, Korallen, Spinnnetzen oder Seerosenblättern vorkommen sowie die Disponierung von Raum-, Bau- und Stadteinheiten nach bioökologischen Richtlinien.

Mit der Übernahme biologischer Bautechnologien aus der Natur sind häufig auch Form-Adaptionen in der Architektur verbunden. Sie führen dazu, dass Gebäude nicht mehr dem klassischen Schema der metrischen Tektonik und Proportionierung entsprechen, sondern eher zoomorphe oder biomorphe Gestaltmuster zeigen. So sieht z.B. die Konzerthalle Parco della Musica in Rom von Renzo Piano wie der riesige Chitinpanzer eines Käfers aus – und ist auch nach dem statischen Schema eines solchen konstruiert. Als Beispiel für eine Inspiration aus der Pflanzenwelt ist die Dachstruktur des Venezuela-Pavillons von Fruto Vivas und Frei Otto auf der Expo 2000 in Hannover zu nennen, bei der sich kinetische Elemente wie Blüten bei Tagesanbruch öffneten und bei Abenddämmerung schlossen.

Neben diesen biotechnologischen und biomimetischen Ansätzen in der zeitgenössischen und zukunftsweisenden Architektur gibt es den noch relativ jungen Bereich der Baubotanik, der bei den visionären Entwürfen eine wichtige Rolle spielt. Bei der Baubotanik handelt es sich um „Lebendarchitektur", die wie eine Pflanze gezüchtet wird und dementsprechend biologische Baukonstruktionen ausbildet, die vom Menschen als Behausung genutzt werden können. Mit diesem Modell einer nachwachsenden und zu 100 % aus Naturmaterialien bestehenden Architektur steht man jedoch noch am Anfang; aber immerhin, die ersten Schritte in diese Richtung sind gemacht.

R&SIE(N)

PARIS, FRANCE

"Fforfutur … Tomorrownow, Retrofutur, Backtothefutur, Nostalgiaofthefutur and Futurofnostalgia … NoFutur, …FforFake."

ISOBIOT®OPE, 2010

Thebuildingwhichneverdies

Shown at the Australian Pavilion,
12th International Architecture Exhibition,
La Biennale di Venezia 2010.

• Isobiot®ope is an urban light lab that points out the respective conditions of light as well as the intensity of solar and lunar radiation.
• Der Isobiot®ope kann ein Lichtlabor in der Stadt sein, das die jeweiligen Lichtverhältnisse sowie die Sonnen- und Mondeinstrahlung anzeigt.

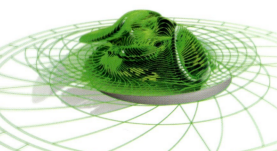

● ENGLISCH   R&Sie(n) presented the room installation Isobiot®ope at the 2010 Venice architectural Biennale as a fragment of their project, called "thebuildingwhichneverdies". The Isobiotrope is a kind of light lab, which can test and measure the human physiological response to light and darkness. It also can examine the effect ultraviolet rays have on the human body as well as on human metabolism over a time-range of 24 hours. The observatory follows the orbit of the moon and determines its position by rotation. Sunlight is absorbed by fluorescent pigments and photovoltaic cells and then transformed into energy. The fluorescent components on the outer surface function as UV sensors and detectors, thus showing the intensity of the UV rays that have an effect on human beings and all other forms of life during the daytime. This makes the glass components indicators of the dangers of the sun and the concentration of ozone in the stratospere. Inside the light lab, the physiological and metabolistic consequences of light and UV rays can be measured by day and by night.

R&Sie(n)´s light lab is a model which could also be imagined as architecture, if scaled up. It offers a way to combat light pollution in our cities and create light conditions in the interiors of our buildings that try to be in harmony with the natural metabolism.

● DEUTSCH   R&Sie(n) waren 2010 auf der Architektur-Biennale in Venedig mit der Rauminstallation Isobiot®ope vertreten, ein Fragment ihres Architekturprojektes „thebuildingwhichneverdies". Der Isobiot®ope ist eine Art Lichtlabor, das die menschliche physiologische Anpassung an Licht- und Dunkelzustände testen und messen kann. Weiterhin ist es möglich, innerhalb von 24 Stunden die Auswirkungen der UV-Strahlung auf den menschlichen Körper sowie auf den menschlichen Stoffwechsel zu untersuchen. Das Observatorium kann die Mondlaufbahn verfolgen, indem es seine Position durch Rotation ermittelt. Die Strahlung der Sonne wird über phosphoreszierende Pigmente und fotovoltaische Zellen aufgefangen und in Energie umgewandelt. Die phosphoreszierenden Komponenten auf der Außenfläche fungieren als UV-Sensoren und -Detektoren und zeigen die UV-Intensität an, die tagsüber auf die Menschen und alle Lebensformen einwirkt. Auf diese Weise werden die Glaskomponenten zu Indikatoren für die Gefahren der Sonneneinstrahlung und die Entwicklung der Ozonkonzentration in der Stratosphäre. Im Inneren des Lichtlabors könnten die Auswirkungen von Licht und UV-Einstrahlung auf die menschliche Physiologie und den Stoffwechsel bei Tag und bei Nacht gemessen werden.

R&Sie(n) hat mit diesem Lichtlabor ein Modell geliefert, das in größeren Dimensionen auch als Architektur vorstellbar ist und dazu beitragen könnte, der Lichtverschmutzung in unseren Städten entgegenzuwirken und im Innern unserer Bauten Lichtverhältnisse zu schaffen, die dem natürlichen Stoffwechsel der Bewohner möglichst angemessen sind.

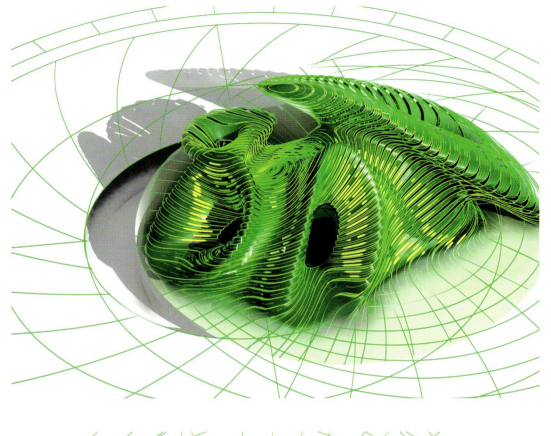

• Inside Isobiot®ope people can test and check out the effects of light, darkness, and UV rays on their bodies and metabolisms.
• Im Inneren des Isobiot®ope könnten Menschen die Wirkung von Licht, Dunkelheit und UV-Strahlung auf ihren Körper und Stoffwechsel testen und kontrollieren.

• R&Sie(n) is an architectural firm based in Paris and founded in 1989 by François Roche and Stéphanie Lavaux. In their eyes, architectonic identity is an unstable concept, which can only be defined by temporary shapes. Phytogenic and bio-dynamic processes are integral parts of their work. R&Sie(n) want to give reality and fiction the same priority and to describe geographic situations and narrative structures in a way that might change both. Their projects are divided into three categories: research as speculation; fiction in practical usage; and practical usage as lifetime.

• R&Sie(n) ist ein Architekturbüro mit Sitz in Paris, gegründet 1989 von François Roche und Stéphanie Lavaux. Sie verstehen architektonische Identität als instabiles Konzept, das nur durch temporäre Formen definiert werden kann, dabei sind pflanzliche und biologisch-dynamische Prozesse wichtige Bestandteile. R&Sie(n) versuchen, dem Realen und Fiktionalen die gleiche Bedeutung beizumessen und geografische Situationen sowie narrative Strukturen zu formulieren, die beides verwandeln können. Ihre Arbeiten sind in drei Kategorien unterteilt: Forschung als Spekulation, Fiktion als Praxis und Praxis als Lebensdauer.

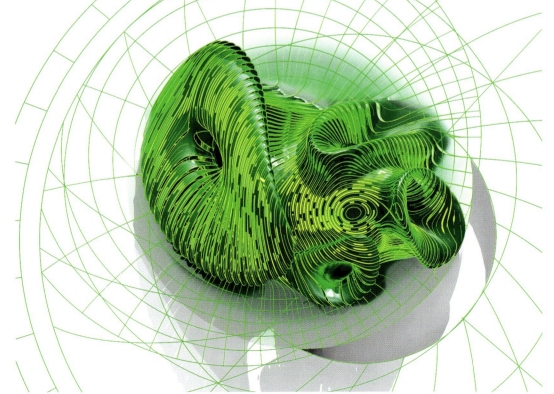

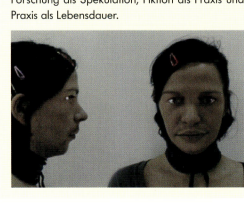

DIGITAL TECTONICS

"The future of architecture will be soft and furry or won't be at all," was Dali's prophecy. Today, this has become a new reality. With genetics, thanks to new biological and digital technologies, human beings can transcend a historical barrier, from merely analogue action at the level of the "surface" to a shaping of the molecular order. Now humans can work at an intramolecular level, towards knowledge of the genetic ordering principles; they gain insight into how the general visible order of biological and digital beings is controlled by biological and digital information chains. One of the main advantages is that the control of these information chains allows the structure, form and "skin emergence", through biological or digital processes, to become architecture. This is done with materials that emerge, i.e. "grow" by themselves, thanks to self-organizing systems, towards more precision, more efficiency, more sustainability. A further aspect is the possibility of fusion and link of these information chains towards what is called biodigital architecture. A vast potential arises in the biological world if we work with DNA as if it was biological software, and in the digital realm if we work with software as if it was digital DNA.

In the 1920s and 30s, when some architects were disposed to systematically configure a modern world, they were stimulated by cultural pressure to fight for proper adaptation to new times and for minimum conditions of decent human existence. Today the urgency is stronger, as it is about the entire planetary subsistence. The question is no longer a simple caprice, nor an intellectual urge. The necessity is global. The whole planet is faced by the danger of ecological death for all mankind. By chance, now in this crucial moment, new technologies of an enormous potential are available: biological and digital techniques, and even a fusion of both, in this instance biodigital architecture. This is an architecture that has incorporated the advantages that become available through the understanding of genetics in both ways, the biological and the digital. It will allow humanity to work towards its ecological survival, this time taking into consideration the needs and values of all regions of the earth.

As the pioneers of modern architecture, who broke with the ancient classical tradition to found a new modern tradition, we are facing the challenge of creating a new tradition of biodigital technologies. For this, it is necessary that people work on three key elements: research, teaching and the professional work itself, as did the founders of modern architecture. We have arrived at a stage where we know that there are sufficient differential parameters to effect an epochal change towards a biodigital architecture.

Alberto T. Estévez

DIGITALE TEKTONIK

„Die Zukunft der Architektur ist weich und behaart oder es gibt gar keine Zukunft", prophezeite einst Salvador Dalí. Heute ist das zu einer neuen Realität geworden. Mit Hilfe der Genetik, dank der neuen biologischen und digitalen Technologien, ist der Mensch in der Lage, eine historische Barriere zu überwinden. Von einer lediglich analogen Gestaltung auf der Ebene der „Oberfläche" schreitet er zur Gestaltung der molekularen Ordnung. Der Mensch kann mittlerweile auf der intramolekularen Ebene arbeiten und hat sein Wissen auf genetische Ordnungsdimensionen erweitert. Er hat herausgefunden, inwieweit die allgemeine sichtbare Ordnung biologischer und digitaler Wesen von biologischen und digitalen Informationsketten bestimmt wird. Einer der Hauptvorteile ist, dass die Kontrolle über diese Informationsketten es erlaubt, mittels biologischer und digitaler Prozesse aus Strukturen, Formen und „Hautbildungen" Architektur entstehen zu lassen. Das lässt sich mit „selbst-wachsenden" Materialien bewerkstelligen, die auf der Basis selbst-organisierender Systeme eine Entwicklung zu größerer Präzision, Effizienz und Nachhaltigkeit ausbilden. Einen weiteren Aspekt bilden Möglichkeiten der Fusion und Verbindung der erwähnten Informationsketten zur sogenannten biodigitalen Architektur. So wie sich auf dem Gebiet der Biologie ein enormes Potenzial eröffnet, wenn man DNS als biologische Software verwendet, ergeben sich in den digitalen Bereichen weitreichende neue Möglichkeiten, indem man Software so benutzt, als handele es sich um digitale DNS.

Die Architekten, die sich in den 20er- und 30er-Jahren des 20. Jahrhunderts an die Gestaltung der modernen Welt machten, reagierten auf einen starken kulturellen Druck, der die richtige Anpassung an die neuen Zeiten sowie Minimalbedingungen für eine würdige menschliche Existenz forderte. Heute ist die Situation noch viel dringlicher, denn es geht um den Fortbestand des gesamten Planeten. Wir haben es nicht einfach mit einer Laune oder einem geistigen Bedürfnis zu tun, sondern mit einer globalen Notlage. Die Erde ist mit der Gefahr des ökologischen Untergangs der Menschheit konfrontiert. Es ist ein glücklicher Zufall, dass in dieser Situation neue Technologien mit enormem Potenzial verfügbar sind: biologische und digitale Technologien und sogar die Verschmelzung derselben, im vorliegenden Fall zur biodigitalen Architektur, die die Vorteile der biologischen und der digitalen Auffassung von Genetik miteinander vereint. Dadurch eröffnet sich der Menschheit die Chance, auf neue Weise für ihr ökologisches Überleben zu sorgen und diesmal die Bedürfnisse und Wertvorstellungen aller Regionen der Erde zu berücksichtigen.

So wie die Pioniere der modernen Architektur mit der klassischen Tradition brachen, um eine moderne Tradition zu gründen, sind wir heute mit der Herausforderung konfrontiert, eine neue Tradition der biodigitalen Technologien zu etablieren. Dazu bedarf es, wie bei den Begründern der modernen Architektur, dreier Elemente: Forschung, Unterricht und eigentliche berufliche Arbeit. Wir haben ein Stadium erreicht, in dem wir wissen, dass ausreichend Differenzparameter vorhanden sind, um den epochalen Wandel zu einer biodigitalen Architektur einzuleiten.

Alberto T. Estévez

TERREFORM ONE

NEW YORK, USA

"It is not only deciphering our ecological issues but returning to a system of perpetuity. This future vision unfolds a truly breathing interconnected metabolic urbanism."

„Es geht nicht nur darum, unsere ökologischen Fragen zu klären, sondern auch darum, zu einem System dauerhafter Beständigkeit zurückzukehren. Unsere Zukunftsvision dreht sich um einen wahrhaft atmenden, umfassenden metabolischen Urbanismus."

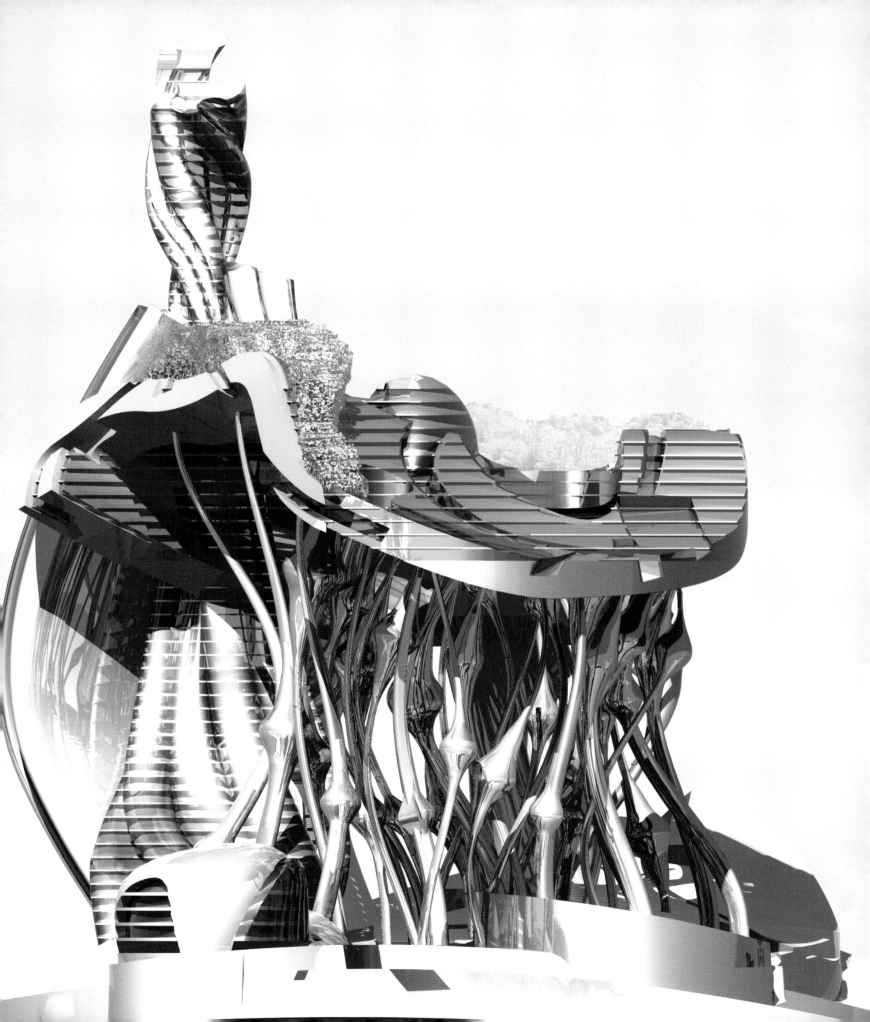

PERISTALTIC CITY, 2008

Circulatory Habitat Cluster for New York, USA

With Mitchell Joachim, Neri Oxman

• Peristaltic City is the vision of a vertical urban building whose spatial configurations constantly change due to the peristaltic movements of hoses made from carbon nanopipes.
• Peristaltic City ist die Vision eines vertikal orientierten städtischen Gebäudes, dessen Raumkonfigurationen durch peristaltische Bewegungen von Schläuchen aus Kohlenstoff-Nanoröhren ständig wechseln.

● ENGLISCH Peristaltic City is a highrise, composed of a cluster of sliding pod-like rooms. The outer surfaces of these pods alter the spatial dimensions of their interiors by peristaltic movements. A soft, flexible, enclosed, and non-mechanical body is arranged around volumetric structures. Hoses, reinforced with fabric, are responsible for the peristaltic activity. Thus, the modules made of carbon nanopipes are able to exercise a structured movement that is symbiotically linked with an urban scaffolding. Mitchell Joachim from Terreform One describes the project as follows: "By contrasting a dynamic spatial apparatus with the traditional organization of core and space, we have abolished the dichotomy of cycle and inhabitable surroundings. We did away with typological stacking, as experience shows that in these cases the individual floors will simply be assigned to different social functions. Instead, we suggest a spacial disposition, allowing heterogeneous and not only organized movements as criteria for a dynamic unification."

● DEUTSCH Die Peristaltic City ist ein hohes Gebäude, das aus einem Cluster verschiebbarer hülsenartiger Räume besteht. Die Außenhäute der Hülsen verändern durch peristaltische Bewegungen die Dimensionen der Räumlichkeiten im Innern. Diese weiche, anpassungsfähige, abgedichtete und nicht-mechanische Konstruktion umschließt volumetrische Strukturen. Textilverstärkte Schläuche machen die peristaltische Tätigkeit möglich. Die Module aus Kohlenstoff-Nanoröhren sind in der Lage, eine strukturierte Bewegung auszuführen, die in symbiotischer Weise mit einem urbanen Gerüst verbunden ist. Mitchell Joachim von Terreform One beschreibt es so: „Indem wir eine dynamische räumliche Apparatur gegen die traditionelle Organisation von Kern und Raum gestellt haben, haben wir die Dichotomie zwischen Kreislauf und bewohnbaren Umgebungen aufgelöst. Typologisches Aufstapeln haben wir abgeschafft, denn die Erfahrung zeigt, dass hier zumeist Stockwerke einfach verschiedenen sozialen Funktionen zugeordnet werden. Als Kriterien für eine dynamische Zusammenfügung schlagen wir stattdessen eine räumliche Disposition vor, die heterogene und nicht nur geordnete Bewegungen zulässt."

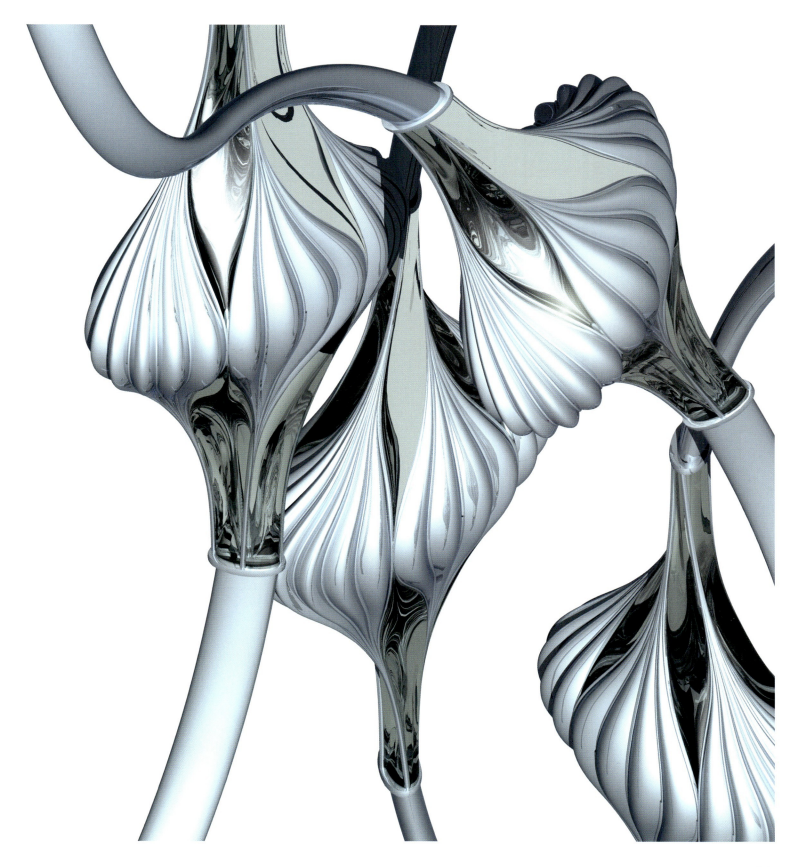

FAB TREE HAB, 2008

Living Graft Prefab Structure

With Mitchell Joachim, Lara Greden, Javier Arbona

- The residential building of the future grows from a tree, consists of 100% living nutrients, and thus is fully integrated into the natural cycle.
- Das Wohnhaus der Zukunft wächst an einem Baum, besteht zu 100% aus lebendigen Nährstoffen und ist damit vollständig in den ökologischen Kreislauf der Natur eingebunden.

- Terreform ONE (Open Network Ecology) in New York is a non-profit organization of designers, architects, artists, and scientists, who advocate green architecture and urban design as well as sustainable and holistic urban planning. The team is headed by the architect and designer, Mitchell Joachim, the co-founder is the architect Maria Aiolova. This unique studio develops innovative solutions and methods in regard to ecological and bionic concepts in the fiels of energy, transport, infrastructure, construction, recycling, food, water, and medial spaces.

- Terreform ONE (Open Network Ecology) in New York ist eine Non-Profit-Organisation von Designern, Architekten, Künstlern und Wissenschaftlern, die sich für grüne Architektur und Gestaltung in der Stadt sowie nachhaltige und ganzheitliche Stadtplanung einsetzen. Der leitende Kopf des Teams ist der Architekt und Designer Mitchell Joachim, Mitbegründerin ist die Architektin Maria Aiolova. Dieses ungewöhnliche Studio entwickelt innovative Lösungen und Verfahren für ökologische und bionische Konzepte in den Bereichen Energie, Transport, Infrastruktur, Bauen, Abfallaufbereitung, Nahrungsmittel, Wasser und mediale Orte.

- ENGLISCH The residential building of the future is supposed to consist of 100% living nutrients. Traditional anthropocentric doctrines are reversed, thus bringing human life back down to earth. The traditional "home" loses its confines and symbiotically blends in with the surrounding eco-system. This new concept of a private home is meant to replace the obsolete design solution of "Habitat for Humanity". Terreform ONE suggests a method to make houses grow out of local trees. A living structure is planted and given an inhabitable shape with the help of computer-generated and reusable scaffoldings. Thus, human residences as well as the natural habitats of animals can be fully integrated into an ecological community.

- DEUTSCH Das Wohnhaus der Zukunft sollte zu 100% aus lebendigen Nährstoffen aufgebaut sein. Traditionelle anthropozentrische Doktrinen werden auf den Kopf gestellt, und das menschliche Leben wird auf den irdischen Boden der Tatsachen zurückgeholt. Das traditionelle „Zuhause" verliert seine Abgrenzung und fügt sich symbiotisch in das umgebende Ökosystem ein. Dieses neue Konzept des Eigenheims soll die veralteten Designlösungen von „Habitat for Humanity" ablösen. Terreform ONE schlägt ein Verfahren vor, mit dem Behausungen aus heimischen Bäumen gezogen werden können. Eine lebende Struktur wird eingepflanzt und durch computergefertigte, wiederverwendbare Gerüste in eine bewohnbare Form gebracht. Dadurch wird es möglich, dass auch menschliche Wohnungen wie natürliche Behausungen von Tieren vollständig in eine ökologische Gemeinschaft integriert werden können.

DESIGN AS A RESOURCE FOR ALL RESOURCES

Design insight is by definition a view, concept, or anticipation of events which evolves beyond any given existing boundaries. This notion may be interpreted in many different ways, each foregrounding particular resources and processes describing the next event. In America, we need radical new strategies to assist in solving our current global resource calamity. As of now, the earth's biosphere suffers from an unremitting state of trauma. We require precise prescriptions that cover a wide scope to alter this massive dilemma.

It is not only deciphering our ecological issues but returning to a system of perpetuity. This future vision unfolds a truly breathing interconnected metabolic urbanism. How does it reify from statistics to architectural form? What does the future look like for America's cities? Design insight is our resource to solve society's resource limitations. America is the lead creator of waste and consumer of fossil fuels on the earth. We make approximately 30% of the world's trash and toss out 0.8 tons per U. S. citizen per year. Ungracefully, our American value system is somewhat distressed.

Value has devolved into feats of rampant affluenza and mega products scaled for super-sized franchise brands, big box retail, XXXL jumbo paraphernalia, etc., encapsulating a joint race for ubiquity and instantaneity in the U.S. mindset. Where does it all end up? Gertrude Stein pointed out: "Away has gone away". The first step we must take is reduction; a massive discontinuation of objects designed for obsolescence. Then we need a radical reuse plan. Our wastefulness is immense, what is our action plan? We forecast resourceful strategies for people to fit symbiotically into their natural surrounds.

To achieve this, all things possible are considered. We design the scooters, cars, trains, blimps, as well as the streets, parks, open spaces, cultural districts, civic centers, business hubs that comprise the future metropolis. For centuries cities have been designed to accommodate the drama of our human will. We have joined the ranks of delivering a new sense of the city, one that privileges the drama of nature over anthropocentric whims. We are constantly vying for a profound clairvoyant perspective. We desire to preview a likeness of our collective future yet untold. Our insight views design not only as a philosophy that inspires visions of sustainable resourcefulness but also a focused scientific endeavor. The mission is to ascertain the consequences of fitting a project within our natural environment. Solutions are derived from numerous examples; living material habitats, waste reuse, smart infrastructure, and mobility technologies. These iterations succeed as having activated ecology both as a productive symbol and an evolved artifact. Current research attempts to establish new forms of knowledge and new processes of practice at the interface of design, computer science, structural engineering, and biology.

Mitchell Joachim and Maria Aiolova (Terreform ONE)

DESIGN ALS MITTEL ALLER MITTEL

Gestaltung befasst sich per Definition mit einer Sicht, einem Konzept oder der Antizipation von Ereignissen und bewegt sich jenseits vorhandener Grenzen. Der Begriff lässt sich auf viele Weisen interpretieren, von denen jede bestimmte Mittel und Prozesse in den Vordergrund rückt, die das nächste Ereignis beschreiben sollen. In Amerika brauchen wir radikale neue Strategien, um die gegenwärtige unheilvolle Ressourcentwicklung auf der ganzen Welt zu überwinden. Schon jetzt leidet die Biosphäre der Erde unter einem Trauma, dessen Ende nicht abzusehen ist. Um aus diesem Dilemma herauszukommen, sind präzise Rezepte nötig, die auf breiter Basis wirken.

Es geht nicht nur darum, unsere ökologischen Fragen zu klären, sondern darum, zu einem System dauerhafter Beständigkeit zurückzukehren. Unsere Zukunftsvision dreht sich um einen wahrhaft atmenden, umfassenden metabolischen Urbanismus. Doch wie können aus Statistiken architektonische Formen werden? Wie wird die Zukunft amerikanischer Städte aussehen? Im Design sehen wir ein Mittel zur Lösung der Ressourcenbeschränkungen. Die USA sind weltweit der größte Verursacher von Abfall und der größte Verbraucher fossiler Brennstoffe. Hier entstehen ungefähr 30 % des Abfalls auf der Welt – jeder US-Bürger produziert im Jahr 0,8 Tonnen davon. Sehr zu unserer Schande ist das amerikanische Wertesystem aus den Fugen geraten.

Werte wurden abgelöst von zügelloser Überflussmentalität sowie von Megaprodukten für überdimensionierte Franchise-Marken, für den Big-Box-Einzelhandel, für XXXL-Jumbo-Krimskrams usw. Das ist ein Wettlauf um augenblickliche Omnipräsenz im kollektiven Bewusstsein der USA. Wo soll das hinführen? Gertrude Stein hat einmal gesagt: „Weg ist weg." Der erste Schritt, den wir gehen müssen, ist Reduktion, ist rasches Einstellen von Dingen, die für schnelle Überalterung gemacht wurden. Dann brauchen wir einen radikalen Wiederverwertungsplan. Unsere Verschwendungssucht ist immens, welche Maßnahmen ergreifen wir dagegen? Wir erarbeiten kreative Strategien, mit denen sich Menschen symbiotisch in ihre natürliche Umwelt einfügen.

Um dies zu erreichen, wird über alle möglichen Dinge nachgedacht. Wir entwerfen Zweiräder, Autos, Züge, Luftschiffe, dazu die Straßen, Parks, Freiflächen, Kultur- und Bürgerzentren, Wirtschafts-Drehkreuze, die die zukünftige Metropole ausmachen. Über Jahrhunderte wurden Städte entworfen, die das Drama des menschlichen Willens beherbergten. Wir haben uns eingefügt in die Reihen derer, die der Stadt einen neuen Sinn geben wollen, einen, der das Drama der Natur über anthropozentrische Marotten stellt. Wir streiten ständig für eine profunde, hellsichtige Perspektive. Wir sehnen uns danach, unsere gemeinsame noch unerzählte Zukunft abzubilden. In unserem Verständnis ist Design nicht nur eine Philosophie, die zu kreativen und nachhaltigen Visionen führt, sondern auch ein zielgerichtetes wissenschaftliches Unterfangen. Wir sehen es als Auftrag an, zu bestimmen, welche Konsequenzen die Umsetzung eines Projekts für unsere natürliche Umwelt haben kann. Lösungen werden aus den verschiedensten Bereichen abgeleitet: Lebensräume für lebende Materialien, Wiederverwertung von Müll, intelligente Infrastruktur und Technologien für Mobilität. Diese Verfahren zeigen, dass sich Ökologie sowohl als produktives Symbol als auch als fortgeschrittenes Werkzeug etabliert hat. Die aktuelle Forschung versucht, neue Formen des Wissens und neue praktische Verfahrensweisen an der Schnittstelle von Design, Informationstechnologie, Bautechnik und Biologie zu verankern.

Mitchell Joachim und Maria Aiolova (Terreform ONE)

ONL
ROTTERDAM, THE NETHERLANDS

DIGITAL PAVILION, 2006
Seoul, Korea

"With our uncompromising realized work we present a theory and practice of architecture based on the principles of swarm behaviour, which builds from the provocative assumption that all building components must be designed to be active actors."

„Die kompromisslosen Arbeiten, die wir bisher realisiert haben, offenbaren einen theoretischen und praktischen Architekturansatz, der auf den Prinzipien des Schwarmverhaltens fußt, ausgehend von der provokativen Annahme, dass alle Gebäudeteile als aktive Komponenten entworfen werden müssen."

● ENGLISCH   With its Digital Pavilion for Seoul, Korea, ONL has devised a complex and flexible sytem of robots to control interacting installations. Exploring the interior of this pavilion is like a tour through the inside of a living installation. Visitors find themselves in the middle of the heart of technology, a ubiquitous computing with all its potential. The installations interact with the public as well as with each other. One installation, for example, generates important data, which are then fed into another installation. Each visitor is individually identified by the robotic system, which generates an unmistakable profile, while the person takes a look around the different floors of the pavilion with its interactive and interacting installations. Thus, each visit becomes a unique experience, because the installations never repeat their exact shape or content. Visitors' movements and streamed contents constantly adapt them to real time. People's interaction with the installations turns the building itself into a living installation. The cell-like divisions of the rooms inside the pavilion have been derived from a 3D Voronoi diagram alogrithm.

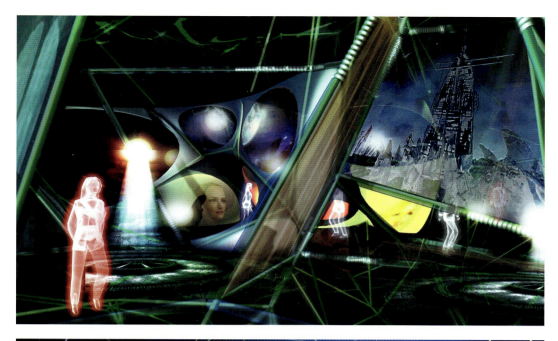

- Digital Pavilion is an entirely computer-controlled exhibition space with interacting installations.
- Der Digital Pavilion ist ein vollständig computergesteuerter Ausstellungsraum mit interagierenden Installationen.

- The architect, Kas Oosterhuis, and the artist, Ilona Lénárd, head the multidisciplinary design firm ONL, where architects, artists, web designers, and programmers explore the merging of art, architecture, and technology on a digital platform. ONL stands for collaborative, non-standard, and emotive design. It is a firm, where the real and the digital worlds meet. Its references include a wide range of projects in various fields of expertise. ONL uses the File-to-Factory system (F2F), which is a state-of-the-art design method, to realize projects like the CET Cultural Center in Budapest oder the Al Nasser HQ Office Tower in Abu Dhabi.

- Der Architekt Kas Oosterhuis und die bildende Künstlerin Ilona Lénárd leiten das multidisziplinäre Designbüro ONL, in dem Architekten, bildende Künstler, Webdesigner und Programmierer auf einer digitalen Plattform die Verschmelzung von Kunst, Architektur und Technik erkunden. ONL steht für kollaboratives, non-standard und e-motive Design; ein Büro, in dem reale und digitale Welten aufeinandertreffen. Die Referenzen umfassen eine Vielfalt von Projekten in unterschiedlichsten Kompetenzfeldern. ONL arbeitet mit dem File-to-Factory-System (F2F), eine hochmoderne Entwurfsmethode zur Umsetzung von Bauprojekten wie z. B. dem CET Cultural Center in Budapest oder dem Al Nasser HQ Office Tower in Abu Dhabi.

● DEUTSCH   Mit dem Digitalen Pavillon für Seoul in Korea hat ONL ein komplexes, anpassungsfähiges Robotersystem entworfen, das interagierende Installationen lenkt. Die Erkundung des Innenlebens dieses Pavillons erlebt man wie einen Rundgang durch das Innere einer lebendigen Installation. Der Besucher befindet sich mitten im Herzen der Technologie: Es handelt sich um ubiquitäres Computing mit seinem ganzen Potenzial. Installationen interagieren mit dem Publikum, aber auch mit anderen Installationen; so produziert z. B. eine Installation wichtige Daten, die in eine andere Installation eingespeist werden. Jeder Besucher wird vom Robotersystem einzeln identifiziert, und es wird ein jeweils unverwechselbares Profil erstellt, während er die verschiedenen Etagen des Pavillons mit seinen interaktiven und interagierenden Installationen erkundet. Jeder Besuch ist ein einzigartiges Erlebnis, da die Installationen niemals ihre genaue Form oder ihren Inhalt wiederholen. Sie sind durch die Bewegungen des Besucherstroms und die gestreamten Inhalte ständig an die Echtzeit angepasst. Indem das Publikum mit den Installationen interagiert, wird das Gebäude zu einer lebenden Installation. Die zellartige Raumaufteilung im Inneren des Pavillons ist von einem 3D-Voronoi-Diagramm-Algorithmus abgeleitet.

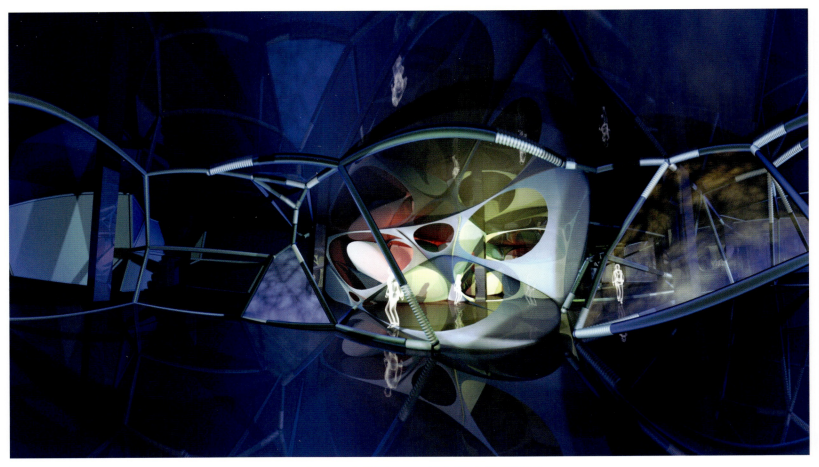

• Exploring the interior of this pavilion is like a tour through the inside of a living installation.
• Die Erkundung des Innenlebens dieses Pavillons erlebt man wie einen Rundgang durch das Innere einer lebendigen Installation.

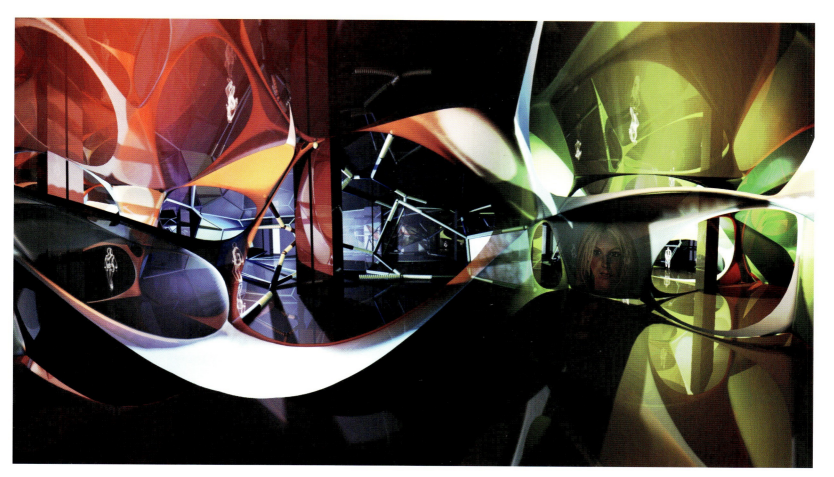

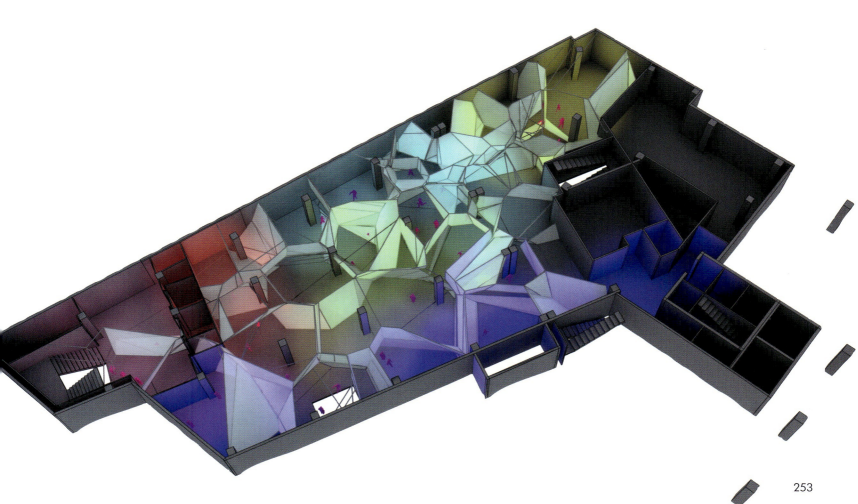

DCA – DESIGN CREW FOR ARCHITECTURE
PARIS, FRANCE

"The future is uncertain. The future is probably worrying. But architecture is a vision of a future that we master and which is therefore reassuring."

„Die Zukunft ist ungewiss. Die Zukunft ist wahrscheinlich besorgniserregend. Architektur ist jedoch die Vision einer Zukunft, die wir beherrschen und die deshalb beruhigt."

FRESHWATER FACTORY, 2010

Almeria, Spain

Special mention, eVolo Competition 2010

• The Freshwater Factory is a projected freshwater tower on 12,000 square metres of the Spanish coast, where saltwater is turned into freshwater by mangrove orchards that grow in sperical greenhouse.
• Die Freshwater Factory ist ein Projekt für einen Süßwasserturm an der Küste Spaniens auf 12.000 m², bei dem durch Mangrovenplantagen in kugelförmigen Gewächshäusern salziges Brackwasser zu Süßwasser aufbereitet wird.

● ENGLISCH This rural project, a highrise functioning as a freshwater tower, is projected for the coastal region near Almeria in southern Spain, where a lot of Europe´s produce is grown throughout the year. As greenhouses cover more then 90% of the region, it is nicknamed "sea of plastic". DCA´s architects suggest a radical and sustainable new approach to this phenomenon that guarantees a reliable water supply for the future and also meets the needs of the local farmers: a freshwater tower, which will irrigate the fields with processed water. The tower consists of round reservoirs, filled with brine, and sperical greenhouse, where mangroves grow. These plants thrive in salt water, while producing freshwater. The total diameter of the tower is one hectare. One hectare of mangroves yield 30,000 liters of freshwater a day. The processed water is pumped into freshwater reservoirs and from there to the fields.

• Sperical greenhouses with mangroves and water reservoirs are stacked up to form a tower and turn saltwater into the freshwater needed to irrigate the fruit and vegetable fields.
• Kugelförmige Gewächshäuser mit Mangroven und Wassertanks werden zu einem Turm aufgestapelt und ermöglichen die Aufbereitung von Salzwasser zu Süßwasser, das zur Bewässerung der Obst- und Gemüsefelder dient.

• The young firm Design Crew for Architecture was founded in Paris in 2003 by the four architects Nicolas Chausson, Gaël Desveaux, Jiao Yang Huang, and Thomas Jullien. They think of their firm as a lab and believe in creating interdisciplinary links. DCA aims at becoming the functional core of an interdisciplinary network of knowledge. In 2005 DCA was awarded the first prize in the competition for "Europan 8", a projected residential and recreational center in Prague.

• Das junge Büro Design Crew for Architecture besteht seit 2003 und hat seinen Sitz in Paris. Die vier beteiligten Architekten sind Nicolas Chausson, Gaël Desveaux, Jiao Yang Huang und Thomas Jullien. Sie betrachten ihr Büro als Laboratorium und sind davon überzeugt, dass es viele Anknüpfungspunkte zu anderen Disziplinen gibt. DCA hat sich zum Ziel gesetzt, der funktionale Kern eines interdisziplinären Wissensnetzwerks zu werden. 2005 gewann DCA den ersten Preis beim Wettbewerb zu „Europan 8", einem geplanten Wohn- und Freizeitzentrum in Prag.

• DEUTSCH Dieses Projekt eines Hochhauses auf dem Land als Süßwasserturm ist in der südspanischen Küstengegend bei Almeria angesiedelt, in der das gesamte Jahr über ein großer Teil des Obstes und Gemüses für ganz Europa angebaut wird. Gewächshäuser bedecken mehr als 90% des Bodens dieser Region und geben ihr den Spitznamen „Plastikmeer". Die Architekten von DCA schlagen eine vollkommen neue Antwort auf dieses Phänomen vor, im Sinne einer nachhaltigen Entwicklung und mit Bezug auf die in Zukunft aufkommenden Anforderungen an die Süßwasserversorgung und die Bedürfnisse der Landwirte: ein Süßwasserturm, der das Anbauland mit aufbereitetem Wasser bewässert. Der Turm besteht aus runden Tanks, die mit salzigem Brackwasser gefüllt werden, und kugelförmigen Gewächshäusern mit Mangrovenpflanzungen. Mangroven haben die Fähigkeit, im salzigen Brackwasser zu wachsen und dabei Süßwasser auszuschwitzen. Die Gesamtfläche des Turmes beträgt einen Hektar. Ein Hektar Mangrovenpflanzen können pro Tag 30.000 Liter frisches Süßwasser produzieren. Das aufbereitete Wasser würde über Pumpen und ein Rohrleitungssystem in Frischwassertanks und von dort aus auf die zu bewässernden Felder transportiert.

HWKN
NEW YORK, USA

"We believe that architectural form has the potential to communicate a positive message about changes in society."

„Wir glauben, dass die architektonische Form das Potenzial besitzt, eine positive Botschaft über die Veränderungen in der Gesellschaft auszusenden."

METREEPOLIS, 2008

• MEtreePOLIS, the bionic city of the future, will be overgrown with thriving mega-plants, which serve as energy suppliers.
• Die bionische Stadt der Zukunft, MEtreePOLIS, wird von wuchernden Megapflanzen bewachsen sein, die als Energielieferanten dienen.

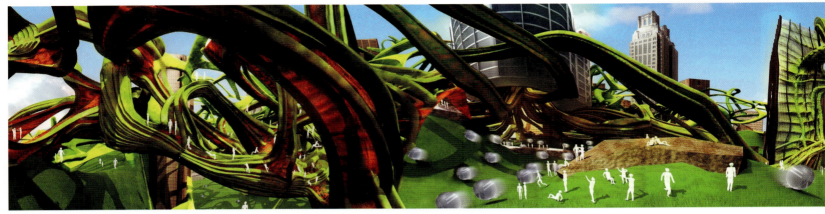

- Historic urban architecture will be integrated into the new system of Power Plants by becoming overgrown.
- Historische Stadtarchitekturen werden durch Bewuchs in das neue urbane System der Power Plants eingebunden.

● ENGLISCH   MEtreePOLIS is a concept for a bionic urban structure in the 22nd century. This urban project adopts the latest findings of genetic engineering to project a visionary growing of urban mega-plants. According to HWKN, technical progress will open up the possibility to integrate photosynthetic molecules into an electronic device, thus turning genetically manipulated plants into energy producers. The urban landscape will become something like a forest, where energy producing plants (Power Plants) form the highest region, creating a canopy of treetops. These plants tap into natural sources of energy and make them usable for the city´s infrastructure. Power Plants will also convert the conventional cityscape into a green jungle with an integrated architecture. Streets erode and are overgrown with moss that forms their new surface. A fleet of hydrogen-powered vehicles moves through those streets, only choosing the most energy-efficient route. The heritage of the urban planning of the past becomes part of a new bio-organism. The surviving historical buildings adapt to the biological pattern of plants, living on the energy it provides. This merger of nature and cityscape also offers a high recreational potential for its inhabitants, who will live in a direct symbiosis with the Power Plants.

- HWKN was founded in New York by the architects Matthias Hollwich and Marc Kushner in 2007. Matthias Hollwich had been working for OMA in Rotterdam, Eisenman Architects, and Diller + Scofidio in New York before. Marc Kushner was employed at J. Mayer H. Architekten in Berlin and Lewis Tsurumaki Lewis (LTL) in New York. HWKN´s philosophy is based on the notion that it is possible to solve the most pressing social, economic, and ecological problems of the present and the future with radical as well as simple architectural solutions. In this context, the human factor plays a major role. However, they are convinced that the ecological mistakes and damage of the past can only be undone with the help of active progress and innovative concepts.

- HWKN wurde 2007 von den Architekten Matthias Hollwich und Marc Kushner in New York gegründet. Matthias Hollwich arbeitete davor bei OMA in Rotterdam sowie Eisenman Architects und Diller + Scofidio in New York. Marc Kushner war Mitarbeiter bei J. Mayer H. Architekten in Berlin und Lewis Tsurumaki Lewis (LTL) in New York. HWKNs Philosophie basiert auf der Idee, dass es möglich ist, die dringlichsten sozialen, wirtschaftlichen und ökologischen Probleme der Gegenwart und Zukunft mit radikalen, aber ebenso einfachen architektonischen Ansätzen zu lösen. Dabei spielt die Berücksichtigung des menschlichen Faktors für sie eine große Rolle. Andererseits sind sie aber auch überzeugt, dass man nur durch aktive Progression und innovative Konzepte die ökologischen Fehler und Schäden der Vergangenheit wiedergutmachen kann.

- DEUTSCH MEtreePOLIS ist der Entwurf für eine bionische Stadtstruktur im 22. Jahrhundert. HWKN greift aktuelle Erkenntnisse der Gentechnik auf und projektiert auf diese Weise die visionäre Züchtung von städtischen Megapflanzen. Nach Ansicht der Planer wird der technische Fortschritt die Integration fotosynthetischer Moleküle in einem elektronischen Gerät ermöglichen. Dadurch werden gentechnisch veränderte Pflanzen zu Energieerzeugern. Die Stadtlandschaft kann so als eine Art Wald verstanden werden, dessen oberste Schicht, also die Baumkronen, aus energieliefernden Pflanzen (Power Plants) gebildet wird. Diese Pflanzen verwerten natürliche Energiequellen und machen sie für die städtische Infrastruktur nutzbar. Entsprechend würden diese Power Plants auch das konventionelle Stadtbild in eine grüne Dschungellandschaft mit integrierter Architektur verwandeln. Die Straßen würden erodieren und mit einen neuen Belag aus nachwachsendem Moos erhalten. Ein Strom von wasserstoffbetriebenen Fahrzeugen würde sich durch die Landschaft bewegen und nur auf den energieeffizientesten Routen fahren. Die Hinterlassenschaften der städtebaulichen Vergangenheit werden Teil eines neuen Bioorganismus werden. Die erhaltenen historischen Gebäude werden sich dem biologischen Pflanzenraster anpassen und von der Energie leben, die es liefert. Diese Verschmelzung von Natur und Stadtlandschaft birgt darüber hinaus ein hohes Erholungspotenzial für die Bewohner, die in direkter Symbiose mit den Power Plants leben.

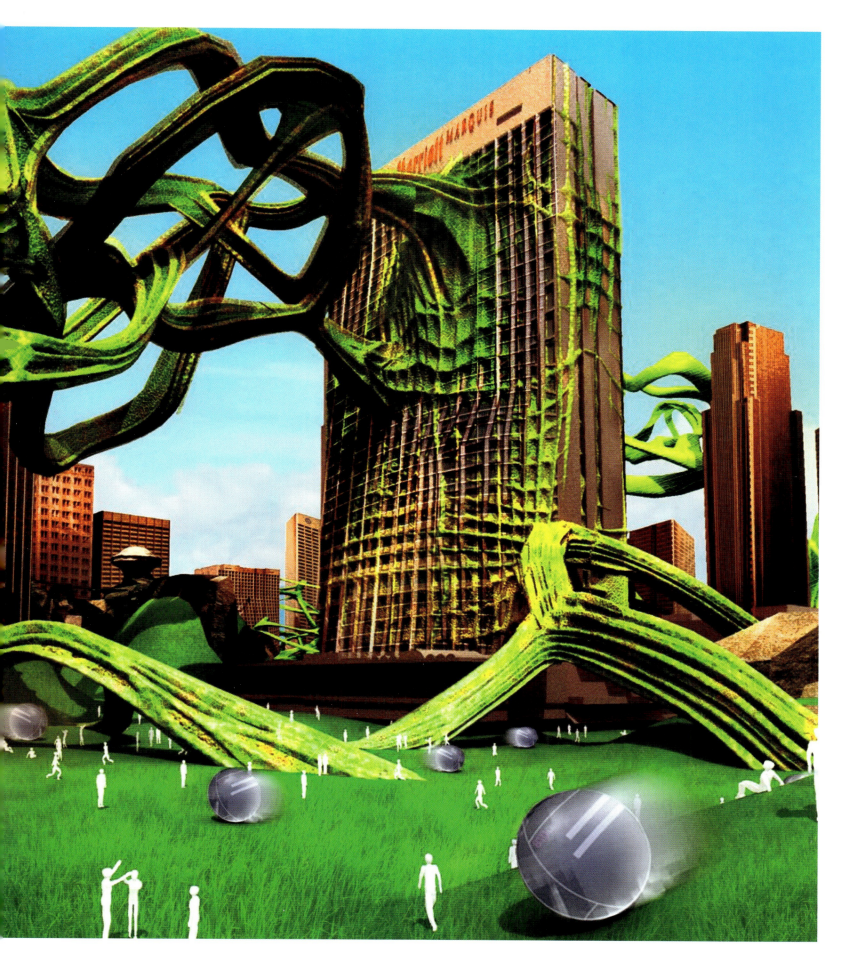

A POSSIBLE MANIFESTO

In 2050 people will probably no longer feel any need for architecture. In 2050, a plausible time frame and a realistic horizon, if we have not radically come to grips with the environmental, social and symbolic problems that are dramatically emerging, architecture will seem like the superfluous art of a luxury couturier. In 2050, if architecture does not seriously change its direction, it will seem like an anachronistic practice connected to past millennia, too slow to provide answers in a fluid present, too rigid to establish a dialogue with the desires of a society in constant evolution.

The world around us is changing profoundly and produces desires, urgent questions that await answers, experiments, visions, also from architecture. We no longer know what to make of an individualistic, autobiographical, condescending and cynical architecture, deaf to the world that surrounds it, narcissistic, that continues to consume territory and resources in a senseless way without offering, in exchange, solutions suitable for a new time.

We are seeking imperfect, thoughtful, generous, epic works capable of opening up unexpected perspectives, not just serving a present that is already past. We imagine an architecture capable of generating works that are the offspring of new political and social thinking about reality, that stand up against that dark self-destructive urge the human species is pursuing with such obstinacy. Architecture has to produce theories independent of the age and the consumer mentality, but it also has to investigate what it means to generate forms and spaces in a fluid, mobile, unstable time. We have to break free of the paralyzing melancholy of the 20th century and its modern heroes. We are the products of a much longer, more sophisticated and complex history, and we need to recover the rich, fertile legacy that can help us to produce evolved, mature fragments of future.

We need to reactivate an unprecedented dialogue with our history. This new millennium will have to be devoted to the patient, loving recovery of what has been lost, constructing original archives, not mausoleums of repressed memory but places of living experimentation, of intense creativity without preconceived notions, in which heritage, histories and desires can converge. In the 20th century we continued with a systematic process of destruction of resources and depletion of our (biological and cultural) heritages; what can activate architecture so that this new century can be devoted to the radical cleaning of what we have boorishly defiled? Our relationship with Nature as a living entity that must be carefully investigated must change. But what horizons can architecture explore, beyond the conventional rhetoric of necessary sustainability?

As big cities gradually grow, the areas of wild, abandoned, autonomous nature will also increase. At the same time, climate change and the resulting processes of desertification and gradual reduction of the coasts will impose completely different logics of settlement that all still require exploration. We have been accustomed to seeing history as a constant flow of growth (demographic, economic, of wellbeing) that incessantly produces goods and places. But how should architecture behave when faced with parallel phenomena of metropolitan hyper-densification in certain areas and demographic regression in others? What models can be applied? What visions can be proposed to political and economic decision-makers?

Architecture has to get back into the flow of life, constructing new narratives, welcoming spaces that become stories people can share, places that gently re-establish our ways of living in the city and the landscape, suggesting different, alternative modes, as opposed to the traditional models of colonization of space. Architecture ought to contribute to imagine new collective spaces in which to nurture differences, to embrace conflicts in order to transform them into dialogues, to recognize diversity as a basic genetic legacy, to contribute to the formation of secular, tolerant, open identities. What contribution can architecture make to an evolved idea of welfare that can combine quality of urban space with scarcity of available resources? We will no longer be able to afford to consume more territory, to add works to works. This is a fundamental political priority to which architecture must make its technical and cultural contribution. We will have no need to construct new "modern" objects in order to live in our age, but we can aptly reinterpret the heritage we possess, working on it from the inside, modifying with force, increasing density, demolishing with clarity, freeing spaces without feeling the need to immediately fill them back up.

Empty space becomes more and more a resource of design and experimentation, in reaction against the horror vacui that has devastated the last century. In an almost present future where flows of information, energy and resources will be available spread equally in an open-source mode, our way of inhabiting space and transforming it will radically change, forcing us to imagine new models of settlement and sharing of public and private spaces. The cities and territories we inhabit will be considered and used, to an increasing extent, as digesting bodies, living organisms, metabolisms active round the clock that will modify the geography of places, of our experiences and ways of inhabiting and utilizing public and private space.

We need to demand an unprecedented form of "gentle radicalism" from architecture, to bring it back into the world as an art / technology aware of its social role, as the vehicle of generous, destabilizing visions. An architecture that is able to build the places to be inhabited by the fragile humanity of this new millennium. Only in this way, perhaps, can architecture avoid vanishing by the year 2050.

Luca Molinari

EIN MÖGLICHES MANIFEST

Im Jahr 2050 werden wir Architektur wahrscheinlich nicht mehr brauchen. Wenn wir bis dahin, also innerhalb eines absehbaren und realistischen Zeitrahmens, die auf dramatische Weise wachsenden ökologischen und sozialen Probleme nicht radikal angehen, wird Architektur wie die überflüssige Kunst eines Luxus-Modeschöpfers wirken. Wenn die Architektur nicht ernsthaft ihre Richtung wechselt, wird sie 2050 eine anachronistische Praxis sein, die an den vergangenen Jahrtausenden festhält. Zu langsam, um auf die ungewisse Gegenwart zu reagieren, zu starr, um in einen Dialog mit den Wünschen einer sich stets entwickelnden Gesellschaft zu treten.

Die Welt um uns herum ändert sich zutiefst, erzeugt Wünsche und wirft drängende Fragen auf, die von der Architektur Antworten, Versuche und Visionen erwarten. Wir wissen nichts mehr anzufangen mit einer individualistischen, autobiografischen, rechthaberischen und zynischen Architektur. Einer Architektur, die taub gegenüber der Umgebung ist, narzisstisch, weil sie unaufhörlich Land und Ressourcen auf sinnlose Art und Weise verbraucht, ohne im Gegenzug angemessene Lösungen für ein neues Zeitalter zu bieten.

Wir suchen unvollkommene, nachdenkliche, großzügige, epische Bauten, die unerwartete Perspektiven eröffnen, die nicht einfach im Dienst einer Gegenwart stehen, die bereits vergangen ist. Wir stellen uns eine Architektur vor, die Bauten hervorbringt, die Früchte eines neuen politischen und sozialen Denkens über die Wirklichkeit darstellen, und die sich dem dunklen Wunsch nach Selbstzerstörung, den die Menschheit beharrlich verfolgt, entgegenstellt. Die Architektur muss zeit- und konsumunabhängige Theorien produzieren, sich aber auch mit der Frage beschäftigen, was es bedeutet, Formen und Räume in einer unklaren, mobilen, instabilen Zeit zu schaffen. Wir müssen uns von der lähmenden Traurigkeit des 20. Jahrhunderts und seinen modernen Helden befreien. Wir sind das Produkt einer viel längeren, anspruchsvollen und komplexen Geschichte, und wir müssen uns auf unser reiches fruchtbares Erbe besinnen, das uns fortgeschrittene und reife Fragmente der Zukunft entwickeln lässt.

Es gilt, einen völlig neuen Dialog mit unserer Geschichte aufzunehmen. Das neue Jahrtausend wird sich der geduldigen und liebevollen Wiederaufarbeitung dessen widmen, was wir verloren haben, also originale Archive gründen, nicht Gedenkstätten der unterdrückten Erinnerung, sondern Orte lebendiger Experimente und intensiver aufgeschlossener Kreativität, an denen das Erbe, die Geschichte und Wünsche aufeinandertreffen. Im 20. Jahrhundert haben wir die systematische Zerstörung und Erschöpfung unserer biologischen und kulturellen Ressourcen kontinuierlich vorangetrieben. Was könnte die Architektur dazu beitragen, dass sich dieses neue Jahrhundert der gründlichen Reinigung dessen widmet, was wir rüpelhaft verschmutzt haben? Unsere Beziehung zur Natur als lebendige Einheit muss sich ändern, es ist notwendig, sie sorgfältig zu prüfen. Aber welche Horizonte jenseits der üblichen Rhetorik der notwendigen Nachhaltigkeit wird die Architektur erforschen?

Nach und nach werden die großen Städte wachsen und ebenso die verlassene und autonome Wildnis. Gleichzeitig werden der Klimawandel und die daraus resultierende Wüstenbildung und zunehmende Küstenverringerung eine ganz neue Siedlungspolitik erfordern, die erforscht werden muss. Wir haben uns daran gewöhnt, die Geschichte als konstanten Wachstumsprozess (demografisch, wirtschaftlich, sozial) zu sehen, der ständig Güter und Orte produziert. Aber wie muss sich die Architektur gegenüber parallelen Phänomenen wie Hyper-Verdichtung in Ballungsräumen und Bevölkerungsregression in anderen Gegenden verhalten? Welche Modelle soll sie anwenden, welche Visionen politischen und wirtschaftlichen Entscheidungsträgern vorschlagen?

Die Architektur muss in den Lebensfluss zurückkehren, muss neue Geschichten erfinden, einladende Räume, die zu Geschichten werden, die die Menschen teilen können; sie muss Orte schaffen, die unsere Art, in der Stadt und auf dem Land zu leben, behutsam neu etabliert, indem sie den traditionellen Methoden der Raumbesiedlung andersartige, alternative Möglichkeiten entgegenstellt. Die Architektur muss an der Vorstellung neuer öffentlicher Räume mitwirken, Vielfalt fördern und sich Konflikte zu eigen machen, um sie in Dialoge umzuwandeln, Vielfalt als wesentliches genetisches Erbe anzuerkennen und somit dazu beizutragen, weltliche, tolerante und offene Identitäten zu bilden. Welchen Beitrag kann die Architektur zur entstandenen Wohlfahrts-Idee beisteuern, der fähig ist, urbane Raumqualitäten mit den verfügbaren, knappen Ressourcen zu vereinen? Wir können es uns nicht länger leisten, mehr und mehr Land zu verbrauchen und Bauten anderen Bauten hinzuzufügen. Architektur muss in technischer und kultureller Hinsicht an dieser zentralen politischen Priorität mitwirken. Um in unserer Zeit leben zu können, müssen wir keine neuen „modernen" Bauten erschaffen, sondern das vorhandene Erbe bestmöglich interpretieren, es von innen heraus neu gestalten, mit Nachdruck variieren, verdichten oder auch entschieden abreißen, um so Raum zu schaffen, ohne diesen sofort wieder auszufüllen.

Im Entwurfs- und Versuchsprozess kommt die Leere als Reaktion auf den Horror Vacui, der die Architektur im letzten Jahrhundert bestimmt hat, immer mehr zum Tragen. In einer fast gegenwärtigen Zukunft, in der der Informations-, Energie- und Ressourcenfluss überall gleichmäßig (als Open Source) zur Verfügung stehen, wird sich unsere Art, den Raum zu bewohnen und ihn zu transformieren, grundlegend ändern, und uns dazu zwingen, neue Modelle der Besiedlung und Aufteilung von privaten und öffentlichen Flächen zu entwickeln. Die Städte und Gebiete, in denen wir leben, werden zunehmend als Verdauungskörper, lebende Organismen und permanent aktive Metabolismen gesehen und genutzt und verändern so die geografische Beschaffenheit der Orte, unserer Erfahrungen und der Art, wie wir öffentlichen und privaten Raum bewohnen und nutzen.

Wir müssen uns für einen völlig neuen „sanften Radikalismus" einsetzen, der die Architektur als Form der Kunst/des Bauingenieurwesens in die Welt zurückbringt und der ihre soziale Rolle sowie ihre Bedeutung als Mittlerin von freizügigen, umwälzenden Visionen bewusst macht. Eine Architektur, die in der Lage ist, für die fragile Menschheit des neuen Jahrtausends bewohnbare Orte zu erschaffen. Nur auf diese Weise wird vielleicht die Architektur im Jahr 2050 nicht verschwunden sein.

Luca Molinari

BIBLIOGRAPHY
LITERATUR

Aldersey-Williams, Hugh: Zoomorphic. New Animal Architecture. London 2003.

ACO Severin Ahlmann (Ed.): Schnittstelle_architektur_wasser. Büdelsdorf, Dortmund and Hamm 2011.

Bahamón, Alejandro; Pére, Patricia; Campello, Alexandre: analogien. Moderne Architektur und Pflanzenwelt. Munich 2008.

Böhme, Gernot: Architektur und Atmosphäre. Munich 2006.

Börries, Friedrich von: Klimakapseln. Überlebensbedinungen in der Katastrophe. Berlin 2010.

Böttger, Matthias; Borries, Friedrich von; Heilmeyer, Florian (Ed.): Bessere Zukunft? Auf der Suche nach den Räumen von Morgen. Berlin 2008.

Callenbach, Ernest: Ecotopia. New York 1990.

Daniels, Klaus: Low Tech – Light Tech – High Tech. Bauen in der Informationsgesellschaft. Basel, Boston and Berlin 1998.

Davis, Mike: Wer baut uns jetzt die Arche? Das Gebot zur Utopie im Zeitalter der Katastrophen. Munich 2008.

De Bruyn, Gerd and Trüby, Stephan (Ed.): architektur_theorie.doc. texte seit 1960. Basel, Boston and Berlin 2003.

European Climate Foundation: Roadmap 2050. A Practical Guide to a Propsperous Low-Carbon Europe. The Hague 2010.

Friedman, George: The Next 100 Years. A Forecast for the 21st Century. New York 2010.

Friedman, Yona: Machbare Utopien. Absage an geläufige Zukunftsmodelle. Frankfurt/Main 1983.

Greer, John Michael: The Ecotechnic Future: Envisioning a Post-Peak World. Gabriola Island, Canada 2009.

IBA Hamburg. Haus der Zukunft. ARCH+ 198/199. Zeitschrift für Architektur und Städtebau. Mai 2010.

Johansen, John M.: Nanoarchitecture. A new Species of Architecture. New York 2003.

Kaku, Michio: Physics of the Future: How Science will shape Human Destiny and our Daily Lives by the Year 2100. New York 2011.

Klanten, Robert and Feiress, Lukas (Ed.): Beyond Architecture. Imaginative Buildings and Fictional Cities. Berlin 2009.

Klanten, Robert; Feiress, Lukas (Ed.): Utopia Forever. Visions of Architecture and Urbanism. Berlin 2011.

Kuhnert, Nikolaus a. o.: Post Oil City. Die Stadt nach dem Öl. Die Geschichte der Zukunft der Stadt. ARCH+ 196/197. Zeitschrift für Architektur und Städtebau. Januar 2010.

Leach, Neil (Ed.): Digital Cities. London 2009.

Leach, Neil and Yuan, Philip (Ed.): Scripting the Future. London Forthcoming.

Meyhöfer, Dirk (Ed.): Water Enjoyment. Sustainable Quality, Technology and Design. Düsseldorf 2011.

Nachtigall, Werner: Bau-Bionik. Natur, Analogien, Technik. Berlin, Heidelberg and New York 2003.

Olthuis, Koen and Keuning, David: Float! Building on Water to Combat Urban Congestion and Climate Change. Amsterdam 2010.

Portoghesi, Paolo: Nature and Architecture. Milan 2000.

Ragon, Michel: Wo leben wir morgen? Mensch und Umwelt – Die Stadt der Zukunft. Munich 1963.

Ryan, Zoë: Building with Water. Concepts, Typology, Design. Basle 2010.

Schwarzenbach, René; Rentsch, Christian and Lanz, Klaus (Ed.): Mensch Klima! Wer bestimmt die Zukunft? Zurich 2011.

Sterlin, Bruce: Tomorrow Now. Envisioning the Next Fifty Years. New York 2002.

Topham, Sean: Where's my Space Age? The Rise and Fall of Futuristic Design. Munich, Berlin, London and New York 2003.

Wenzel, Petra and Lippert, Werner (Ed.): Der Traum vom Turm. Exhibition catalogue. NRW-Forum Kultur und Wirtschaft. Düsseldorf 2004–2005. Ostfildern-Ruit 2004.

Woods, Lebbeus: Utopia? New York 2009.

PHOTO CREDITS
FOTONACHWEIS

P. 14–19: B+U
P. 21–23: The Why Factory
P. 27–37: MAD
P. 41–43: FloodSlicer
P. 45–47: RAG Urbanism
P. 49–51: ARCHI-TECTONICS
P. 54–57: raumlaborberlin
P. 59–64: J. MAYER H. Architects (p. 63: Jens Passoth; Floto + Warner)
P. 69–71: Nabito Architects and Partners
P. 71 (portrait): Sebastiano Palumbo
P. 72–73: Joanna Borek-Clement
P. 73 (portrait): Jason Miller
P. 74–77: LAVA
P. 77 (portrait): Tom Kovak
P. 81–85: Courtesy of Faulders Studio
P. 87: LABscape
P. 87 (portrait): Tecla Tangorra
P. 89–91: Luca d'Amico, Luca Tesio
P. 92–99: Mass Studies
P. 103–105: Paul-Eric Schirr-Bonnans
P. 106–109: Werner Sobek
P. 109 (portrait): A.T. Schaefer
P. 110: Philippe Rahm Architectes
P. 112–113: Brøndum & Co
P. 113 (portrait): Schlomoff
P. 116: Architecture and Vision/Background image courtesy of NASA
P. 118–119: Architecture and Vision
P. 119 (portrait): © Ideami
P. 120–123: Foster + Partners
P. 123 (portait): Croci and du Fresne
P. 124–129: carlorattiassociati
P. 131 (portrait): Rainer Horsch
P. 131–133: Studio Massaud
P. 137–141: Christophe DM BARLIEB
P. 142–147: Marcosandmarjan
P. 145 (left portrait): Paul Smoothy
P. 148–153: MVRDV
P. 151 (portrait): Allard van der Hoek
P. 155–163: Vincent Callebaut Architectures
P. 164–169: IwamotoScott Architecture
P. 172–173: JNStudio/Jung Min Nam
P. 175–177: Luc Schuiten
P. 178–181: Antoine Damery
P. 181 (portrait): Nathan Stribley

P. 182–185, 189: Bjarke Ingels Group
P. 186–187: Bjarke Ingels Group + Glessner
P. 193: ARUP
P. 194: FloodSlicer
P. 195: ARUP
P. 197–199: © Jacques Rougerie/SeaOrbiter ®
P. 202–203: Pauley Interactive
P. 205–209: EMERGENT Tom Wiscombe LLC & KOKKUGIA LLP
P. 211–213: Phu Hoang Office
P. 214–219: Biothing
P. 221–223: Scott Lloyd, Aaron Roberts (room 11) and Katrina Stoll
P. 225–229: OFF Architecture
P. 231, 233 below: Ben Statkus (Statkus Architecture), Daniel Agdag, Melanie Etchell, William Golding, Anna Nguyen, Joel Ng
P. 233 above: FloodSlicer
P. 237–239: R&Sie(n)
P. 243–247: Mitchell Joachim
P. 251–253: ONL [Oosterhuis_Lénárd]
P. 255–257: DCA – Design Crew for Architecture
P. 259–263: HWKN

INDEX

ARCHI-TECTONICS
11 Hubert Street
New York, NY 10013, USA
www.archi-tectonics.com

ARCHITECTURE AND VISION
Hohenstaufenstrasse 10
80801 Munich, Germany
www.architectureandvision.com

ARUP
Level 10, 201 Kent Street
Sydney NSW 2000, Australia

BJARKE INGELS GROUP
Nørrebrogade 66d, 2nd floor
2200 Copenhagen N, Denmark
www.big.dk

BIOTHING
www.biothing.org

JOANNA BOREK-CLEMENT
www.joannaborek.com

B+U
834 S. Broadway SUITE # 502
Los Angeles, CA 90014, USA
www.bplusu.com

VINCENT CALLEBAUT ARCHITECTURES
119, rue Manin
75019 Paris, France
www.vincent.callebaut.org

CARLORATTIASSOCIATI
walter nicolino & carlo ratti
Corso Sella 26
10131 Turin, Italy
www.carloratti.com

CDMB ARCHITECTS
Hirtenstrasse 10, 10178 Berlin, Germany
www.barlieb.com

LUCA D´AMICO
Corso Vittorio Emanuele 37
10125 Turin, Italy

ANTOINE DAMERY
www.adesigner.fr

DESIGN CREW FOR ARCHITECTURE (DCA)
36 boulevard de la Bastille
75012 Paris, France
www.d-c-a.eu

DICKSON DESPOMMIER
Environmental Health Science of Columbia University
60 Haven Ave., Room 100
New York, NY 10032, USA
www.verticalfarm.com

EMERGENT Tom Wiscombe
2404 Wilshire Boulevard, Suite 8D
Los Angeles, CA 90057, USA
www. emergentarchitecture.com

ALBERTO T. ESTÉVEZ
Genetic Architectures Research Group & Office
(ESARQ, Universitat Internacional de Catalunya)
Inmaculada 22
08017 Barcelona, Spain

FAULDERS STUDIO
1571 Ninth Street
Berkeley, CA 94710, USA
www.faulders-studio.com

FOSTER + PARTNERS
Riverside, 22 Hester Road
London SW11 4AN, UK
www.fosterandpartners.com

FLORIAN HEILMEYER
Weserstrasse
Berlin-Neukölln, Germany

PHU HOANG OFFICE
536 Court Street, Suite 2
Brooklyn, NY 11231, USA
www.phuhoang.com

HWKN
281 Fifth Avenue
New York, NY 10016, USA
www.hwkn.com

CRISTOPH INGENHOVEN
Plange Mühle 1
40221 Düsseldorf, Germany
www.ingenhovenarchitects.com

IWAMOTOSCOTT ARCHITECTURE
729 Tennessee Street
San Francisco, CA 94107, USA
www.iwamotoscott.com

JNSTUDIO
J. NAM ARCHITECTURE DESIGN & RESEARCH
166 Terrace Street # 301
Boston, MA 02120, USA
www.jnamstudio.com

KOKKUGIA
6/Wellington Court
6 Shelton Street
London WC2H 9JS, UK
www.kokkugia.com

LABSCAPE
306W, 38th Street, Suite 1504
New York, NY 10018, USA
www.labscape.org

LAVA
Laboratory for Visionary Architecture Europe
Heilbronner Strasse 7
70174 Stuttgart, Germany
www.l-a-v-a.net

MAD
3rd Floor West Tower, No.7
Banqiao Nanxiang, Beixinqiao
100007 Beijing, China
www.i-mad.com

MARCOSANDMARJAN
15 Vicars Close
E9 7TH London, UK
www.marjan-colletti.blogspot.com

MASS STUDIES
Fuji Bldg. 4F
683-140 Hannam 2-dong Yongsan-gu
Seoul 140–892, Korea
www.massstudies.com

J. MAYER H. ARCHITECTS
Bleibtreustrasse 54
10623 Berlin, Germany
www.jmayerh.de

MCGAURAN GIANNINI SOON
10–22 Manton Lane
Melbourne Victoria 3000, Australia
www.mgsarchitects.com.au

LUCA MOLINARI
viapiranesi srl
Via G.B. Piranesi 10
20137 Milan, Italy
www.ymag.it

MVRDV
Dunantstraat 10
PO Box 63136
3002 JC Rotterdam, The Netherlands
www.mvrdv.nl

NABITO ARCHITECTS AND PARTNERS
c/Ramon Turró 11
Tercer C.A.P.
08005 Barcelona, Spain
www.nabit.it

OFF ARCHITECTURE
168 rue Saint-Denis
75002 Paris, France
www.offarchitecture.com

ONL
Essenburgsingel 94c
3022 EG Rotterdam, The Netherlands
www.oosterhuis.nl

PHIL PAULEY
Somerset House
South Wing, Strand
London, WC2R 1LA, UK
www.philpauley.com

PHILIPPE RAHM ARCHITECTS
12 rue Chabanais
75002 Paris, France
www.philipperahm.com

RAG URBANISM
Richard Goodwin
61 James Street
Leichhardt
Sydney NSW 2040, Australia

RAUMLABORBERLIN
Am Flutgraben 3
12435 Berlin, Germany
www.raumlabor.net

ROOM 11
Studio VIC
3rd floor, 105 Victoria Street
Fitzroy Victoria 3065, Australia

JACQUES ROUGERIE
Péniche Saint Paul
Port des Champs-Elysées
75008 Paris, France
www.rougerie.com

R&Sie(N)
20 rue des Maronites
75020 Paris, France
www.new-territories.com

PAUL-ERIC SCHIRR-BONNANS
2 avenue Barthou
35000 Rennes, France
www.paulericschirrbonnans.com

LUC SCHUITEN
Avenue Huart Hamoir 83a
1030 Bruxelles, Belgium

SMAQ
Kastanienallee 10
10435 Berlin, Germany
www.smaq.net

WERNER SOBEK
Albstrasse 14
70597 Stuttgart, Germany
www.wernersobek.com

STUDIO MASSAUD
7 rue Tolain
75020 Paris, France
www.massaud.com

TERREFORM ONE
33 Flatbush Avenue, 7th Floor
Brooklyn, NY 11217, USA
www.terreform.org

THE WHY FACTORY
TU Delft, Faculty of Architecture
Julianalaan 132–134
2628 BL Delft, The Netherlands
www.thewhyfactory.com

JOHN WARDLE ARCHITECTS
Level 10, 180 Russell Street
Melbourne Victoria 3000, Australia
www.johnwardlearchitects.com